D1563435

Modern Southeast Asia Series

James R. Reckner, *General Editor*

Operation Passage to Freedom

★★★★★★★★★★★★★★★

Operation Passage to Freedom

The United States Navy in Vietnam, 1954–1955

★★★★★★★★★★★★★★

Ronald B. Frankum, Jr.

Texas Tech University Press

This book is typeset in Century Old Style Standard. The paper used in this book
meets in the mininum requirements of ANSI/NISO Z39.48-1992 (R1997). ∞

Designed by Kaelin Chappell Broaddus

Library of Congress Cataloging-in-Publication Data
Frankum, Ronald Bruce, 1967–
Operation Passage to Freedom : the United States Navy in
Vietnam, 1954–1955 / Ronald B. Frankum, Jr.
p.   cm. — (Modern Southeast Asia series)
Includes bibliographical references and index.
ISBN-13: 978-0-89672-608-6 (hardcover : alk. paper)
ISBN-10: 0-89672-608-8 (hardcover : alk. paper)
1. Operation Passage to Freedom, 1954–1955. 2. Evacuation of
civilians—Vietnam (Democratic Republic) 3. Humanitarian assistance,
American—Vietnam. 4. Political refugees—Vietnam. I. Title.
DS556.9.F69 2007
959.704'1086914—dc22   2006039810

Printed in the United States of America
07 08 09 10 11 12 13 14 15 / 9 8 7 6 5 4 3 2 1

Texas Tech University Press
Box 41037
Lubbock, Texas 79409–1037 USA
800.832.4042
ttup@ttu.edu
www.ttup.ttu.edu

CONTENTS

Illustrations ix

Maps xi

Tables xiii

Series Editor's Foreword xv

Preface xix

Chapter 1 The Road to Geneva 1

Chapter 2 The Growing Crisis 16

Chapter 3 Organizing the Passage 40

Chapter 4 A Mass of Humanity, August 1954 58

Chapter 5 Challenges by Land, August 1954 96

Chapter 6 Hanoi to Haiphong: The Circle Closes 115

Chapter 7 Resettling a Nation 142

Chapter 8 Hanoi to Haiphong: A Country in Transition 158

Chapter 9 Transitions and Change 179

Conclusion The Bamboo Curtain Falls 196

Appendixes

Appendix A Ship and Craft Designations and Descriptions 211

Appendix B Ship and Craft Loading Capacity—Personnel 213

Appendix C U.S. Ships and Craft Involved in Operation
Passage to Freedom 214

Notes 219

Bibliography 237

Index 247

ILLUSTRATIONS

★★★★★★★★★★★★★★★

Fig. 2.1.   Refugee camp organization chart.   31

Fig. 2.2.   Staff organization chart for Staging Center Haiphong.   32

Fig. 4.1.   Vietnamese refugees aboard USS *Menard*.   69

Fig. 4.2.   A "helping hand" during Operation Passage to Freedom. 70

Fig. 4.3.   The first debarkation of Vietnamese refugees in Saigon. 72

Fig. 4.4.   Vietnamese Catholic priests overseeing the preparation
             of rice.   73

Fig. 4.5.   Vietnamese refugees being served food, August 1954.   74

Fig. 4.6.   Instant friends.   76

Fig. 4.7.   Refugee groups at Phom Xa railway station, Haiphong.   78

Fig. 4.8.   A ladder is lowered to a French LSM, August 1954.   80

Fig. 4.9.   Reception committee passing out welcome packages.   81

Fig. 4.10.   Delousing of Vietnamese refugees before boarding.   84

Fig. 5.1.   View of the debarkation point in Saigon.   100

Fig. 5.2.   Refugee camp in South Vietnam.   103

Fig. 6.1.   PMU team dust soldiers with DDT before they board.   118

Fig. 6.2.   Ceremony aboard USS *Menard*.   123

Fig. 6.3.   American sailor helps feed a small refugee.   131

Fig. 6.4.   Welcoming speech at the arrival of the one hundred
             thousandth refugee.   132

Fig. 6.5.   Vietnamese Catholic priests served as leaders and
             interpreters.   136

Fig. 8.1.   Winner of the beard contest among the sailors.   173

Fig. 8.2.   A small boy lends a helping hand.   174

MAPS

Map 1.1. Indochina in 1954, showing the Demarcation Line
          between the North and the South   13
Map 3.1. Haiphong and Its Harbor   45
Map 3.2. Underwater Demolition Team Survey of Do Son
          Peninsula   47

TABLES

★★★★★★★★★★★★★★★★

Table 2.1. Estimated Costs for Refugee Resettlement in the Saigon
            Area (in Piasters)   29
Table 3.1. Task Force 90 Organization Structure   42
Table 5.1. Estimated Space Available for Evacuees in South
            Vietnam   98
Table 6.1. Number of Days Each Ship Type Served in the
            Operation   139
Table 7.1. Refugee Status in Central Vietnam   150
Table 8.1. Central Vietnam Refugee Census   171
Table 9.1. North Vietnamese Refugees Evacuated to South
            Vietnam as of November 26, 1954, and Repartition of
            Refugees in Resettlement Areas   187
Table 9.2. Task Group 90.8, January 1955   195
Table 10.1 Evacuation Totals, May 1955   205

SERIES EDITOR'S FOREWORD

Few events in American history have generated as much emotion, as much division, and as many long-term impacts for American society as our nation's involvement in Vietnam, Laos, and Cambodia in the latter half of the twentieth century. Texas Tech University Press' Modern Southeast Asia Series is intended to facilitate an open dialogue about the Vietnam War and its lessons, with contributions reflecting all points of view.

In this work, Ronald B. Frankum, Jr., recounts events surrounding America's first major, direct involvement with the Vietnamese people. For those who went south in 1954 and 1955, it is easy to conclude they sought the simple things in life: an opportunity to work the land, to raise a family in peace, and to worship as they saw fit. Unfortunately for those who made the long trip south, and for those native to the South, such simple aspirations proved remarkably difficult to achieve.

In the summer of 2004, while I was leading a student study trip through Vietnam, we had the occasion to drive the highway from Rach Gia on the Gulf of Thailand to Long Xuyen on the Mekong's lower branch, the Hau (Bassac) River. I hadn't traveled this highway since 1969, when I was a part of an armed convoy of Vietnamese military vehicles heading south to the coastal city, so I observed the passing scene with great interest. A few miles north of Rach Gia we passed through the village of Cai Son. As we drove through, I was pleasantly surprised to see rising in the center of the town a magnificent new Roman Catholic church. Indeed, the structure was imposing, cathedral-like, and it drew on architectural lines that would be quite familiar to American Catholics. Cai Son, it turned out, was one of the areas in which the Ngo Dinh Diem resettled Catholics from the North. In this work, Dr. Frankum carefully examines the events of 1954 and 1955 that resulted in the establishment of a vibrant Catholic community at Cai Son and similar communities in a number of other locales throughout the Republic of Vietnam.

The essence of the situation in 1954 was that, having sustained a major defeat at the strategic Dien Bien Phu on the border between Laos and North Vietnam, the French at Geneva agreed to a series of provisions designed to end the First Indochina War. A "temporary military demarcation" line was established at the seventeenth parallel, with a communist government established in the North and a noncommunist government in the South. The Geneva Accords included a provision that individuals in either of the two zones were permitted to freely relocate from one zone to the other during a three-hundred-day period of "regroupment."

Following Geneva, the noncommunist government headed by Ngo Dinh Diem struggled to establish the basic services of a national government for the people of the South, even as the process of regroupment progressed. One can but imagine the challenge of establishing the necessary infrastructure of a national government in the most tranquil of times. But 1954 was not a tranquil time. Of greatest significance for South Vietnam was the flow of approximately eight hundred thousand Vietnamese from the North to the South during the regroupment period. For the Ngo Dinh Diem government and the U.S. Overseas Mission, the arrival of this massive influx of humanity posed significant problems.

The majority of these individuals traveled south by land; however, more than three hundred thousand of them became the temporary guests of the U.S. Navy. Tired, fearing religious persecution, their traditional close ties to the land severed, and subjected to communist propaganda that suggested the American sailors would throw them overboard once the ships went to sea, the refugees nevertheless cast their lot with the American sailors.

In order to capture the largely unrecorded story of the seaborne exodus of North Vietnamese, Frankum conducted extensive interviews with crewmembers of U.S. Navy and Military Sea Transportation Service ships that participated in Operation Passage to Freedom. As Frankum notes, this was the largest such humanitarian sealift in the history of the United States.

But there is much more to this story than just an account of sailors adapting to unique challenges in order to carry out an unusual mission. In fact, the history of our navy is replete with major humanitarian responses to evolving civil crises. Perhaps the most notable recent large-scale humanitarian mission was the navy's response to the remarkable tsunami that devastated regions of South and Southeast Asia in 2004, but in Indochina in 1954 and 1955, the ships of Amphibious Group One responded in truly professional form to the crisis they confronted.

In one of those unconscious aspects of history, the same Amphibious Group One, whose efforts helped so many reach freedom in the South in 1954 and 1955 and helped provide an enlarged political base for Ngo Dinh Diem, a Catholic, stood offshore from Saigon at the end of October 1963 in anticipation of the coup d'etat that resulted in the assassination of President Ngo Dinh Diem and his brother, Ngo Dinh Nhu.

The story of Operation Passage to Freedom, though, as Frankum explains, also involved the even more complex issues of reception and resettlement of the refugees throughout South Vietnam. Frankum's account of the U.S. Overseas Mission's tireless efforts to deal with all of the unanticipated crises related to the relocation of some eight hundred thousand displaced Vietnamese is a story long in need of recognition, and it is one that illuminates America's early involvement in the shaping of the Republic of Vietnam.

James R. Reckner
Texas Tech University

PREFACE

Often I have been asked, as a historian, how I became interested in researching the Vietnam War. The response, perhaps, is not appropriate for these pages; it certainly would take more time and space to convey than what I have available here. What is important, however, is that through my study of the Vietnam War and its origins I have identified several significant events that have not drawn the attention of scholars before. One of those events was the August 1954–May 1955 U.S. naval action Operation Passage to Freedom. The story behind my interest in Operation Passage to Freedom is applicable in this case. Very little has been written about the U.S. Navy in Vietnam in the immediate post–Korean War era, nor has the magnitude of American participation in the resettlement of Vietnam refugees as a result of the 1954 Geneva Conference been explored. I had not realized the extent of American involvement in that critical time in Vietnamese history until I happened to chance upon a photograph depicting a scene from the operation.

Early in 1998, I was sitting at my desk in the Vietnam Archive at Texas Tech University sorting through photographs in the collection of Douglas Pike, a longtime Foreign Service officer who spent several years in Vietnam and a lifetime collecting materials and data on Southeast Asia. A series of photographs among the several thousand in the collection drew my interest, including a black-and-white image of an older Vietnamese woman, in pitiable condition, surrounded by U.S. sailors. The caption on the back indicated that the photograph was one taken during the U.S. naval operation known as Passage to Freedom. I quickly sorted the image with others from the collection, but it continued to play in my mind for the next year or two. Prompted by the expression on the face of the woman, which combined what could only be described as a lifetime of hardship, a recent experience of anguish, and a glimmer of hope, I began

researching the operation. What I learned was rather shocking, as few of
the more significant works on the Vietnam War gave more than a passing
mention of Operation Passage to Freedom.

It was in early 2000 that I resolved to use this operation as a foundation for my next research project. On a Friday, late in the afternoon, after
searching the Internet, I found websites and contact information for the
veterans' associations of a few American ships that had been involved in
the operation, and I sent out a general inquiry to see if I could find anyone
who had participated in the event. The response I received when I returned to work on Monday morning served as a catalyst for this book.

Operation Passage to Freedom was more than a brief paragraph in
the American war in Vietnam. For most Americans, Operation Passage
to Freedom, if thought of at all, was a footnote to the early involvement
of the United States in the war that would consume the nation a decade
later. But to the young men, now in their seventies and eighties, who
moved a nation in 1954 and 1955, Operation Passage to Freedom was a
pivotal point in their lives. Even fifty years later, for many of the sailors
who served aboard those ships of Task Force 90, the event became a
defining one in their lives.

What those sailors accomplished during the three hundred days of
Operation Passage to Freedom changed, forever, the lives of more than
310,000 Vietnamese who traveled on American ships. What the United
States attempted to accomplish during that period significantly altered
the lives of more than 810,000 Vietnamese who chose to move from the
Democratic Republic of Vietnam (DRV) in the north to the Republic of
Vietnam (RVN) in the south. Operation Passage to Freedom established
the United States' moral obligation to the Vietnamese people through its
participation in the event. By assisting the Vietnamese move from North
Vietnam to the south across the seventeenth parallel, which divided communism and noncommunism, the United States committed itself to bet-
terment of those people's lives. Involvement in the moving of a significant
part of a nation established the moral obligation to ensure that those
people's lives would improve under a democratic government, free from
the threat of communism. It was this moral obligation that motivated
American officials on the ground during the operation and propelled the
United States during the Eisenhower administration to help build a nation. It was the failure to uphold this moral obligation during the Kennedy

administration that fed into American escalation of the war in the 1960s. This argument, however, is for another book.

In many respects, Operation Passage to Freedom provides another piece to the puzzle in explaining why and how the initial humanitarian involvement of the United States in Vietnam in the 1950s eventually led to its massive military involvement in the 1960s and 1970s. The humanitarian nature of Operation Passage to Freedom—that is, the assistance to those in need of help—brought the generation of American personnel involved in the naval operation, as well as those involved in the resettlement and rehabilitation of the refugees, a new and different perspective on the role of the United States in the post–World War II Cold War environment. The need and desire to help forged a bond with the Vietnamese. This bond translated to a moral obligation by those who experienced the American operation to see that the refugees received the best care the United States could provide as well as an environment in which they had the possibility of thriving. This moral obligation does not replace or supplant America's primary foreign policy objective of containing communism in Southeast Asia, nor does it take the place of other factors such as the economic cohesion of the region or the establishment of the experiment of democracy in Vietnam to serve as a bulwark against communist encroachment. Operation Passage to Freedom helped to encourage the moral obligation that sought to strengthen the nation of South Vietnam, to better its people, and to satisfy American foreign policy objectives in the region.

This book is organized chronologically whenever possible. The most notable exceptions are during the months of August and September 1954, when the United States was most active on the ground and at sea. I chose to separate the events by land and sea during those two months in order to allow the reader to fully appreciate the magnitude of the operation and the work of the United States Overseas Mission (USOM), which, like the navy's operation, has been relegated to the back pages and footnotes of America's experience in Vietnam during the refugee crisis. Operation Passage to Freedom was one of the largest humanitarian sealifts of its kind in the history of the United States, but the work of the USOM in refugee relief and organizing the infrastructure of a country torn apart by nine years of war and one hundred years of French colonial rule is equally impressive. Historians of this period tend to focus on the rise of Ngo Dinh Diem and his battles with the Cao Dai, Hoa Hao, and Binh Xuyen or the intrigue of Edward Landsdale and the Central Intelligence Agency. Lost is the work of the USOM, which I hope will find its rightful place in history through these pages. Consideration of Operation Passage to Freedom and the work of the USOM as part of America's early experience in Vietnam help to explain why Eisenhower's nation-building experiment was undertaken outside the context of Cold War mentality. I do not dispute the significance of the Cold War in the shaping of American diplomacy in Vietnam; it is paramount to understanding U.S. action and the evolution of the war. I argue that Cold War mentality, coupled with the experience of Passage to Freedom and the emergence of a moral obligation to the Vietnamese people, help to broaden, and perhaps make even more complicated, America's longest war.

Special thanks for this work go to Sherri Lynn Brouillette, my wife, who read through earlier versions of this manuscript and, in addition to editing my faulty prose, asked the questions necessary to make the final version of the book understandable. It takes a unique individual to do this; I am lucky enough to have married one. James R. Reckner, director of the Vietnam Center and Archive at Texas Tech University, also deserves a note of thanks for his encouragement in the project and continued support. The Vietnam Archive continues to be one of the real treasures for historians of the Vietnam War, and under the direction of Reckner and Steve Maxner, my successor at the Vietnam Archive, it promises to achieve more than its most vocal supporters could have imaged. The Naval Historical Center provided a wealth of information on Rear Admiral Lorenzo S. Sabin and the operation as well as financial assistance through the Vice Admiral Edwin B. Hooper Research Grant in 2001. Also, I wish to thank William S. Dudley and Edward J. Marolda of the Naval Historical Center for their kind words and support.

A few veteran sailors deserve a special note of thanks as well. Ted Bobinski (USS *Consolation*), John L. Cole (USS *Calvert*), William A. Greene (USS *Gunston Hall*), Noah Joyner (USS *Estes*), Jack Lemasters (LST-887), Ralph Limon (USS *Telfair*), Russ Macdonald (USS *Montrose*), Fred C. Machado (USS *Montague*), Les and Dorothy Rutherford (USS *Menard*), and Jim Ruotsala (USS *Montrose*) all helped to coordinate the members of their associations for oral history interviews and allowed me access to their association reunions. Robert Mix, who served with

Admiral Sabin, also a willing participant, provided a link to a man I never had the chance to meet and offered encouragement and cajoling, when necessary, to help me get this book finished. Without their help, this book would not be nearly as complete. The names of all the sailors who contributed to the project, through either interviews or personal donations of material, are listed in the bibliography.

This book started as an exploration of the stories of those sailors who served aboard the ships of Task Force 90. It evolved into something much more. To the more than forty sailors I interviewed and the many hundreds who served on the ships of Task Force 90: I hope you will find the story of your humanitarianism inspiring. You should know that I tried to include as many of your thoughts as reasonable. To other readers of this book: the oral history interviews, copies or originals of photographs, slides, letters, and documents reside in the Vietnam Archive at Texas Tech University. This historical event demands preservation, and the Vietnam Archive is the only place I consider safe enough to entrust with the memories and materials of the sailors who made this history.

Operation Passage to Freedom

CHAPTER 1

★★★★★★★★★★★★★★★

The Road to Geneva

By the time of the presidential election of 1952, with its mandate for change that brought Dwight D. Eisenhower into the White House, the United States found itself even more deeply engaged in a Cold War with the Soviet Union. This conflict, which these adversaries fought in the military, diplomatic, political, economic, social, and cultural arenas, had moved beyond the continent of Europe. For many in the new administration, this global threat represented a clear danger to the United States, which had not only the responsibility to defend American values at home and abroad but also an obligation to protect those nations and people who were resisting Soviet communism.

Since the end of World War II, both American and Soviet actions around the world had helped to deepen the distrust between the two postwar powers. George F. Kennan, the chargé d'affaires in Moscow, set the tone of the earlier relationship with his famous February 22, 1946, "long telegram," in which he posited the reasons for Soviet action. Kennan maintained that the United States could not negotiate with the Soviet Union, which he argued was both neurotic in its view of world affairs and driven by a historic sense of insecurity. Indeed, Soviet action in consolidating its control in Poland, Rumania, Finland, Bulgaria, Hungary, Yugoslavia, and Czechoslovakia after World War II affirmed this notion. Never again, as Stalin would argue, would the Soviet Union leave its western borders susceptible to invasion.[1]

This distrust between the Soviet Union and the United States intensified throughout the presidency of Harry S Truman. In Europe, perceived Soviet threats against Greece and Turkey culminated in the pronouncement of the 1947 Truman Doctrine, which enunciated the necessity of protecting governments against insurgencies. Truman reinforced American active internationalism in Berlin when the Soviets initiated a blockade of that city from June 1948 to May 1949 in an effort to force the United States to bend to their will. The lesson learned from the American victory in the Berlin Airlift was never to retreat from the face of communist aggression. Through the Truman presidency, containment became the byword of the day. Once again, Kennan, by then director of the State Department's policy planning staff, in his 1947 *Foreign Affairs* article, "The Sources of Soviet Conduct," argued that the United States must contain the Soviet Union wherever Soviet action threatened interests beyond its borders. With the fall of China in 1949 and the invasion of the Republic of Korea in 1950, the United States became more vigilant of Soviet encroachment in the free world.

By the time Eisenhower became president, the Cold War mentality had become entrenched in American society. Eisenhower was not only faced with the challenge of confrontational Soviet aggression, but he also had to deal with the rise of new nations out of the ashes of the old colonial system. Whereas Truman had remained focused on the ever-present Soviet threat in Europe, Eisenhower recognized that future Cold War battles would be fought in the Third World. It is through these circumstances that American foreign policy leaders developed the "zero-sum" theory; any country that turned away from democracy (a loss for the United States) was a gain for the Soviet Union. This policy tended to ignore the nature of indigenous nationalist movements and assumed that the Soviet Union inspired much of the agitation in the Third World.

In early 1954 the eyes of the average American were not focused on Indochina. Having just completed a three-year military engagement on the Korean peninsula, the American public paid little attention to the struggles of the French in the First Indochina War. It was that region, in Southeast Asia, that would serve as a major test for the administration as a new battle in the Cold War emerged. At the time of Eisenhower's inauguration, the French had been fighting in Indochina for seven years against an insurgency named the Viet Nam Doc Lap Dong Minh Hoi

(Vietnam Independence League), also known as the Viet Minh.[2] During that time France had failed to subdue the Viet Minh and had grown increasingly reliant on U.S. financial assistance to continue its war. As U.S. financial obligations to the French Union forces increased, American officials began to express grave doubts about the viability of France's continued presence in Indochina. Military leaders were reluctant to commit U.S. personnel and resources to the French venture because of limited resources, the nature of the indigenous war, and worry about French resolve to stay the course in the region.[3] The military's opposition to an increased American presence in Indochina was reinforced by the new commander in chief, who required evidence of French resolve in the region before continuing to finance the war. American pressure for action, coupled with a French desire for positive gains, resulted in a new strategy in the Tonkin region that would ultimately lead to the end of French rule in Indochina.

On May 8, 1953, General Henri Navarre replaced General Raoul Salan as the commander in chief of the French Union forces in Indochina. Navarre was determined to refocus French efforts in Indochina, which had, up to that point, been largely static. The Navarre Plan, as it would become known, was designed to consolidate the French position in the south of Vietnam through a strategy of pacification and defense. Once the south was secured—he expected this to occur by the fall of 1954—Navarre planned to use the northern elements of the French Union forces, which would have been consolidated by that point, to launch an offensive against the areas known to be occupied by the Viet Minh. Navarre expected this northern phase to last into 1956, assuming he received the reinforcements requested from the French government.[4]

Yet even before the southern phases of the operation began, the Viet Minh forces under the command of Vo Nguyen Giap disrupted Navarre's timetable. Viet Minh forces in the North began a preemptive attack against the French Union forces who denied their attempts at consolidation. These Viet Minh forces had been using the mountains of Laos as a base of operations and operated between the two countries with impunity. French concerns for the defense of Laos as well as the need to cut off the Viet Minh routes between the two countries led Navarre to devise Operation Castor, a modification to the original Navarre Plan.[5] The importance of Laos and its continued security increased in October 1953 with the signing of the Treaty of Amity and Association with the French, reaffirming the French-Laotian relationship under which Laos acknowledged loyalty to France and its membership in the French Union. With this treaty the protection of Laos became a matter of French honor, and Navarre's Operation Castor offered a solution to the growing crisis with the Viet Minh in northern Vietnam and Laos.

The main goal of Operation Castor was to disrupt the free flow of Viet Minh troops along Route 41 from Laos to North Vietnam. On November 20, Navarre sent six battalions of the Expeditionary Corps into a strategic valley in the Dien Bien district. The French Union forces established their garrison to the northwest of the village of Dien Bien Phu in an area that had served as a fortress in previous years of the First Indochina War. The objective of the garrison was to serve as a blocking force against the Viet Minh. It was expected that the Viet Minh would see this move as a strategic imposition to their northern strategy and thus be forced to confront the French Union forces. The fortress at Dien Bien Phu was designed to confound the Viet Minh and force them to react to the French. With this in mind, the French commander at Dien Bien Phu, Christian Marie Ferdinand de la Croix de Castries, dug in and waited for the Viet Minh to react. A fatal flaw in the French strategy, however, was an underestimation of Viet Minh capabilities. Both Navarre and de Castries failed to anticipate that the Viet Minh could move enough personnel to threaten the French Union forces. The French also maintained that it would be impossible to move siege artillery up the steep slopes surrounding the valley fortress. They were proven wrong.

For Ho Chi Minh, political leader of the Vietnamese resistance, and his military commander, Vo Nguyen Giap, Dien Bien Phu offered a unique opportunity to change the course of the war. Neither the French nor the Viet Minh were willing to make concessions to end the hostilities. A Viet Minh victory at Dien Bien Phu, mused Ho and Giap, might force France to reconsider the cost of having an empire in Indochina and precipitate French withdrawal from the region. Consequently, at the end of December, Ho and Giap decided that they would confront the French at Dien Bien Phu and set about a plan to encircle the fortress and, using weapons from the stockpile of World War II lend-lease equipment captured by the People's Republic of China (PRC) during the Korean War, force the French to action. Navarre responded to the challenge and ordered that

Dien Bien Phu be held at all costs. Thus, the decisive battle for Indochina that would decide the fate of the French colonial empire in Asia commenced in the remote area of Dien Bien Phu. By the end of January, the Viet Minh achieved their objective. The French at Dien Bien Phu were cut off, and relief columns were ambushed along the road from Hanoi.[6] With the increase of antiaircraft artillery and control of the high ground, Giap was able to devise his strategy for victory.

As the battle waged at Dien Bien Phu, Ho Chi Minh made it known that he would entertain a political solution to the Indochina situation. The French National Assembly then began to pressure Prime Minister Joseph Laniel to begin negotiations, led by Pierre Mendes-France, with the Viet Minh. With pressure from those in opposition to the war, the Laniel government agreed to enter negotiations on the Indochina situation toward a possible solution to the problem. The French agreed to hold talks during the already scheduled Geneva Conference on the Korean armistice and the future of that peninsula. These negotiations, agreed to by Ho Chi Minh and the Democratic Republic of Vietnam (DRV), were to begin on May 8. With the agreements, the Viet Minh established a timetable from which their struggle at Dien Bien Phu would be orchestrated. For Ho Chi Minh and Vo Nguyen Giap, it was imperative to achieve some semblance of victory at Dien Bien Phu before the commencement of negotiations at Geneva. By the end of February, the Viet Minh had managed to set into place, with the help of the PRC, enough troops and supplies to begin significant offensive operations, which were designed to overrun the fortress. Giap, however, remained cautious of a frontal assault on the fortified French position until he could ensure victory. He thought that this had been achieved a few weeks later when, on March 13, the Viet Minh launched their assault. After an intense artillery barrage, the Viet Minh forces charged the outlying French outposts, achieving both a tactical surprise and early gains. These advantages were balanced by a high cost paid in casualties. Giap reformulated his strategy on March 17 into a more protracted siege of the fortress and began construction of forward trenches to minimize the area of exposure for Viet Minh troops when they launched their frontal assaults. The tactic was cautious but effective, as the French Union forces were not prepared or able to maintain their defensive positions for a prolonged siege. By the end of March, the situation had reached a critical level when the French found it increasingly difficult to continue their resupply of troops by air. As the situation deteriorated on the ground in Indochina, the French turned to the United States for possible solutions to this crisis.

The United States had not been passive about the French situation in Indochina, nor had it remained a silent observer of events as they unfolded in the early days of 1954. The dilemma for the United States was how to respond to the crisis in a way that complemented Eisenhower's New Look military strategy and Secretary of State John Foster Dulles' brinksmanship tactics. By the end of March, the United States recognized that it needed to take a more active role, though that role had not yet been defined. When Dulles addressed the Overseas Press Club of America on March 29, he outlined the themes of American foreign policy toward Indochina, cautioning the PRC against intervention in Indochina while warning the Viet Minh that the United States would deny them control of Vietnam. He called for a coalition to counter communism in Southeast Asia, suggesting that this threat, if left unchecked, would have grave consequences for the region's noncommunist countries. Dulles proposed a policy of United Action by which nations directly concerned with the crisis in the region, but specifically the United States and Britain, would form a coalition and contribute military personnel to the French effort in Indochina to stave off looming disaster at Dien Bien Phu and help defeat the Viet Minh.[7]

United Action took on a more serious tone on April 3, when Dulles and Chairman of the Joint Chiefs of Staff Arthur Radford met with key congressional leaders to explain the policy.[8] The meeting, which focused on an American response to the deteriorating situation at Dien Bien Phu, outlined the significance of Indochina to Southeast Asia and Cold War policies. Dulles argued that a settlement with the Viet Minh would weaken America's strategic position in the world; it is important to note that only five years had passed since the loss of China to communism during the Truman administration. Just as that loss severely hampered Truman's foreign and domestic policy, Dulles argued, the loss of Indochina would result in a weakening of allied resolve to defend against communist insurrection and a turning point in the Cold War. The battle for Indochina was more than a struggle for the survival of French colonialism. It was a significant battle in the Cold War and critical for American prestige and power. More than just an objective of foreign policy, the Indochina situation took on the aura of moral obligation for the United States to assist those nations under the threat of communist insurgency as well as to continue the American diplomatic tradition of providing assistance to any nation that required American aid. This was an obligation hurt by the fall of China to communism in 1949 and the stalemate during the Korean War, which successfully defended that country, but at a terrible loss of life and resources.

This concept of moral obligation remained vivid during the debate on United Action and the American response to the Dien Bien Phu crisis. In pressuring the British to become active in the defense of the French position, Eisenhower, in a personal appeal to Prime Minister Winston Churchill, reminded him of the failures before World War II: "We failed to halt Hirohito, Mussolini and Hitler by not acting in unity and in time."[9] Even with the French weakening, Eisenhower believed that Britain and the United States, united, could turn a desperate situation positive. The failure of resolve—the failure to fulfill the obligation as a protector of the free world—was not lost on Churchill. For Eisenhower, the former supreme commander of Allied forces in Europe during the war, this appeal was more than words; it was the basis of his foreign policy toward Indochina. The moral obligation theme was publicly reinforced during an April 7 presidential message to the American people, during which Eisenhower introduced his version of the domino theory: "You have a row of dominoes set up." he began. "You knock over the first one, and what will happen to the last one is the certainty that it will go over very quickly."[10] Eisenhower continued by mentioning the 1949 fall of China to the communists and warned that no more land or people could be lost in Asia.

The situation at Dien Bien Phu continued to deteriorate during the latter part of April. The United States provided limited assistance to the French, but, beyond materials and transport of men, there was little it could accomplish without congressional authorization. On April 22, 1954, Dulles and ambassador to France C. Douglas Dillon met with French foreign minister Georges Bidault and French army chief of staff General Paul Henri Romuald Ely in Paris. Both Bidault and Ely believed the situation at Dien Bien Phu was hopeless. They suggested that nothing would save the situation except a massive air intervention from the United States, referring to Operation Vautour (Vulture), which proposed using U.S. aircraft to launch an air attack on Viet Minh positions surrounding the beleaguered fortress.[11] When Dulles questioned the practicality of more planes when there were not enough men to maintain them, Bidault denied this problem. Bidault indicated that he favored internationalizing the war if it meant rescuing Dien Bien Phu. He argued that the United Kingdom could not provide much help and should not be considered as the United States contemplated the situation.

Dulles reported this to Eisenhower, who responded accordingly. There could be no American action without allied inclusion. Eisenhower suggested to Dulles that he make sure the British government appreciated the precarious situation and the peril of French collapse in the region. "The British must not be able merely to shut their eyes," Eisenhower contended, "and later plead blindness as an alibi for failing to propose a positive program."[12] At a morning meeting on April 23, 1954, Bidault told Dulles that the situation at Dien Bien Phu was desperate. The French had expended their last reserves in a failed attempt to regain Point Huguette, one of the strategic strong points that surrounded the fortress. Navarre had informed Bidault that there were two options: a massive B-29 bomber attack or a cease-fire request for all of Indochina.[13] When Bidault offered Dulles the two French options—negotiated peace or internationalization of the war—the secretary of state explained that air intervention was impossible.

At dinner that night, Dulles reported to Eisenhower that British foreign secretary Anthony Eden doubted the British would cooperate should the United States enter the fight in Indochina. The United Kingdom feared another world war. Bidault, at the same dinner, told Dulles that if the United States intervened at Dien Bien Phu and the French fortress fell, then the French would continue the fight as a matter of honor. If the United States failed to become involved militarily and the fortress collapsed, then there would be no option but defeat, withdrawal, and a change in the French government toward the left.[14] Bidault, in many respects, used this diplomatic maneuver to place the burden of Dien Bien Phu, a continued French presence in Indochina, and the survival of a pro-Western French government on the United States. This ploy had long been a suspicion in American circles. It did not change the situation's outlook, only its urgency.

In an April 25, 1954, meeting, Eden suggested to Dulles that it would be better to keep the communists guessing about the Allies' next move should the conference fail.[15] Because he believed that Dien Bien Phu was lost, any military assistance to the fortress now would be ineffective and costly. At the conference, Eden offered the French all the diplomatic support they needed to keep them in Indochina until the parties involved reached an adequate settlement. After that, the United Kingdom would join in guaranteeing the settlement while it agreed to plan secret military measures with the United States to defend Thailand and the rest of Southeast Asia should the French capitulate at the conference. Although Dulles agreed that air intervention at Dien Bien Phu was futile, Eden's newest stance disheartened him. Dulles asserted that French capitulation in Indochina was likely because of the British position.[16] It was important, from Dulles' perspective, to ensure that the French believed the British and Americans would support them more after the fall of the fortress than they had earlier. At this point Eden agreed to disagree, stating that, while he realized the United Kingdom's position was not what Dulles wished, it was as far as he and the British government would commit.[17]

While at Geneva, Dulles seems to have been wavering back and forth on the new form of United Action. On April 25, 1954, he sent a telegram to Acting Secretary of State Christian Herter in which he stated that armed intervention by executive action was not warranted. The uncertainty of the French government in maintaining power provoked Dulles to say that the United States could not intervene. It would be embarrassing to the U.S. government to go into Indochina only to have its actions repudiated by the French.[18] The next day, Dulles chided the narrow British approach. The United Kingdom, he complained, minimized the collective approach and maximized the risks and potential requirements.[19] He would warn Churchill of the adverse congressional and public opinion associated with the United Kingdom's position of standing against the United States, but he expected no change in the British stance.

The situation became more complicated after Dillon met with Réne Pleven, French minister for national defense. Pleven told Dillon that the French would make every effort to hold on to Dien Bien Phu for at least three more weeks. The French hoped the United States would use that period to overcome internal political obstacles and resolve any lingering doubt in order to become more active in Indochina.[20] This French request occurred even though Pleven believed the United States would not react without British concurrence, but Pleven either did not understand the congressional restrictions forced upon Dulles or did not fully comprehend the minimal effect of the latest French change of heart. The French move was too little, too late.

The French fortress at Dien Bien Phu finally fell on May 7, 1954. While the military loss was recoverable, the political repercussions were decisive to French government and army morale. In a speech after the fall, Dulles provided for the possibility of intervention in Indochina.[21] Dulles made sure the French ambassador to the United States, Henri Bonnet, understood that the United States was prepared to talk about internationalization of the conflict when the French were ready.[22] He assumed the French would be prepared to negotiate as soon as the communists revealed their terms at Geneva.

With the United Kingdom no longer a key participant in United Action, the affair took on a new level of seriousness. In a telegram to the American embassy in Paris, Dulles outlined the new conditions for intervention.[23] The French and Indochinese would have to make a formal request to the United States. Dulles had already stated that this would happen when the communists revealed their position. Thailand and the Philippines must agree to participate immediately. Australia and New Zealand would join after the Australian election if the United States invoked the ANZUS Treaty. There was reason for Dulles to believe these conditions would be met. The United States would bring this matter to the United Nations, but this was a formality. The Allies needed to agree on a command structure and process to train the indigenous troops. Evidently, the United States would take the lead in this matter. Finally, France would have to agree to the independence of the Associated States as well as keep troops intact in Indochina during United Action. Dulles did believe the French would internationalize the war and make an "honorable" arrangement with the Associated States to preserve French prestige. While Dulles had envisioned what must be done in Indochina, there was still no indication as to how it would be done. This remained the obstacle for Australia and the U.S. Congress, neither of which would unconditionally support Eisenhower and Dulles.

At the Geneva Conference, the situation remained unchanged, primarily because of French maneuvers to strengthen their position during negotiations. Bidault told Eden that the United States and France were working out an agreement to send three American divisions to Indochina should the conference fail. While Bidault said he regarded this move as "distant thunder" that might help the conference, the French used the story to try to reestablish control at the conference.[24] Reports circulated at Geneva that reinforced the notion of American deployment of infantry. One report concluded that Eisenhower and Dulles were conditioning the American public and Congress to the idea of intervention in Southeast Asia and argued that there was no great opposition to the use of ground forces in the next conflict despite the results of two recent world wars.[25] Allied fears were shortly put to rest. On June 7, 1954, Dulles instructed the American ambassador to France, C. Douglas Dillon, to inform Prime Minister Joseph Laniel that the French must stop talking about the employment of U.S. Marines in the Tonkin Delta. If they did not, the State Department might issue a denial that would cause much embarrassment.[26] As the Geneva Conference progressed, the likelihood of United Action decreased dramatically.

The United States would not act without French commitments, and the French were not forthcoming. Dulles allowed the French to use the United States, but only to keep the communists guessing at the conference. He realized they were seeking only the best possible settlement for themselves. The possibility of United Action ended, in Dulles' mind, on June 20, 1954, when the French government obtained a cease-fire agreement in Indochina. That agreement then led to the Geneva Agreements of July, 20–21, 1954, and the creation of the two Vietnams, Laos, and Cambodia.[27] There was little the United States could accomplish militarily without allied and congressional support. United Action had a slight chance of occurring without communist aggression and no chance of proceeding while the United States continued to project a confused policy toward Vietnam, and French actions indicated that its time in Indochina was at an end. While Eisenhower and Dulles might have had the opportunity to prevent the Viet Minh's total victory, they were not able to thwart the advance of the enemy. Both Dulles and Eisenhower would blame the intransigence of the United Kingdom and the faltering of the French government for the failure in Indochina.

American commitment to the Vietnamese would not end with the fall of Dien Bien Phu or the settlement at Geneva, however. Instead, these events ushered in a new era of U.S. commitment to Vietnam, one that would formulate as a result of the Geneva Agreements and the exodus of Vietnamese from the North to the South.

The Geneva Conference concluded on July 20, 1954, with a cease-fire agreement to begin in North Vietnam at 7:00 a.m. on July 27, 1954; in central Vietnam at 7:00 a.m. on August 1, 1954; and in South Vietnam at 7:00 a.m. on August 11, 1954. Under the terms of the Geneva Agreements, Vietnam was divided into two temporary zones, with a provisional line running along the Son Ben Hai River to Bo Ho Su and, from there, due west to the Laotian border. With the DRV and its People's Army of Vietnam or Viet Minh forces to the north and the Republic of Vietnam with the remnants of a defeated French army and a young Vietnamese military to the south, the two Vietnams emerged divided along the seventeenth parallel. The North fell within the Viet Minh sphere of influence and organized into the DRV, while the Republic of Vietnam formed to the south of the Demilitarized Zone and, with the support of the United States, began to fashion into a viable member of the international community opposed to communism.

The agreement resulting from the 1954 Geneva Conference provided for the cessation of all hostilities and the peaceful reintegration of North and South through the process of elections to take place no later than July 21, 1956, two years after the signing of the Final Declaration of the Geneva Conference. Of the delegates at the conference, only France and the DRV signed the document (the former by Brigadier General Henri Delteil) for the commander in chief of the French Union forces in Indochina; the latter by Vice Minister of National Defence of the Democratic Republic of Vietnam Ta Quang Buu for the commander in chief of the People's Army of Vietnam. For the United States, the final agreement represented anything but a successful conclusion to the negotiating process. Article eight of the final declaration stated, "The provisions of the agreements on the cessation of hostilities intended to ensure the protection of individual and of property must be most strictly applied and must, in particular, allow everyone in Viet-Nam to decide freely in which zone he wishes to live."[28] Article fourteen of the agreement outlined the political and administrative measure for the regrouping of personnel on either side of the seventeenth parallel. Section (d) of this article stated, "From the date of entry into force of the present Agreement until the movement

CHINA

Wenlan • • Kaihua
Gejiu •
Simao •
Lao Cai
Phong
Saly •
Dien Bien Phu •
Luong
Nam Tha •
Muong Sai •
Samneua •

Xinjing •
Nanning •

Gui Xian •

CHINA
Yulin •

Yen Bai •
NORTH VIETNAM
Lang Son •
Viet Tri •
Hoa Binh •
Hanoi •
Hon Gai •
Hai Phong •

Zhanjiang •

Nam Dinh •

LAOS

Luang
Prabang •
Xiangkhoang •
Sayaboury •

Nam Binh •

Thanh Hoa •

HAINAN
ISLAND

Gulf of Tonkin

Vientiane •
Nong Khai •
Udon
Thani •
Nakhon Phanom •

Vinh •

Dong Hoi •

Phitsanulok •

Khon Kaen •

Muong
Xepon •
Savannakhet •

Vinh Linh •
DEMILITARIZED ZONE
Cam Lo • • Quang Tri City
Khe Sanh •
Hue • • Phu Bai
An Hoa • • Da Nang

THAILAND

Surin •
Nakhon
Ratchasima •

Ubon
Ratchathani •
Si Sa Ket •
Warin
Chamrap •

Saravane •
Pakse •
Attopeu •

Tam Ky • • Chu Lai
• My Lai
Dak To •
Kontum •

Sara Buri •

Bangkok
Aranyaprathet •

Sisophon •

Pleiku •
• Qui Nhon
An Khe •

Siem Reap •
Battambang •
Pursat •

Stoeng Treng •
Lomphat •

**SOUTH
VIETNAM**
• Tuy Hoa

CAMBODIA
Kompang
Thom •
Kompong
Cham •

Ban Me Thuot •

• Gia Nghia

Nha Trang •
Cam Ranh •

Phnom Penh
Kompong
Speu •

Phuoc
Binh •
Tay Ninh •
Bao Loc •

Da Lat •

Phan Rhang •

Gulf of Thailand

Kompong
Sam •
Kampot •
Ha Tien •
My Tho •

Saigon
Long Binh •
Vung Tau •

Phan Thiet •

Rach Gia •
Can Tho •

Bac Lieu •

CON SON

South China Sea

Indochina in 1954,
showing the DMZ

Map 1.1.

of troops is completed, any civilians residing in a district controlled by one party who wish to go to live in the zone assigned to the other party shall be permitted and helped to do so by the authorities in that district." Article fifteen of the agreement gave residents from both sides of the newly divided Vietnam a maximum of three hundred days for the withdrawal and transfer of military forces, equipment, and supplies from any given region. Theoretically, during the evacuation of French troops from North Vietnam, Vietnamese civilians would have the opportunity for free passage to the South.

The result of these three articles was the massive migration of Vietnamese from north to south as well as smaller movement from south to north. Operation Passage to Freedom, or Operation Exodus, as named by South Vietnam, saw the movement of more than 810,000 Vietnamese from north of the seventeenth parallel to south of it. The movement of people and the logistical nightmare of resettling the population in the war-torn South challenged the United States in what would be considered the first major humanitarian effort to aid the Vietnamese people.

Those Vietnamese who made the decision to leave their homes in the North did so for many reasons. Approximately one-third of the people who fled were Catholics and left as a result of Viet Minh treatment of those who followed the Church. They were also encouraged to leave by their village priests, who often served not only as their spiritual leaders but also their guides and translators during the passage and organizers of their new villages once they settled in the South. Another significant group to flee was those who had assisted the French in their colonial conquest of the region. These individuals feared their future in the North, and rightfully so. Once they were identified by the Viet Minh they underwent varying degrees of torture and degradation. Many ethnic groups, such as the Chinese Nung, departed their ancestral homes for fear of Viet Minh retribution and for the prospects of a better future in the South. Others left because members of their family or village had made that decision. No reliable surveys were conducted during this period to assess motivation, although many refugee stories confirm these motivations. Indeed, it would have been difficult as well as demanding of time and resources to gather this data. Americans involved in this operation perceived that it was a flight from communism that motivated the Vietnamese; that was enough for them to dedicate the time and energy necessary to fulfill their end of the passage to freedom.

This episode in Vietnamese history would also have a profound effect on those Americans who experienced it. The plight of the Vietnamese people escaping the rule of the DRV was one filled with danger and hardship. The desire of those Vietnamese fleeing communism in the North was not lost on the Americans. Coupled with the embedded Cold War mentality that had developed in the previous decade, the mass exodus of Vietnamese demanded an American response. Operation Passage to Freedom was the result, but American interests in the region would continue beyond the transfer of Vietnamese from the North to the South. American experiences and actions during the operation entrenched the notion of moral obligation by the United States toward the new Republic of Vietnam and reinforced early American commitment to building a nation below the seventeenth parallel that would be able to withstand the threat of its communist neighbor and emerge as a responsible, active member of the international community.

The American sailors who participated in Operation Passage to Freedom were the first Americans many Vietnamese had ever seen. These bluejackets were only doing the job assigned to them, but they represented so much more. They were the first contact, ambassadors for the United States participating in one of the largest evacuations the world had ever seen. This humanitarian effort would be overshadowed by U.S. involvement in Vietnam in the 1960s and 1970s, but the effect on those who participated and those who were evacuated has stood the test of time.

CHAPTER 2

The Growing Crisis

From the end of the Geneva Conference to the formal commencement of U.S. assistance in the evacuation of French and Vietnamese personnel during Operation Passage to Freedom, the focus of concern for those present in Indochina was the growing refugee problem. The need for organization and coordination among units responsible for assisting in the relocation, resettlement, and reemployment of refugees surfaced as the number of displaced persons increased. Without a formal request by the French or Vietnamese for assistance in transporting evacuees, the best the American organizations could do was plan and prepare for the inevitable problems and obstacles that would result from the influx of people from the North.

The United States had a few agencies that could manage the emerging situation in Indochina. The Foreign Operations Administration (FOA) was the most appropriate, having been created in 1953 to coordinate all American foreign economic and technical assistance programs. Because it also was involved in the coordination of mutual security activities, it was well suited to assist in the organization of the Vietnamese evacuees as they assumed refugee status upon arriving in the South. When the Mutual Security Act of 1954 terminated the FOA through Executive Order 10610 on May 9, 1955, its successor, the International Cooperation Administration, continued to play a role in the development of South Vietnam. During Operation Passage to Freedom, however, it was the FOA that coordinated the American relief effort to the Vietnamese refugees. Under the FOA, the Special Technical and Economic Mission (STEM) and United States Overseas Mission (USOM) each would play a valuable role in the South Vietnamese nation-building experiment.

The problem of displaced people from the First Indochina War (1945–1954) had scarred the countryside, from the Tonkin Delta to the Mekong Delta. The war had scattered the refugees, who fled the conflict as well as Viet Minh and French mistreatment, throughout Indochina. While the problems of this population would pale in comparison to the refugee situation in August 1954, the U.S. officials learned many lessons and gained valuable experience by conducting field trips and assisting those in need. From January 16 to 19, 1954, STEM members Herman J. Holiday, chief of the Community Development Division, and Dr. Hildrus A. Poindexter of the Health and Sanitation Division visited refugee camps in Lakhorne, Thailand, to determine the needs of Laotian refugees resettled there as a result of the war.[1] There had been a reported five thousand Laotian refugees in the village of Lakhorne, but the team found only five hundred; the other forty-five hundred had been returned to Savannakhet to assist with the military operations as civilian aides. Holiday and Poindexter found the refugees in need of rice and medical supplies, both of which were to be supplied under a Laotian community development project. Malaria was the most prevalent medical problem, although the sole Laotian nurse in charge of medical care, Madame Manivnanh, provided a long list of medical supplies required for the proper treatment for those under her care. Holiday and Poindexter discovered, during the course of this field trip, that the refugee problem in small doses was quite manageable. Even with a lack of food and medical supplies, the existing level of care was adequate as long as the refugees could be returned to their original homes in a timely manner. The question of a dramatically larger number of displaced persons, many of whom sought permanent resettlement, was not considered. In the early days of 1954, with the development of the great fortress in the northwest of Vietnam at Dien Bien Phu and a recent French promise of a swift end to the conflict, the division of Indochina was inconceivable. There was no reason for the French to plan contingencies for the transportation and care of refugees.

Although the French had not really prepared for the refugee resettlement, field trips by members of USOM to North Vietnam yielded additional information regarding how the United States might respond to the refugee population. On January 25, USOM representatives conducted a field trip to the province of Bui Chu, which contained 365 villages.[2] Only 16 of these villages were considered secure by daylight. Of the province's 440,000 citizens, 103,000 resided within the 16 villages, all of which were grouped around the central town of Bui Chu. Carter de Paul, USOM special representative to North Vietnam; William L. Haid of the Community Development Division; and R. Bruce Salley of the Health and Sanitation Division went to Bui Chu to assess the conditions of the area and recommend appropriate action for the problems they observed. Unlike the refugee camp visited in Laos, Bui Chu was situated in the middle of the conflict between the French Union forces and the Viet Minh forces. It was unlikely that the eight to ten thousand refugees in the city of Bui Chu would be able to return to their homes unless the French Union forces achieved a significant victory at Dien Bien Phu. The area observed, therefore, resembled more closely the daily conditions of North Vietnam. There was one hospital with eighty-five beds to serve the entire province. As a result, the hospital experienced severe overcrowding, with two or three patients per bed. Another situation that foretold the difficult conditions the United States might face with increased participation in the evacuation was the Quonset hut hospital built with U.S. aid. The hospital had been completed earlier and was ready for occupation except for lack of a water tank and furnishings. A Vietnamese physician was ready to supervise the hospital once it had the last two items. Until the visit by the American representatives, however, there was no knowledge of the missing two items, nor was it understood that the hospital was not in use. The inability to determine, then communicate needs in order to maximize use of American resources plagued early U.S. involvement in Indochina.

Even when American resources were deployed, they did not always provide the greatest benefit. American aid had provided a thirty-three kilowatt generating plant to Bui Chu, but it was not in use because the cost of fuel was greater than the revenue brought in by those who used the electricity. Vietnamese officials could not raise the price for electricity because the increased price would force existing customers to go back to gas lamps. The Vietnamese needed additional financial aid to connect the plant with additional customers, which would bring enough revenue in to pay for the fuel to run the generators. As a result, the generator was useless unless more customers were added to the grid to offset the price of fuel to produce electricity. The North Vietnamese Office of Social Action agreed to pay the difference in fuel costs to keep the plant operating while additional customers were connected and others were educated on the advantages of electricity. The representatives recommended seeing the project through and improving the safety conditions of the generator. The representatives recommended an additional two million piasters[3] from available American aid to enable the province to complete existing projects, provide blankets and other relief supplies, and help build an additional water tower in the new village of Ngoc Huu to supply newly arriving refugees in Bui Chu province. Again, without U.S. intervention the problem would not have come to the fore, and the generator would have remained idle. The lessons learned during this field trip were threefold. First, the refugee problem in the North was growing, and with that growth the importance of coordinated aid was paramount. Second, previous American aid projects needed follow-up to ensure that they were complete and operational. Finally, Carter de Paul maintained that much of the goodwill generated from promises of aid was lost because of delays in releasing emergency relief funds. "The refugee may appreciate a smile and kind words," he argued, "but he can't eat them and they don't keep his children warm."[4]

Other field trips to the central part of Vietnam provided recommendations for helping the refugees, foreshadowing the need after the Geneva Conference. After the postponement of a trip to Tuy Hoa by USOM Representative Haid, he was able to report on the activities of the Office of Social Action around Hue.[5] Haid visited An Nong, Phu Bai, and Gia Le, where approximately twelve hundred and fifty families had been displaced as a result of French efforts to deprive Viet Minh forces of shelter and tribute. During his visit Haid learned of a program that provided prefabricated shelters that refugees constructed themselves. He recommended that STEM support this effort and develop similar programs as the need for shelter increased. Another problem he observed was that refugees needed to be retrained in order for them to become self-sufficient in their new environment. He recommended establishing artisan schools and cooperatives for greater production as well as providing the salaries for Vietnamese social workers involved in the refugee effort. As after the visit to Bui Chu, Haid recommended streamlining the funding of relief projects, arguing that "homeless and hungry people can't appreciate red tape."[6] These recommendations served as the model for initial U.S. aid to Vietnam.

A field trip to points south of Hue on April 2 provided a further glimpse into the growing concern of the refugee crisis.[7] The STEM special representative for central Vietnam, Richard C. Matheron, visited the province of Quang Binh to inspect refugee and resettlement camps established as a result of the increased Viet Minh fighting in the area. Under a tighter than usual French escort, which included a tank, a half-track, and two 6 x 6 GMC trucks loaded with French Union soldiers, the party traveled from Dong Hoi thirty-two kilometers south to Phu Viet, visiting Thach Xa Ha during the inspection. Lessons learned during this trip, relevant to future resettlement after Geneva, were significant. Matheron witnessed less than adequate sanitary facilities, overcrowding, and other characteristics prevalent during the previous field trips to refugee and resettlement areas. During the one-and-one-half-hour trip from Dong Hoi to Phu Viet, Matheron reviewed extensive rice cultivation areas, some of which were in use, though many went uncultivated because of Viet Minh threats or the lack of tools and work animals necessary to make the work profitable. A few Viet Minh could disrupt an entire region with their presence and the threat of violence and intimidation. That Matheron had to conduct his field trip with an armed escort helped to reinforce this point.

It was during this trip that the chief of the province, Nguyen van Tich, informed Matheron that refugees received rice and fish for only five days after resettlement. Because it took nearly six months for a rice harvest to mature, the refugees did not have enough food before they could become self-sufficient. Although land was plentiful and equipment and supplies for cultivation were within reach, emergency relief needed to be extended until refugees could provide for themselves. This was not a short-term program; rather, it was one that required a long-term commitment to ensure that those displaced would receive the necessary aid and support to guarantee their survival. Matheron recommended an extension of existing American foreign aid to include emergency food supplies for agricultural refugees for a period of at least six months. These supplies would greatly aid the refugee population as well as secure American goodwill with the local officials and displaced population.

A follow-up field trip at the end of July showed little progress toward the objectives, concluding that "there had been too much talking and too little action."[8] The Vietnamese had relied on schools in Quang Tri, Dong Ha, and Tourane (Danang) to house the refugees rather than construct buildings in reception centers to handle the influx. Matheron also found the Vietnamese unconcerned with the vaccination and sanitary environment in central Vietnam. He recommended that STEM approve the National Emergency Relief Project from the Ministry of Social Action when it was presented and suggested that STEM send a health technician and a qualified refugee to travel among the reception areas to provide assistance and advice. More important, Matheron warned that U.S. naval authorities in Saigon needed to be ready for a request from the Vietnamese for assistance in transporting and caring for the evacuees. It was evident to him that the Vietnamese were not capable of dealing with the situation, while the French appeared to be unwilling to make the necessary commitments.

As the military situation began to fall apart, especially after the defeat of the French at Dien Bien Phu and the refusal of the United States to come to their aid during the crisis, the refugee situation took a turn for the worse. In addition to the military defeat, the emotional setback was tremendous, as many within the Vietnamese community realized that, as insecure as their current situation seemed to be, their future was equally uncertain. These military and psychological factors, as well as a breakdown of coordination and administration, contributed to the urgency of the situation. For example, medical supplies intended for Tay Ninh did not reach the refugees and, instead, were being sold to the Viet Minh. To combat nonshipment or the diversion of supplies to other than intended sources, it was recommended that a full accounting of the supplies shipped be matched against supplies received and distributed.[9]

With the fall of Dien Bien Phu on May 7 and the collapse of the French Union forces in the Tonkin Delta, the refugee crisis took on a new look, as military personnel and their families joined the civilian refugee population in search of more secure territory. At the end of June, the French started a program of resettlement that consolidated specific villages in order to free housing for French Union forces. The program called for the relocation of twenty-five thousand families in fifty villages. While the French army provided transportation and had enough food stockpiled in

Haiphong, it did not have sleeping mats or clothing to help the displaced families, nor did it have the financial means to provide for these materials. The Vietnamese had recommended another thirty thousand families for relocation to the Hanoi, Gia Lam, and Huan Long areas, though the French were against the idea because it would congest those cities and hamper military movement. Another forty thousand families of civilians were expected to relocate as a result of French consolidation, and according to a USOM report dated June 25, the total number of families affected could reach two hundred thousand in the event the war intensified.[10]

To coordinate their efforts, the French and Vietnamese established an emergency committee consisting of Vietnamese and French experts from social services, public health, and psychological warfare offices. USOM officers agreed to assist this committee from behind the scenes and provide whatever assistance was required within the mission's means. Each USOM member involved in the emergency committee deliberations planned procedures to provide all elements of living for at least sixty thousand people for a period of four months. On June 28, USOM representative to North Vietnam Gerald Strauss reported on the exodus of French Union troops from Nam Dinh and Phu Ly.[11] Strauss estimated that four hundred seventy-five thousand would evacuate these southern provinces to French Union strongholds in the Tonkin Delta region. Strauss and Herman Holiday recommended the release of ten million piasters to take care of immediate requirements. A few days later, the preliminary number of refugees from the southern provinces was greatly reduced down to thirty-five thousand known refugees and perhaps as many as twenty thousand others who might join the exodus. The original figure of ninety-five thousand families, or four hundred seventy-five thousand people, came from French sources, which argued that the number represented the total number of families and people they, and the Vietnamese, wanted to relocate. Neither country had the means to transport and care for such a large volume of individuals. The potential for a major refugee problem reached the FOA on July 3 as its director, Harold E. Stassen, requested data on the situation and the likelihood that the Vietnamese government would request aid exceeding the $250 million allocated for 1955 fiscal year funds.

This was almost immediately followed by a request from USOM Saigon for the release of 30.8 million piasters to serve as a six-month loan to the Vietnamese government. The government needed to stockpile supplies, including four thousand tons of rice, ten thousand cases of condensed milk, and six thousand tons of coal, at Haiphong (one-third) and Hanoi (two-thirds) in case these major cities were isolated as the French collapsed. USOM released 31 million piasters for stockpiling supplies but suggested that it delay release of the money until after July 20 in order not to be misconstrued by the negotiators in Geneva. USOM did not want those at the conference who were opposed to American influence in Indochina to use this event as a pretext for delaying the settlement or as propaganda to sway international opinion regarding U.S. motives in the region.

As the deliberations regarding the stockpiling of supplies in Hanoi and Haiphong continued, the concern about equipment in territories directly threatened became an issue. In Son Tay the USOM had constructed an irrigation system with a $75,000 diesel motor along with two million piasters for installation. As fighting approached Son Tay, the question became whether the motor and other equipment remain, be sabotaged, or be destroyed so the Viet Minh could not take advantage of it.[12] The relocation of the French Union troops and their dependents signaled a change in the USOM, as the new objective appeared to be assisting the Vietnamese government in relocating and resettlement.

From July 6 to 9, a team of four from USOM, led by Dr. Poindexter, visited the maritime zone around Haiphong where refugees were concentrating.[13] The purpose of the trip was to observe vaccination and inoculation efforts and determine the public health needs for the refugees and inhabitants. Haiphong had been a city of one hundred thousand during World War II, and its infrastructure had remained constant while it had grown to more than two hundred fifty thousand by 1953. It was a logical resettlement area because of the access to the sea as well as the concentration of French Union forces there after the fall of Dien Bien Phu. Joining the investigating team were Daniel Weiner, sanitary engineer; L. J. Smith for public works; and Michael Adler for community development. There were approximately ten thousand refugees in Haiphong and another seventeen thousand in surrounding provinces. For the most part, the programs to vaccinate and inoculate were organized and proceeding adequately. In Kien An province, Poindexter found the greatest variety of disease, such as trachoma, dysentery, several skin diseases, rheumatism, headaches, and fever. With eighty villages and approximately three hundred fifty-six thousand inhabitants, the province had few medical personnel and only one civilian hospital.

In Haiphong the team visited six locations, including the general hospital, the venereal disease treatment center, the construction site of the maternity-dispensary unit, and the maternity unit in the industrial part of the city. The team observed that Haiphong was adequate for refugee resettlement with its present infrastructure. It required only first aid kits and qualified nurses to take care of the refugee population and conduct vaccination and inoculation programs. For the surrounding areas, they recommended two additional doctors with transportation and a team of nurses and supplies to finish the vaccinations and inoculations. Preventive medicine recommendations also included two DDT teams to systematically spray the houses in the provinces and first aid kits and first aid assistants for each concentration of two thousand refugees. The team learned that the area that could potentially become the embarkation zone for a major civilian relocation operation was suitable, though at its capacity. It was the best that the Tonkin Delta had to offer for an evacuation, however.

Another concern was the staff members of STEM, USOM, and other missions who were in the direct path of the Viet Minh advance. In early June 1954, the mechanisms were set in motion to ensure that personal effects of the Americans were transported to the South, anticipating the loss of the North. On July 1, the acting director of USOM, Paul Everett, instructed Strauss to begin shipping all classified and nonessential materiel to Saigon. Everett authorized the release of funds to Strauss to purchase emergency equipment, food, and fuel for the mission in the North in case the situation deteriorated further. Everett also ordered emergency supplies to the North for the mission to distribute, giving Strauss the option to place whatever he deemed necessary on the return flight.[14] On July 10, Everett informed U.S. ambassador to Vietnam Donald R. Heath that STEM planned to stop all road and bridge work in the North except for Route 5 between Hanoi and Haiphong.[15] STEM also planned to extend the wharf in Haiphong and insert three barges as well as improve the Gia Lam airport. These projects would assist the French in their immediate crisis and prove valuable five weeks later when the first U.S. Navy ship began participating in the evacuation. On July 16, Everett advised Strauss that he should transport as much as possible of the aid supplies, vehicles, and equipment from the Hanoi area to the Haiphong area before July 20, the proposed end date of the Geneva Conference. Five days after the signing of the agreement, however, equipment had not been transferred, and in a letter Carter de Paul requested Strauss to delay evacuation of equipment until further consultation with Washington concluded.

Following the signing of the Geneva Conference agreements on July 21, Poindexter and Richard Matheron, STEM representative to central Vietnam, visited the Vietnamese officials in Hue who were in charge of refugee affairs.[16] The general tenor in Hue was one of comfort and elation after learning that the seventeenth parallel would be the dividing point between North and South Vietnam. Hue, the imperial capital, fell in the southern zone. While the government officials in Hue were resigned to the inevitable division of their country and relieved of their political position, the focus of concern turned to the refugee situation and the role Hue would play in the emerging crisis.

An estimated one hundred thousand refugees in central Vietnam required assistance. This did not include refugees from North Vietnam who might wish to travel to the South. In Quang Binh province, there were an estimated fifty thousand people, half of whom were Catholic, who were expected to relocate south of the seventeenth parallel. Two reception areas were planned for central Vietnam: Dong Ha for those traveling by land and Tourane for those traveling by sea. For refugees from North Vietnam, Nha Trang was also being considered as a staging area. Poindexter and Matheron observed that central Vietnam had enough medicine to take care of the immediate needs of the refugees, with a few exceptions, though there were not enough personnel to handle the influx of refugees and administer the resettlement programs. Although the staging areas had fresh water, none had sanitary facilities or adequate housing to handle the number of refugees anticipated, nor did the supply of rations to help the relocated amount to more than a week's worth of food.

On July 28, Dr. Poindexter and his team visited Tourane to observe the first group of refugees from Quang Binh province; approximately five thousand had arrived by boat in the week since the closing of the Geneva Conference. Although the regional and local governments had made considerable progress in meeting the refugees' needs, there was still a considerable way to go before all requirements were met. The refugees arriving in Tourane were not immunized, nor were they afforded proper medical care, because there were no medical personnel to meet them. In Dong Hoi, the team found five hundred refugees crowded into a building and awaiting the cease-fire to reach the city before they left. This group was also in need of medical care but did not have medical personnel to assist. Because of the lack of medical personnel in central Vietnam, especially around the staging areas, Poindexter requested that at least one American technician remain in the region for a limited time to assist in the medical care program. The United States already had a medical care plan organized and integrated into the Vietnamese refugee program but did not have the personnel to execute it. An American representative would provide a stronger liaison between the Vietnamese and the United States, ensuring that adequate and proper supplies reached the areas where they were most desperately needed.

The government of the Republic of Vietnam played a significant role in areas turned over by the Viet Minh. The evacuees evaluated the government in its handling of their relocation and resettlement. How Saigon dealt with the situation determined the extent to which the refugees would support the government against the Viet Minh. There was a strong belief among Americans in Indochina that the American economic aid program should act immediately to provide impact programs in areas south of the seventeenth parallel that had been occupied by the Viet Minh. The psychological effect of having the immediate presence of the Vietnamese government meeting the needs and desires of the newly liberated inhabitants was too powerful a propaganda tool to ignore, however. The quick establishment of Republic of Vietnam sovereignty in the formerly occupied areas would further solidify the new South Vietnamese government as it faced the challenges brought about by the Geneva Conference. It was important for U.S. officials to supply American economic aid to the Vietnamese government behind the scenes and not associated with the French military. Working behind the scenes would strengthen the government and quell rumors that the United States was attempting to replace the French as a colonial power, while disassociation from the French military would negate the appeal and arguments of Viet Minh sympathizers who remained south of the seventeenth parallel.

By the end of July, as focus centered on what to do with the growing number of refugees in both North and central Vietnam, the U.S. missions and the Vietnamese government developed several plans. On July 28, USOM Saigon received three documents from the minister of public health and social action related to the evacuation of military and civilian personnel from North Vietnam. These documents revealed that the Ministry of National Defense had ordered the evacuation of all army personnel from the North, with those in good physical condition to remain in Haiphong to assist in the evacuation and remain until the end. In addition to the army, the ministry decided to evacuate all army dependents as well as any officials and their families who wished to leave. Finally, students, youth, and members of political, religious, or social groups—such as trade unions—and civilians were given the opportunity to leave the North. The ministry set up a priority system that deviated from the traditional policy of women and children first. Medical personnel would receive priority in order to organize medical centers, and youth leaders and young, healthy, unmarried people would join them to help establish reception centers to organize the people. Once established in the North, these groups would move to the South to create similar structures at the debarkation areas. The second wave of refugees would be made up of high-grade technicians and their families. These people, who would be good propaganda sources for the Viet Minh if they remained in Hanoi, would come from leadership positions in the community, such as teachers, lawyers, and public servants. The next to final installment of people, before the civilian population, would come from religious and political groups and the military. These leagues and groups would provide the leadership infrastructure lacking at both the embarkation and debarkation areas.[17]

As the evacuation began, tents were one of the first items requested by the Saigon government from the United States, as Harold Stassen, director of the Foreign Operations Administration, would learn on July 29. The FOA, in coordination with the U.S. Department of Defense, began shipping tents from the reserve stocks in Japan on July 31. By August 5, FOA had arranged for two thousand tents to shelter forty thousand refugees. These tents were used in the South in resettlement centers and constructed by Vietnamese, with American tools, to aid those displaced during the war and voluntarily after the war.[18]

The Vietnamese government had devised a plan for the refugee community upon its arrival in the South. The objective was to receive the refugees, provide temporary assistance, and then resettle them in areas where they could adapt themselves and engage in agriculture, animal husbandry, and handicraft. The new population had a predominantly anticommunist political philosophy and would become a significant force in areas previously occupied by the Viet Minh. The Vietnamese government planned to establish receiving centers in the schools in Saigon, Cholon, Gia Dinh, and Thu Dau Mot before resettlement. Refugees were to be sorted into areas south of the seventeenth parallel depending upon their profession, with special consideration given to those in civil service professions such as doctors and lawyers. For civilians and artisans, the Vietnamese government planned to take over regions for resettlement in Nha Trang, Phan Thiet, the Central Highlands, Tay Ninh, and Thu Dau Mot. In those areas the Vietnamese government organized artisan and industrial centers for their new inhabitants. Propaganda played an important role in the Vietnamese government's scheme for organizing the refugee population.[19]

The political advantages of the influx of more than eight hundred thousand people, most of whom were Catholic, would provide a tremendous boost to the Diem government and a stabilizing force in traditionally unfriendly areas. Of these more than eight hundred thousand estimated new arrivals, three hundred thousand were Vietnamese military personnel who had been fighting in the North and their dependents, while thirty thousand were government officials and their families and patriotic groups.[20] The Vietnamese government had planned on feeding all refugees for a period of ten days. Those with professions that would easily adapt to the existing South Vietnamese economy would become responsible for their own subsistence after that, while the Vietnamese government would support the rest of the population until the completion of their rehabilitation, or a maximum of ninety days. The Vietnamese government had plans to create one hundred thousand housing units— enough for each family—as well as provide the tools and financial support for artisans and agriculturists to start their trades after resettlement.

Using similar formulas, the Vietnamese government estimated an additional sum of 350 million piasters for the refugee population in central Vietnam to handle the approximately one hundred thousand refugees expected to flow across the seventeenth parallel. It was clear to those in the USOM that the Vietnamese government did not have the financial

Table 2.1. Estimated Costs for Refugee Resettlement in the Saigon Area (in Piasters)

Cost for feeding all refugees for the first ten days in the South at 12 piasters per person per day	84,000,000
Cost of feeding the civilian population for ninety days at 12 piasters per person per day	367,200,000
Cost of creating one hundred thousand housing units at 6,000 piasters per unit	600,000,000
Cost of providing material aid such as bedding, household utensils, and dishes at 600 piasters per family	50,000,000
Cost of providing tools of the trade for refugees such as working tools, draft animals, seeds for planting, fertilizer, and money advances	377,800,000
Cost to fight the psychological war	10,000,000
Cost to fund a core of refugees as leaders in the evacuation population to ensure a smooth and safe operation	11,000,000
Total Estimated Costs	1,500,000,000

means to fund all of their relocation and resettlement schemes. At some point the Vietnamese government would have to call upon the United States for assistance. While those in Vietnam expected the call, many outside the region had no warning of the great demands to which they would be expected to respond. An American criticism of the Vietnamese plan emerged on July 28. It argued that the plan was simple, lacked details, and suffered from a functional decentralization that doomed it from the start.[21] Specifically, the critique mentioned the failure to provide security in the embarkation area and maintained that the resettlement outline would cause unnecessary harm to many who participated in the first wave of transport, as many of the facilities necessary for such a large-scale resettlement would not be available when they left North Vietnam. An American counter-plan was considered and delivered a few days later.

In the U.S. plan, the original design of the reception center would be based upon camps. Each camp was designed to have a capacity of fifteen hundred people and a staff of forty-six. Each camp director would hold responsibility over and provide supervision of the camp, including accounts for all property, supplies, and monies, and would report to the director of services to refugees, health, and social action. Reporting to the camp director, the deputy director would implement all instructions, coordinate operations, handle supplies and services, inspect and assess camp activities, direct internal security, allocate space, and control all movement into and within the camp. The director's administrative section would have a total of five people, and a transportation assistant, cashier accountant, and secretary recorder would round out the staff. The remainder of the camp organizational structure would consist of health and sanitation, welfare service, maintenance and supply, and educational training sections.

The Health and Sanitation Section, a total of four personnel under the direction of the health officer, would be responsible for providing adequate medical and sanitation services and facilities. This would include first aid; identification and referral of serious medical cases; inspection of washing, bathing, and cooking facilities; control of insect and pest populations; and provision of services for pregnant and nursing women, midwifery, and other medical needs as they arose. A first aid assistant, sanitary engineer, and infirmary nurse would support the health officer. The Welfare Service Section also would have a staff of four and, under the direction of the welfare officer, would provide psychological services to the camp inhabitants as well as cash relief, supplementary food and clothing, counseling, and mail services and would attend to the special needs of children. The welfare officer would receive support from a relief supply assistant, warehouse distributor, and caseworker counselor. The Maintenance and Supply Section, under a property officer, would maintain all camp buildings, equipment, and facilities. The property officer would distribute the food rations and maintain the cooking, washing, and bathing facilities. The property officer would have assistance from a plumber, a carpenter, a garbage collector, two kitchen helpers, and an electrician helper. The final section, Education and Training, would be the largest of the five sections, with a staff of twenty-six under the direction of an education officer. This section would be responsible for educational, recreational, and instructional opportunities through formal classes, library and hobby shop facilities, and organization of games, sports, movies, and traditional folklore plays. The education officer would receive support from ten teachers, three nursery assistants, a librarian, ten sports leaders and assistants, a theater assistant, and ten craft assistants, depending upon the size of the camp. In addition to the sections, one unit chief per one to two hundred people, elected from the camp inhabitants, would act as a liaison between the refugees and the camp administration and its sections.[22]

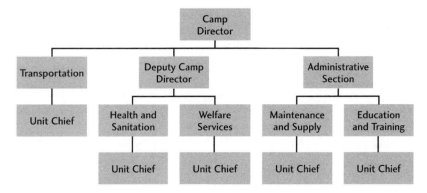

Fig. 2.1. Refugee camp organization chart.

It was very important to keep accurate accounts of refugees as they entered the camps and embarked on their passage to freedom for several reasons, including basic bookkeeping to assess and report the flow of refugees to determine shipping in the North and debarkation requirements in the South. To keep track of the disorganized group, every person or head of household had to fill out the Refugee Registration Record (RRR #1) form within twenty-four hours of arriving in the registration area. It was hoped that this thirty-one-question form would provide the necessary data to learn from where the refugees came, their status, and how they received assistance once within the camp. Initial plans called for each Vietnamese to sign a declaration of his anticommunist beliefs and his desire for evacuation, resettlement, and reemployment. The declaration also relieved the Vietnamese government of liability for loss of property. The planners intended to submit the data from the RRR #1 to French and Vietnamese authorities for security clearance before the refugees passed a security interview, but this plan proved impractical as the evacuation began and a sea of Vietnamese entered Hanoi and Haiphong.[23]

Once the Vietnamese were ready for transport to the South, they entered the staging area in Haiphong. Like the reception center, the staging area had a distinct structure. It was under a director who had overall supervision and acted as liaison with the local and national governments, military representatives, and U.S. agencies involved in the operation. The director also worked with the ship escort officer to select and prepare the Vietnamese to embark and to provide information pertinent to the

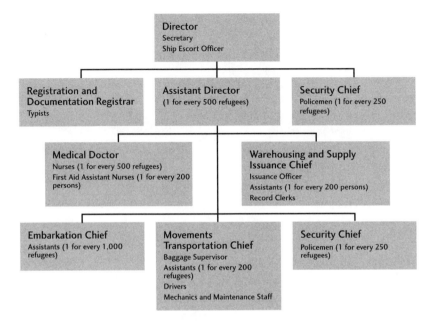

Fig. 2.2. Staff organization chart for Staging Center Haiphong.

refugees' voyage. The director was also supported by a registrar, security chief, doctors and nurses, embarkation chief and staff, transportation chief and staff, warehouse and supply chief and staff, and maintenance chief and staff. The number of personnel depended upon the number of refugees anticipated in the staging center.[24]

During the formation of the American response, several field trips in and around Hanoi and Haiphong supplied more data on the size and seriousness of the evacuation process. On July 28, the refugee situation in Haiphong took on a more definite perspective as more members of the U.S. missions were able to inspect the area and procedures were set in place to handle the refugees.[25] It was clear from this visit, as well as the many others carried out over the waning days of July 1954, that the Vietnamese would not be able to handle the care of the refugee population without significant assistance from the United States and, if possible, France. In An Duong district, there were more than four thousand militia and their families waiting to arrive in Haiphong. These refugees had nothing left, having spent their resources to travel to An Duong district. To take care of the refugee population, American officials ordered rice and dry fish for a period of ten days from the stockpiles in Hanoi, promising more once the chief of social services provided information on what his office needed to continue feeding the people. American officials also ordered an additional 18,848 tons of rice, 1,200 tons of dry fish, 600 kilograms of salt, and 1,200 pieces of clothing to help the Vietnamese in An Duong. Despite these immediate relief efforts, there was a constant danger of starvation for those amassing around the Haiphong area. The French sent 1,000 tons of rice to Haiphong, which arrived on July 28, but an additional 500 tons were required to handle the needs of the refugees expected in Haiphong. The Vietnamese Relief Committee in Haiphong also required assistance in developing rooms around Haiphong, supplying water to reception camps, and improving sanitation facilities throughout the area. The Haiphong camps had approximately twenty thousand refugees at the end of July—more than they could handle. Even when food was distributed, there were not enough pans to cook the meals, as those who fled the Viet Minh left with only that which they could carry over long distances. It was apparent that the reception camps in the North needed to relieve the refugee population by transporting them to the South before additional refugees entered the camps. Failure to transport refugees to the South would result in unacceptable overcrowding in the camps and a growing sentiment of disappointment and discouragement among the refugees. U.S. officials observed that Haiphong Social Services did not have the resources to meet their objectives despite their best intentions and, without U.S. personnel to aid in the process, had little likelihood of success.

Likewise, in the South, there was little chance of Vietnamese and French success without some direct aid by the United States in the resettlement and relocation operation. One example is that of a simple tool for survival, the hoe. In a highly agricultural country, the hoe is a common, crucial tool in ensuring survival. The Agricultural Service for South Vietnam relied on STEM for its supply of ten thousand hoes. Without U.S. financial aid, the Vietnamese government would not have been able to furnish these and other tools necessary for agricultural success.[26] These same hoes still had not been delivered by August 20, despite the urgent need for them in camps around Cap St. Jacques, Nha Trang, and Saigon.

On August 2, Herman J. Holiday reported to Michael H. B. Adler, special assistant of USOM, on the condition of the refugee camps in Hanoi and Haiphong.[27] Holiday had spent a week touring the camps and visiting Vietnamese officials to assess refugee care and evacuation conditions. He noted that the final results of the Geneva Conference had virtually eliminated Vietnamese interest in the care of the refugees around Hanoi and Haiphong. He tried to introduce a system of registering and certifying refugees based on earlier plans but found that it was impossible. He correctly foresaw this failure as a fundamental problem for the Vietnamese, as it left them with no factual information about the people who were to be introduced into the southern economy. The South Vietnamese government would not be able to coordinate the reemployment of farmers, factory workers, and white-collar workers without any knowledge of their talents before they arrived in Saigon. Refugees would be sorted after arrival, causing undue frustration and hardship after so long a journey. Finally, without proper registration it would be impossible to determine the number of people who wished to leave the Tonkin Delta and coordinate facilities to handle the influx. Holiday seemed determined to work with the Vietnamese officials to resolve this dilemma, but he lamented the limitation of his position. Without an official American policy to back him, and considering the emotional state of the Vietnamese in the Tonkin Delta, his influence and authority were not strong. Holiday noted that American interference, even in a behind-the-scenes capacity, would only add to the general confusion existing in the North, and he cautioned against direct assistance to the French, who were in charge of handling the actual movement of Vietnamese.

The organized movement of refugees to Hanoi started on August 1 with the arrival of seventy truckloads of refugees, approximately nine hundred people, from the province of Bac Giang, to the east of Hanoi. Because no organized camps existed, the refugees were sheltered in the Hanoi Trade School until they were transported to Haiphong on August 5. To receive the refugees and organize their movement to Haiphong, the Vietnamese organized a committee of seven to oversee the movement. Holiday noted that the committee was more prone to discussion than action and was hampered by the French, who showed no interest in providing sufficient transportation to move the refugees to Haiphong before August 10—the cutoff date for movement from the outlying provinces to Hanoi. Holiday also learned that, because of Viet Minh intimidation, the committee had experienced trouble finding drivers to move the refugees the twenty-five miles between Hanoi and Haiphong. On August 2, the estimated number of Vietnamese planning to leave the North was three hundred thirty thousand, although the largest group, the farmers, remained the hardest to count because it was questionable whether they could be reached before the deadline. Holiday promised to provide a better estimate as more refugees arrived.

Holiday ended his report with a warning that the disorganization in the South might overshadow that in the North if preparations for the new arrivals did not improve. He cited the story of four thousand Catholics transported by the French from Haiphong to Saigon ten days earlier. Neither Action Sociale nor the Catholic clergy nor the French in Haiphong knew what had happened to those people. If coordination was the key to the operation, the operation was doomed to fail without serious improvement in its organization.

Holiday's report came as no surprise to those in USOM who had traveled to North Vietnam. On the same day Holiday submitted his report, the deputy chief of the Health and Sanitation Division, Dr. Bernard W. Rosenburg, informed Dr. Le Van Khai, director general of health in Saigon, that the American Aid Economic Mission had designated Rosenburg as a public health official and Daniel J. Wiener as a sanitation engineer to work with the Vietnamese in the Departments of Health and Social Action.[28] Although the U.S. officials agreed on the need for intervention in the growing refugee problem, there was still some confusion among the various departments within USOM on how best to organize and coordinate for maximum effect. One case in particular was brought forth by Holiday, who objected to the actions of C. A. Mann, chief of the Program and Requirements Division, when he committed 3.5 million piasters for construction of a refugee village in the district of Go Vap, as well as the consolidation of various refugee projects, without consulting with the Community Development Division. Holiday's division had been assisting the Vietnamese officials in their plans to resettle refugees in Go Vap since the Geneva Conference. The disagreement, beyond a mere "turf" war, illustrates the difficulties U.S. officials would have as early plans for relocation and resettlement progressed.

At the conclusion of the Geneva Conference, the Vietnamese government in the South was disorganized and ineffective in coordinating with the French and Americans. These obstacles were intensified by the sheer magnitude of the problems presented and anticipated with the entrance of up to one million refugees from the North.[29] The ability of the United States to coordinate efforts, despite the example just cited, in these early, confused days is best shown by quick response requests for supplies received. On August 3, Dr. Poindexter, after a meeting in Hue to discuss the arrival of refugees from the North to that city, requested fifty bottles each of terramycin, aureomycin, glycyrrhiza, aspirin, Brown's mixture (an opium compound used to suppress coughs and treat bronchitis), and sulfasuxidine as well as two thousand tubes of antismallpox vaccine and four thousand bottles of anticholera vaccine with glycerin. The STEM office in Saigon received the request the next day and was able, with the help of the Ministry of Health, which provided the smallpox and cholera vaccines, to ensure the arrival of this desperately needed medicine by August 6. For a country ravaged by nine years of war, divided, and in turmoil, this simple act—repeated several times over the ensuing months— is testament to the ability of USOM and its dedicated staff.[30]

An examination of the 12,550 refugees gathered in Tourane on August 6 foretells much about the population to follow.[31] Only 11 percent of the refugees were men—this a result of the fact that most men were in military service—while 23 percent were women and 66 percent were infants and children. Fishermen or families of fisherman made up one-third of the refugees, and the majority of the rest were laborers. Catholics made up 93 percent of the refugee population, and 86 percent considered themselves poor. To aid the refugee population, STEM had four health and sanitation teams in Tourane to assist in their welfare, including a DDT spray team that had already begun work. The remaining three teams— for trachoma control, malaria survey, and health education—had not yet begun their work among the refugee population.

The staff received reinforcements from the FOA on August 5, when Director Stassen announced the temporary transfer of two experts on refugee and resettlement programs to assist in the evacuation. Richard R. Brown, director of the Escapee Program Office of Field Coordination in Frankfurt, Germany, and James H. Campbell, FOA Far East refugee adviser in Hong Kong, arrived in Indochina to work with the acting USOM director, Paul Everett, in coordinating efforts with Vietnamese officials responsible for the reception, care, and resettlement centers. Both men brought with them a wealth of experience and knowledge in large-scale resettlement operations and helped further solidify the American humanitarian presence in Indochina.[32]

The arrival of the FOA experts marked a turning point in future U.S. involvement in the evacuation of refugees from North Vietnam. On August 6, the Joint Chiefs of Staff met with representatives of the State Department to discuss U.S. relations with the Associated States of Indochina.[33] During the course of the meeting, Admiral Robert B. Carney stressed the importance of the evacuation of North Vietnam and the potential pressure placed upon the U.S. Navy to provide assistance in transportation. Admiral Carney worried that the French would not be able to handle the transportation of the refugees. Although the navy had begun preliminary studies on the number of potential refugees, the problems of Haiphong and Hanoi as embarkation ports, and coordination with the French, he urged those present to consider a more detailed study of the evacuation and tight coordination between the State Department and the Department of Defense. A specific concern was the removal of U.S. equipment in the North before the eighty-day and three-hundred-day deadlines. Haiphong had an estimated capacity of forty-five hundred tons per day, but there was no guarantee that enough shipping or shore laborers would be available to meet that capacity. Everett echoed these concerns to President Ngo Dinh Diem in a letter dated August 6 when he outlined U.S. plans to remove all items of military or industrial use from the North while leaving any items used primarily for civilian or humanitarian purposes.[34]

American military equipment had been present in Indochina since 1950 when, as a result of the Korean War, the United States acted to shore up its defense in Asia against the appearance of communist encroachment. On December 23, 1950, the United States had entered with France, Cambodia, Laos, and Vietnam into an agreement for mutual defense assistance in Indochina.[35] Under this agreement the United States provided materiel to French Union forces in their battle against the Viet Minh, consistent with the overarching policy of containment governing U.S. action at the time. Under Public Law 329 (Eighty-first Congress), the United States had provided tanks, vehicles, and other armament to the French Union, and there was great concern that none of that aid fall into the hands of the communists as a result of the Geneva Conference and the withdrawal of the French and Vietnamese forces from the Tonkin Delta. Admiral Carney also worried that without a coordinated effort in the North, many refugees seeking transport would return to their homes if the embarkation areas in Hanoi and Haiphong did not provide basic necessities for refugees as they awaited their movement to the South.

Another report circulating through USOM consisted of notes, taken by Poindexter, that provided insight not only into the care of the refugees but also into the political advantages for both the United States and the new Vietnamese government with the coming influx of Vietnamese from the North.[36] Of primary concern was ensuring that all refugees and those displaced by the war receive emergency medical care from representatives of their own government, if appropriate. This would help to improve the Vietnamese perception of their government in times of crisis. If the government satisfied the need for food, clothing, shelter, and immunization against infectious diseases, its position and status among the refugees would increase. Poindexter believed that the refugees and others directly involved in the operation would gain a sense of pride in the new government if its organization and execution of the evacuation proceeded without obstacles. A successful operation would lead to more efficient resettlement and reemployment of those from the North. Poindexter argued that the United States could assist in this effort by providing the necessary supplies, organization, and infrastructure to the Vietnamese government in the South.

The logical contribution of the Division of Health and Sanitation was professional training and supplies. Along with Poindexter, Doctors Kotcher, Stage, and Weiner could provide the bulk of the expertise of training and advising. These doctors would train nurses and first aid workers for the reception camps as well as supply immunizations and emergency first aid kits to their Vietnamese counterparts. The division could also contribute equipment and expertise for a cleaner supply of drinking water, sanitary cooking facilities, and proper bathing and washing structures. Preventive medicine would also include appropriate disposal of body wastes and refuse generated by the refugees—both responsible for the spread of contagious disease. Finally, the control of insects and rodents in the camps would aid the overall containment of disease. It was the opinion of Poindexter that the United States would provide the expertise to train and advise the Vietnamese to handle these situations as they became a concern. Although the United States would play a prominent role in the beginning, the strategy was to replace the Health and Sanitary Division staff with Vietnamese and emphasize the efficiency of the Republic of Vietnam in caring for their new citizens.

There is no question that, during the period leading up to the formal request for evacuation assistance from the Republic of Vietnam, the Vietnamese and French effort was not coordinated. For the United States, it became necessary to provide some coherent national organization to ensure some type of order out of the chaos that had developed in the preceding months. Before the conclusion of the Geneva Conference, the Vietnamese government had failed to handle the relatively simple refugee problem that had resulted from the French fighting. Action Sociale in North Vietnam provided the minimum comforts of shelter, though it gave little to no medical or social care to those dislocated by the fighting. Refugee camps suffered from disorganization of administration, failure to anticipate needs, and inability to track or control the flow of individuals to and from their area. The Vietnamese government attempted to handle the situation through traditional means without applying the necessary administrative and medical controls to minimize the inherent obstacles.

The signing of the agreements left Vietnam in a critical situation, with the Vietnamese government unable to comprehend the impending crisis. It was apparent from those involved in the situation that without external assistance the Vietnamese government would fail in the evacuation process and lose a unique opportunity to gain more than eight hundred thousand new and devoted citizens in the South. For a newly emerging country with a formidable adversary to the North and a limited amount of time to accomplish its objectives, the necessity of external assistance—especially from the United States—became more critical.

CHAPTER 3

★★★★★★★★★★★★★★

Organizing the Passage

After receiving word that the U.S. Navy would become a significant participant in the operation to transport Vietnamese refugees, French civilians, and military from the newly created DRV in the North to the Republic of Vietnam in the South, the first order of business was the creation of a coherent operational plan to organize and anticipate the unforeseen. Aboard USS *Estes* (AGC-12) in Yokosuka, Japan, Rear Admiral Lorenzo S. Sabin and his staff created Operation Order 2-54—the outline of what would become Operation Passage to Freedom.[1] Admiral Sabin had received command of Task Force 90 with the primary goal of transporting personnel, equipment, and vehicles from North Vietnam before the three-hundred-day deadline. It was a daunting challenge, and although the admiral had no direct experience in this type of operation, he did have several decades of naval experience on which to rely. One of the first tasks, and second only to the gathering of intelligence, was the creation of an operational order to serve as a guideline for conducting the operation. The final order, produced on August 11, 1954, took less than one week to create, but it withstood the duration of the operation with minimal changes—a credit to Admiral Sabin and his staff.

The 114-page document provided for the conduct and support of the evacuation of French Union forces with their equipment; Vietnamese, French, and other civilians who wished to leave the North; and all Mutual Defense Assistance Program (MDAP) equipment by sea.[2] As commander of Task Force 90, Admiral Sabin recognized the need for close contact and coordination with French officials in both North and South Vietnam should the operation have any chance for success. As he would learn—in conjunction with the many U.S. personnel involved in the operation—this would be one of his most pressing challenges.

Operation Order 2-54 outlined the organization of Task Force 90 with specific detail to the embarkation and debarkation units. The operation called for four high-speed transports (APDs), eight attack transports (APAs), four attack cargo ships (AKAs), four dock landing ships (LSDs), eighteen tank landing ships (LSTs), two repair ships (ARLs), twelve utility landing craft (LCUs), and one underwater demolition team (UDT). See Appendix A for ship designations and descriptions—all organized as shown in Table 3.1.[3]

Although the order called for all ships of the Amphibious Group Western Pacific and required elements from Military Sea Transportation Service (MSTS) shipping, the admiral's staff was unsure of the total number of military and civilians they might carry to the South, with estimates ranging between two and seven hundred thousand.[4] Although the range was large, the estimate of an initial one hundred thousand per month was fairly accurate, though the plan called for a marked increase as the operation became established—an increase that, for a variety of reasons, failed to materialize. The orders also called for maintaining a minimum number of ships in the established embarkation and debarkation areas at any one time, while all ships would have the ability to sail independently after they were loaded—a process they hoped would run on a twenty-four-hour timetable.

The objective area for embarkation was Haiphong, although the primary area of embarkation for ships with low draft would be the Do Son Peninsula, approximately twenty miles south of the mouth of the Haiphong River and sixty miles east of Hanoi. These areas afforded the best possible conditions for the operation in the North. The operation order called for one group of control vessels and parties to be stationed on the western side of the Do Son Peninsula and one on the eastern side. A third group would station itself at the mouth of the Cua Cam River, while the final group was ordered to conduct roving operations in all three areas to provide assistance as needed. All AKAs and APAs were directed to furnish their boat groups to supplement the available lighterage. In order to avoid confusion, each of the lighters would fly a color flag to match the beach to which it was assigned.

Table 3.1. Task Force 90 Organization Structure

90	Amphibious Group Western Pacific	R. Adm. L. S. Sabin COMPHIBGRP 1
90.0	Special Task Group	R. Adm. L. S. Sabin COMPHIBGRP 1
90.0.1	Flagship Unit	Capt. J. W. Waterhouse Commander, USS *Estes*
90.0.2	Tactical Air Control Unit	Cdr. A. Trusso Commander, TACRON 1
90.0.3	Administrative Command, Amphibious Group Western Pacific	Cdr. J. W. Higgins, Jr. COMADCOMPHIBGRUWESTPAC
90.0.4	LCU Unit	Lt. Cdr. V. C. Thomas COMLCURON 3
90.0.4.1	LCU Element ABLE	Lt. (JG) W. E. Roberts COMLUCDIV 31
	LCU-539 LCU-877 LCU-1236 LCU-1421 LCU-1446 LCU-1451	
90.0.4.2	LCU Element	Lt. (JG) D. M. Blemaster COMLCUDIV 33
	LCU-531 LCU-810 LCU-1273 LCU-1374 LCU-1378 LCU-1396	
90.1	Reconnaissance and Control Group	Cdr. A. E. Teall COMPHIBCONDIV 12
90.1.1	Control Unit	Cdr. A. E. Teall COMPHIBCONDIV 12
	USS *Knudson* (APD-101) USS *Wantuck* (APD-125) USS *Begor* (APD-127) USS *Cavallaro* (APD-128)	
90.1.2	Reconnaissance Unit	Cdr. A. E. Teall COMPHIBCONDIV 12
	APD as assigned UDT as assigned	
90.2.1	Transport Unit ABLE	Capt. W. C. Winn COMTRANSDIV 13
	USS *Calvert* (APA-32) USS *Magoffin* (APA-199) USS *Telfair* (APA-210) USS *Montrose* (APA-212) USS *Andromeda* (AKA-15) USS *Skagit* (AKA-105)	

Table 3.1. Task Force 90 Organization Structure *(continued)*

90.2.2	Transport Unit BAKER	Capt. B. N. Rittenhouse COMTRANSDIV 14
	USS *Bayfield* (APA-33) USS *Mountrail* (APA-213) USS *Okanogan* (APA-220) USS *Menard* (APA-201) USS *Algol* (AKA-54) USS *Montague* (AKA-98)	
90.2.3	Landing Ship Dock Unit	Capt. P. W. Mothersill COMLSDRON 1
	USS *Comstock* (LSD-19) USS *Epping Forest* (LSD-4) USS *Tortuga* (LSD-26) USS *Whetstone* (LSD-27)	
90.3	Landing Ship Group	Cdr. F. W. Logsdon COMLSTRON 3
90.3.1	Landing Ship Unit ABLE	Lt. Cdr. E. C. Thomas COMLSTDIV 33
	LST-516 (F) LST-758 LST-772 LST-803 (H) LST-854 LST-855	
90.3.2	Landing Ship Unit BAKER	Lt. Cdr. L. H. Bartsch COMLSTDIV 12
	LST-692 (F) LST-822 LST-825 LST-845 LST-846 LST-1123	
	Landing Ship Unit CHARLIE	Lt. Cdr. W. W. Hacker COMLSTDIV 14
	LST-887 LST-901 LST-902 LST-1080 (H) LST-1096 LST-1128 (F)	
90.3.4	LSR Unit	Lt. Cdr. R. G. Laurie COMLSRDIV 32
	LSMR-412 (F) LSMR-527 LSMR-536	
90.3.5	Repair Unit	Lt. Cdr. A. D. Parker CO, USS *Atlas*
	USS *Atlas* (ARL-7) USS *Sphinx* (ARL-24)	

Table 3.1. Task Force 90 Organization Structure *(continued)*

90.4	Naval Beach Group	Capt. C. E. Coffin, Jr.
		COMNAVBEACHGRU 1
	Beachmaster Unit 1	
	Boat Unit 1	
	Amphibious Construction Battalion No. 1	
	Underwater Demolition Team 12	
90.5	Troop Training Team, Amphibious	Brig. Gen. A. Shapley, USMC
	Group Western Pacific	CG, TTT PHIBGRUWESTPAC
	Troop Training Team,	
	PHIBGRUWESTPAC	
90.6	Amphibious Task Group ABLE	Capt. B. N. Rittenhouse
		COMTRANSDIV 14

3 APA	2 LSMR
1 AKA	2 APD
1 LSD	1 NBG DET
6 LST	1 UDT DET

92	Mobile Logistical Support	R. Adm. R. A. Gano
92.3	Mobile Logistical Support, Tourane Bay	R. Adm. R. A. Gano
	USS *Ajax* (AR-6)	
	USS *Mispillion* (AO-105)	
	USS *Karin* (AF-33)	
	USS *Sussex* (AK-213)	
	USS *Sharps* (AKL-10)	
92.3.1	Mobile Logistical Support, Haiphong	
	USS *Haven* (AH-12)	
	USS *Reclaimer* (ARS-42)	
93.6	Amphibious Troops Assigned	Commander, 5th Cavalry Regiment
90.7	Amphibious Task Group BAKER	Capt. W. C. Winn
		COMTRANSDIV 13

3 APA	2 LSMR
1 AKA	2 APD
1 LSD	1 NBG DET
6 LST	1 UDT DET

93.7	Amphibious Troops Assigned	Commander, 4th Marine Regiment
	Fourth Marine Regiment (Reinforced)	
90.8	Amphibious Task Group CHARLIE	Capt. P. W. Mothersill
		COMLSDRON 1

3 APA	2 LSMR	1 UDT DET
1 AKA	2 APD	
2 LSD	1 ARL	
6 LST	1 NBG DET	

93.8	Amphibious Troops Assigned	Commander, 9th Marine Regiment
	Ninth Marine Regiment (Reinforced)	

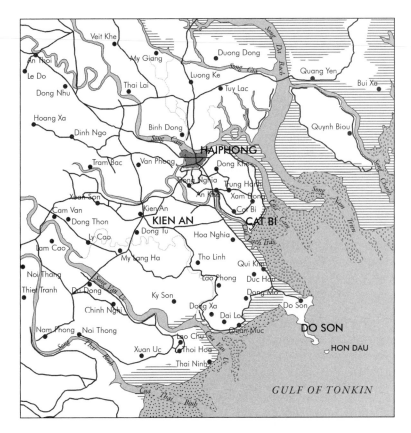

Map 3.1. Haiphong and Its Harbor

Admiral Sabin ordered the Control Unit, under the command of Commander A. E. Teall, to provide information about Haiphong and the Do Son Peninsula. The admiral ordered Teall's unit to conduct hydrographic reconnaissance of the seaward approaches of the landing beaches on the peninsula from the three-fathom line inshore to the high-water mark on the beach. This survey was needed to locate suitable slots and causeway sites for LSTs. The operation order identified Baie de Clateau (Blue Beach) as the most likely area on the east side, with the Yellow Beach and Purple Beach on the west side as the least likely to provide suitable embarkation conditions. The admiral also ordered the unit to conduct reconnaissance of the landing sites north of the Song Da Bach south of Bi Cho and on the Song Bach Dang west of Quang Yen as well as to prepare for demolition and mine clearance as directed.

Haiphong offered the best pier facilities in the DRV, though the depth limitations in the channel restricted APAs and AKAs with maximum loads.[5] These ships, the workhorses of the operation, remained in the anchorage area, while vessels such as the LSMs, LCUs, other landing craft, and lighters shuttled the evacuees as they began their passage to freedom. The responsibility for embarkation fell under the command of Captain W. C. Winn. The first priority of the Embarkation Group was to quickly and efficiently load the evacuees while eliminating potential obstacles from arising as a result of conditions or Viet Minh interference and to screen, select, and control all embarked evacuees. To assist in the process, the Embarkation Control Unit, under the control of the Embarkation Group, provided assets at the ports and beaches to control and supervise loading operations as well as assist in providing liaison with the French officials ashore. Other responsibilities for the Embarkation Group and Control Unit included coordinating all ship movements, assigning anchorage, preparing sailing orders, and working with the Haiphong port director. Finally, the Embarkation Group and Control Unit were required to transport embarked personnel and equipment to the South, provide troop personnel to the Shore Party Unit as required, and provide lighterage and stevedores for unloading the ships in the South. They were also required to acquire passenger lists and cargo manifests for each ship loaded. Each ship was to be loaded to the maximum capacity consistent with its safety and seaworthiness.

APAs, AKAs, and merchant ships were advised that their hold spaces could be required and that the tank decks of the LSTs might be used to berth personnel (see Appendix B for ship loading capacity for personnel). All ships were ordered to construct temporary topside sanitary facilities and conserve water to the best of their ability. Transport ships also arranged to rig temporary ventilation to ensure habitability during the voyage. While ship captains were instructed to use their discretion on the amount of baggage the evacuees could bring with them, animals were prohibited.

In conjunction with the Embarkation Group, the Haiphong port director organized all shipping in the Haiphong area, to include the docking and undocking and beaching and retracting of all vessels involved in the operational area. The Embarkation Group relied on the central control officer for the procurement, coordination, and control of movement of all

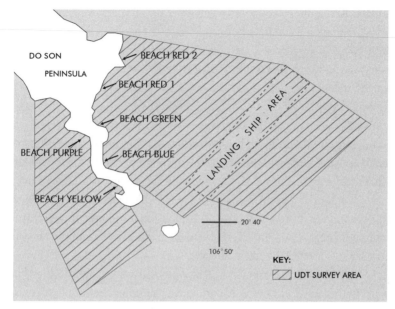

Map 3.2. Underwater Demolition Team Survey of Do Son Peninsula

LCUs and smaller craft on the beaches and on the river control officer for all landing craft in Quang Yen and the Cua Cam and Song Bac rivers leading to Haiphong. The Naval Liaison Section acted as an advisory agency to Commander Teall on naval matters affecting loading operations, arrivals, departures, and sailing orders. Finally, the Naval Beach Group Unit provided overall coordination of beach functions, including reporting on the conditions on the beach, surf reports, and the progress of embarkation operations ashore.

In this type of operation, with the real potential for a Viet Minh attack, Harbor Security played a significant role in the overall efficiency of the Embarkation Group. The threat of surprise attack by swimmers or small craft was the area of greatest concern. To combat this threat, which was enhanced by the likelihood that friendly small craft and swimmers would be in the vicinity, strict procedures were set in place to protect the shipping in Haiphong. All friendly craft were instructed to show dimmed running lights and be prepared to reply to challenges with proper identification. Ships used to transport evacuees and equipment maintained an armed ready boat during the night, and in many cases more than one boat patrolled the vulnerable areas around moored ships. All ships were required to maintain lookouts twenty-four hours a day, with armed sentries at each side as well as bow and stern. To avoid floating debris that might be used to camouflage potential sappers, all ships were warned against dumping trash over the side while in the objective area. Harbor Security Patrol complemented the efforts of the ships to ensure that all U.S. Navy personnel, their ships, and their charges were safe during this most vulnerable time in the operation.

The combined efforts of the individual components in the Embarkation Group and Control Unit allowed for the greatest efficiency possible in this most unusual of naval operations in the post–World War II era. A foreign land and frightened, disorganized people challenged the officers and personnel ashore. Without the professional manner in which they conducted themselves and performed their duties, the operation could never have achieved the great success it did.

The operation order called for all ships to sail independently after loading or, in the event of enemy air or submarine intervention, in a convoy system with appropriate air and surface escort. As the mission progressed and it became apparent that the PRC was not going to aid the Viet Minh in harassing the operation, extreme measures were deemed unnecessary. All ships en route from Haiphong to Saigon and other points south of the DMZ were instructed to travel along the coastal route but remain outside the fifty-fathom curve as far south as possible. The operation order called for each ship to sail at the best possible speed based upon the capabilities of that ship, although it stressed conservation of fuel and water. As a matter of course, each ship was required to tow or be towed, if necessary, and heavy ships were required to fuel smaller ships. Each ship involved in the operation was required to maintain a minimum of readiness while at sea.

In the South, Saigon became the obvious choice for debarkation, as it was not only the seat of government for the newly formed Republic of Vietnam but also the largest metropolitan area south of the seventeenth parallel. As the operation proceeded and the inadequacies of the southern regime surfaced, other ports were established to handle the influx of Vietnamese refugees fleeing from the North. The flexibility of this type of approach to the problem indicated the enormity of this problem in Vietnam, but it also resulted from an inadequate source of intelligence available regarding the Vietnamese people and their country.

In the early 1950s the United States did not anticipate a conflict in Vietnam and therefore did not commit significant intelligence assets in Vietnam.[6] The United States based its planning and intelligence for Vietnam and the military capabilities of the Viet Minh on a June 1954 Commander Naval Forces, Far East (COMNAVFE) Special Intelligence Study for Indochina. Admiral Sabin's staff used this earlier report as a basis for the operation, but the intelligence annex of Operation Order 2-54 demonstrated how little the United States understood the situation in Vietnam from a military perspective. As a member of Admiral Sabin's staff, Robert Mix was involved in the process by which the United States gathered intelligence in advance of the operation.

"We tried to gather all the intelligence we could get a hold of," Mix recalled. "We had intelligence officers on the staff, and we were trying to look to where we could land ships because nobody had ever been to Haiphong before, and we knew nothing about the layout of the land and how we were going to get all these people onto the ships."[7] The French provided much of the available intelligence, though it was often difficult to determine the best way to get that information from the former occupiers of Indochina, who at times seemed reluctant to assist the American effort.

Of utmost significance to the U.S. Navy were the Viet Minh's capabilities at sea and its ability to disrupt the evacuation once it began. The DRV did not possess a naval force, although it did have a number of sail- and motor-powered junks as well as faster vedettes. This force, however, was not designed to confront the French navy, nor was it expected to pose any real threat to the United States. Because the force was used primarily for clandestine merchant marine operations in an effort to bypass French efforts to blockade ports, and the need for that mission effectively ended with the removal of the French navy, the Viet Minh naval threat to the United States' effort was greatly diminished. The Viet Minh were known not to possess an air force, nor were they believed to possess any special weapons, such as atomic or bacteriologic agents. One real threat was the use of mines. Although, as of August 1, U.S. intelligence had discovered no floating mines in the North, it was believed the Viet Minh were capable of deploying such mines in rivers, canals, and shallow waters along the coast—the very areas in which the United States would conduct its operation.

Although naval intelligence characterized Viet Minh capabilities as minimal, Operation Order 2-54 maintained that, with the assistance of the PRC, the Viet Minh could offer significant resistance to U.S. efforts in the region. The most probable Viet Minh action was the use of created incidents, sabotage, strikes, infiltration of agents into the civilian refugees, propaganda, demonstrations, and passive resistance to disrupt or restrict the orderly evacuation of individuals from the North to the South. It was also believed likely that the Viet Minh would continue or increase guerilla activities and harass friendly forces to disrupt the flow of evacuees. The operation order believed the Viet Minh, if assisted by the PRC, were capable of conducting air attacks and mining the waters of the East China Sea, Formosa Straits, and Gulf of Tonkin as well as overwhelming the remaining French and Vietnamese forces in the North before the evacuation's completion. Finally, the navy also thought that submarine attacks, small-scale surprise attacks on U.S. personnel, and amphibious assaults in the Tonkin Delta against embarkation staging areas might be possible, though improbable.

As with any U.S. military operation, there was great need to ensure that task force organization, evacuation plans, and other details of the operation did not find their way to the opposing forces. As a result, the operation order, though it did not censor personal correspondence, did require individual captains to caution personnel against mentioning potentially classified information or any information that might provide the DRV with vital information about the logistics of the evacuation. Because of potential and realized concern that Viet Minh agents would infiltrate the civilian population, all personnel involved with Task Force 90 were cautioned to keep contact with the Vietnamese at a minimum. This would not only limit Viet Minh intelligence but also prevent potential misunderstandings between sailors and civilians based on differences in language and culture. Additionally, navy personnel were warned to anticipate that Viet Minh agents would spread rumors, organize demonstrations, start fires, set explosives, sabotage ship mechanical devices, and steal or destroy U.S. and Vietnamese property to disrupt operations or spread discontent among the evacuees. In addition to the difficulties of moving a nation and the threat of Viet Minh sabotage, there was also the problem of language. Very few Americans spoke French, and far fewer could communicate in Vietnamese, potentially making communication one of the most significant obstacles to the success of the operation.

The operation order called for the assignment of at least one U.S. military linguist to each ship and major unit of Task Force 90. Commanders were allowed the flexibility to interchange these personnel with their commands in the most logical manner to provide for the most efficient use of translators and interpreters in the operation. The navy also anticipated the use of five additional interpreters on each APA and AKA; four of them would be proficient in French and Vietnamese and one in French and English. The United States expected the French translators to act as liaison between the commanding officers of the ships and the evacuees and to be responsible for the control and discipline of the evacuees. As the operation progressed and the French failed to provide the necessary personnel to the U.S. side of the operation, each ship and individual personnel on many ships rewrote this section of the operational order to succeed in the transportation of civilians from the North to the South.

Despite French failures to deliver the promised translators, American personnel involved in the operation were able to overcome the language barrier in a variety of ways. The Vietnamese refugees did not speak English, nor did the sailors understand Vietnamese. French was one common link for many; high school French, however, seldom worked. In some cases, volunteers aboard the transports were asked to act as interpreters. Leo Andrade, a lieutenant junior grade aboard USS *Menard* (APA-201), was one such volunteer, but in his case, as with others trying to make the passage more comfortable for the Vietnamese, his effort fell short of the requirement. Ray Skinner, aboard USS *Montrose* (APA-212), also tried his high school French but also had a hard time understanding the French of the Vietnamese. Skinner would discover that there was another shared language among the Vietnamese and Americans: Latin. Many of the Vietnamese refugees were Catholic, and the priests who led them from the surrounding areas shared that common language with the chaplains aboard the U.S. ships. Latin reemerged as the language of communication in remote Indochina. Fred Machedo, boatswain's mate second class aboard *Menard*, which arrived first in Haiphong, recalled that the Catholic priest aboard the ship communicated with the Vietnamese priests. Louis McCluskey, a hospital corpsman aboard USS *Consolation* (AH-15), remembered the use of Latin during the operation and how odd it was that the dead language was their means of communication.[8]

Not all the ships involved in the operation had the luxury of Latin-speaking personnel. When the language barrier could not be overcome orally, the oldest form of communication took over. James Chapman, boatswain's mate aboard USS *Calvert* (APA-32), recalls:

> About the most successful way of dealing with the people was to make sign languages, make gestures like if you wanted a cigarette, how you'd light the cigarette and stuff like that. If they wanted cigarettes, just hold out cigarettes to them. You had to just act out what you were trying to get across to them and that was about the only way that they could communicate with them because like I say, that chaplain that spoke their language, I don't think I ever saw him. So, the communications with the people would have been what you could come up with in hand gestures and that kind of thing. That was about the only way of communications that you had. But that, believe it or not, turned out to be fairly successful. You could get quite a few points across to them just by motions with the hands and that kind of deal.[9]

Communication was perhaps the most significant day-to-day challenge of those who directly participated in Operation Passage to Freedom. A little ingenuity and a tremendous amount of compassion were enough to overcome the obstacle.

The problems did not end there. The climate of Southeast Asia would also test the Americans. Weather became a significant factor in the evacuation of the military and civilians.[10] Indochina is dominated by monsoon circulation, with a southwesterly monsoon of high temperatures and humidity from June to September and a dry northeasterly winter monsoon from October to March. The climate over the whole of the operation area was characterized as tropical, with high temperatures and humidity. The operation order commented on the potential for rainfall, wind, and typhoons from July to November, but it minimized these natural obstacles to the overall mission. Typhoons were thought to be the principal weather obstacle, and indeed they proved to be during the course of the operation. Several typhoons would disrupt and delay stages of the operation, but they did not result in a significant loss of time over the course of the three hundred days.

The role of the Debarkation Group was as important as that of the Embarkation Group.[11] In the North, the Embarkation Group faced obstacles caused by Viet Minh propaganda and overt intervention as well as French intransigence. In the South, the French continued to be unwilling to accommodate the United States in the evacuation. Although the Viet

Minh threat was significant, the inexperience of the young Republic of Vietnam government and inadequate facilities for debarking and housing the refugee population placed severe strain on the operation from the very first month. Like the Embarkation Group, the Debarkation Group was equal to the task and through American ingenuity and perseverance was able to accomplish its mission.

The operation order called for the Embarkation Group to assist with debarkation efforts, and the commander of the Debarkation Group, Captain B. N. Rittenhouse, was provided with the following guidelines and objectives: After arriving in Saigon and establishing a liaison with French authorities, Rittenhouse and his staff were responsible for unloading all the operation's vessels in Saigon as well as those whose length and draft prohibited entry into the channel leading to the port. This included vessels with a draft more than 30 feet and a length longer than 694 feet. The operation order emphasized quick turnaround, because the navy had a limited amount of time to move an undetermined number of people and equipment. The principal ports in Saigon were the Khanh Hoi and Messageries Maritime Wharves. Khanh Hoi Wharf, located on the west bank of the river approximately 2,100 feet below Arroyo Chinois, was constructed with a masonry wall and a solid fill. It was approximately 3,445 feet long and 24 to 30 feet deep. It could handle up to five Liberty-type ships and two of the Liberty 2 C1-A types. The Messageries Maritime Wharf, also located on the west bank of the river just below the mouth of the Arroyo Chinois, was constructed with open concrete piles and a concrete deck. It was approximately 1,425 feet long and also had a depth of 24 to 30 feet. It could handle one Liberty-type ship and berth two Liberty 2 C1-A types. Both piers were in excellent condition, and it was estimated that a total of twenty-three ships of approximately ten thousand tons displacement could reside at the piers and be moored to the pilings in Saigon. The port also had twenty-four mobile cranes with three- to twenty-ton capacity, two floating cranes with fifty- and ninety-ton capacity, and two small pontoon cranes. With the addition of 114 lighters of 50- to 150-ton capacity and ten tugboats, the facilities at Saigon could handle the majority of the influx of shipping during the operation. As the operation progressed, the port facilities proved inadequate when the French limited U.S. Navy access to berths and the South Vietnamese government failed to organize and disperse the evacuees in a timely manner.

The administrative responsibilities for an operation of this type were immense.[12] Admiral Sabin and his staff implemented a few rules to ensure the orderly movement of evacuees and equipment. Sailors were offered liberty in ports south of the seventeenth parallel at the discretion of the SOPA and with the approval of French and Vietnamese officials. The sailors were instructed, however, not to leave the vicinity of the embarkation and debarkation points. Saigon was the common port for liberty, though as the operation progressed Tourane (Danang) and Cap St. Jacques (Vung Tau) also became areas for rest and recreation. No leave was granted, save for emergency, for the duration of the operation. This did not become a factor, as most ships were on station for only a short period of time. While ashore, no American personnel, including shore patrols in the South, were allowed sidearms; this resulted in some interesting experiences for those assigned to shore patrol duty.

One of the outgrowths of Operation Passage to Freedom was the potential of publicizing the humanitarian nature of U.S. involvement in Vietnam but also the horrors of living under communist rule. The potential for publicity in the operation was unlimited. Photographs and stories of American servicemen providing aid and a safe haven to a large portion of the Vietnamese people who had decided to leave all their possessions, their homes, and sometimes their families to escape communism was strong propaganda. It should be no surprise that the operation order stressed the need for maximum publicity for the role the U.S. Navy would play in the operation. Admiral Sabin and his staff encouraged all units to provide newsworthy stories for relay to the public relations office. The order provided for complete assistance to all media representatives, while accredited American correspondents who joined ships engaged in the operation would be treated as equivalent to the rank of lieutenant commander for messing and berthing. American ships were authorized to transmit stories originated by the civilian press unless commercial facilities existed, and no censorship was to be imposed on civilian-originated releases. It is interesting to note that despite all efforts to make the operation a publicity coup, it failed to sustain interest in the United States.

Although they were not dealing with weather, the Viet Minh, or the press, Admiral Sabin's staff was consumed by the logistical challenges of mounting an operation in an underdeveloped nation. An operation that would involve more than one hundred ships would require advanced logistical planning.[13] The general logistics plan allowed for the initial supply of all ships through normal supply channels with the expectation of an extended operation. It was expected that all ships would avail themselves of every opportunity to replenish to capacity, with large ships providing supplies for smaller ships. The operation order planned to establish a mobile Logistic Support Group at Tourane Bay, halfway between Saigon and Haiphong. Admiral Sabin also anticipated stationing repair ships at both Saigon and Haiphong and relying on the French shore facilities for any emergency repairs. The ships of Task Force 90 were instructed to assist MSTS vessels in order to maintain logistical coherency.

Ships were required to carry ninety days' worth of dry and frozen provisions and were to fill to capacity with fresh provisions and water. All ships were to carry full wartime allowances of ammunition and to fill to capacity with fuel, lubricants, fog oil, ship's store stock, clothing and small stores, spare parts for machinery, ordnance, electronics, and aviation stores. Ships were also to carry a 180-day supply of medical and dental stores. Water was considered one of the most critical items of re-supply. Ships in transit to Haiphong were instructed to limit water expenditures so they would arrive on station with full tanks. Although fresh water was available in a limited quantity in Saigon and from the French navy at Haiphong, it was considered contaminated and safe only after chlorination. Water tankers were anticipated to be available at Tourane in the middle of September. The commander of the Logistics Support Group was also responsible for the transit arrangements of replacement personnel, mail, payment, and recreation during the operation. Another expected problem during the operation was medical care. The enormity of medical problems would not become clear until after the evacuation began, and it is a credit to the Americans that they accomplished as much as they did during the three-hundred-day period.

The medical component of Task Force 90 had the dual role of maintaining the health and welfare of the navy personnel involved in the operation and providing necessary assistance to the refugee population, which was in desperate need of medical attention.[14] The operation order worked on several assumptions in preparing for the mission. First, there was little expectation that the French Union troops and civilians would bring with them adequate medical supplies and equipment. Medical personnel expected people of all age groups with special medical problems in obstetrics, gynecology, pediatrics, and geriatrics and with little to no medical assistance or supplies to aid them. Despite the dire conditions they predicted, navy medical personnel believed that the French Union personnel and MAAG would be able to arrange for the necessary epidemiological screening, appropriate immunizations, and delousing of all personnel in the staging areas before embarkation.

All hospital, command, and transport ships in the operation had medical and dental departments, and additional medical departments were aboard cargo and dock landing ships. Hospital ships also included a fleet epidemiological unit and sanitation personnel, while specialized hospital landing ships (LST[H]) held mobile surgical teams as well as blockloads of medical supplies and equipment. On land, beach medical personnel would handle the screening of evacuees and organize the embarkation camps around Haiphong. For friendly forces, the hospital ships would be used for early surgical and medical care of major illness and injuries. The APA transports would be used to carry these cases and to take on any overflow for primary surgical and medical care in case of major illness and injury should the hospital ship become full or not available. The command, cargo, and dock landing ships and MSTS transports (T-AP) would care for minor illnesses and injuries and handle major illnesses and injuries if their medical departments were capable. Finally, mobile surgical team personnel on tank landing ships would provide care for illness and injury among the embarked personnel in accordance with the capabilities of their medical facilities. These teams would also accommodate ambulance helicopters when needed. On land, the beach medical personnel would provide medical and dental care to the personnel of the Naval Beach Group and its assigned units as well as assist sick and injured civilians in the embarkation area. All ships involved in the operation were ordered to prepare to assist the evacuation of casualties as required. In the event that a refugee died during transportation from the North to the South, captains were required to take all feasible measures to preserve the remains in conformance with the wishes of the family and in accordance with their religious beliefs.

Before arriving on station to conduct the evacuation, all medical personnel received intensive instruction in sanitation, ward techniques, and nursing care of the sick and injured. They also received additional training in preventive medicine and communicable disease control, and all navy personnel were required to be immunized for cowpox, cholera, typhus, typhoid, and tetanus. One real medical concern was dysentery, especially bacillary dysentery of the para-Shigella group. The operation order provided detailed procedures for isolating dysentery in order to limit an epidemic. Despite immunizations for typhus and cowpox, these two diseases continued to be real threats to the military and civilian populations during the operation. To limit typhus all ships were ordered to ensure that embarked personnel were free from lice and mite infestations. The cowpox vaccination was deemed satisfactory to limit the possibly of smallpox. Finally, to combat malaria, which was a threat in the operation because of the climate and mosquitoes found in Indochina, all personnel were required to take chloroquine diphosphate antimalaria suppressive therapy from before they arrived on station until three weeks after they left Indochina.

As will be described later, the medical departments played a major role in the operation from both a military and civilian perspective. Medical personnel provided first-rate care to U.S. Navy personnel involved in the operation so they could continue their duties uninterrupted. Medical assistance to the Vietnamese population—in many cases the first modern medicine they had experienced—provided unparalleled goodwill toward the United States and necessary medical care to a most deserving population of patients.

With the 114-page operational order, the U.S. Navy entered French Indochina with the objective of providing transportation to all those who wished to leave North Vietnam and removing all equipment that might be used for Viet Minh gain. Although the Operational Order seemed simple in construction, the mission was not. Its greatest advantage was its reliance on flexible Task Force 90 personnel. Although Admiral Sabin might not have had prior experience in moving large numbers of civilians, he had enough firsthand knowledge of the navy to allow the personnel under his command to conduct their responsibilities. Over the next ten months, Task Force 90 personnel would show their quality as they conducted the largest civilian evacuation known to that point in naval history and what would become the first and greatest humanitarian effort by the United States in Vietnam.

CHAPTER 4

A Mass of Humanity
August 1954

On August 7, the Vietnamese-French Committee on Evacuation announced that it would begin evacuating the inhabitants of Hanoi and the surrounding province, including all North Vietnamese government employees and professors and staff from universities. For the first two weeks, from August 8 to 20, the plan was to evacuate by air up to 1,440 individuals each day, for a total of about 15,400.[1] The Vietnamese government requested that STEM finance the cost of chartering ships to carry other refugees who wished to leave the North. The Vietnamese government had already found two vessels, each with a 5,000-person capacity, willing to conduct the operation at a cost of $45,000 U.S. per ship per month. Lieutenant Colonel Kaipo F. Kauka, the MAAG transportation officer, informed STEM that the U.S. military would have a ship operating in the area by the end of the week, but Task Force 90 met the needs of the Vietnamese without this charter.

Kauka and Major General John O'Daniel, chief of MAAG, met on August 7 to review the requirements of the evacuation operation and outline the role that MAAG would play during the next nine months. The day after the meeting of the Committee on Evacuation, the chief of naval operations, Admiral Robert B. Carney, informed the commander in chief of the U.S. Pacific Fleet, Admiral Felix B. Stump, that the U.S. government intended to participate in the transportation of Vietnamese from the northern part of French Indochina. The United States made the decision after a request for assistance by South Vietnamese president Ngo Dinh Diem and French military leaders in Indochina. U.S. participation would accomplish several goals. First and foremost, it would move Vietnamese away from Viet Minh and communist influence. The United States also recognized the precarious position of the South and acknowledged the benefits of a population swing of more than eight hundred thousand people, all of whom had already voted against the Viet Minh—and thus communism, in American eyes—by their desire to leave the North. Finally, those conducting America's Cold War could not help but recognize the propaganda value of moving so large a population away from communism by the use of personnel and ships of the U.S. Navy.

General O'Daniel became the overall military coordinator for land-based operations under U.S. ambassador to Indochina Donald Heath. Admiral Sabin, commander of Task Force 90, became responsible for all sea operations during the course of the operation.[2] The admiral was uniquely qualified to head the evacuation operation, and it became one of the pivotal moments in his career and life. During his distinguished career, which had begun in 1917 when he entered the U.S. naval academy, until his transfer to the retired list as a vice admiral on March 1, 1961, the operation was one of his most poignant accomplishments.[3] Admiral Sabin rose through the ranks of the navy during World War II and was involved both theaters, including commands during Tunisia, Sicily, Salerno, and Normandy, where he was the naval officer in charge of Omaha Beach. From the end of the World War II to the period when he assumed command of Amphibious Group One and became commander of Task Force 90, he distinguished himself as commander of Destroyer Flotilla One in the Far East and chief of staff to Commander Destroyers, Pacific Fleet. As rear admiral, the rank he held during Operation Passage to Freedom, he served as inspector general of the MSTS, as vice commander of the MSTS, as commander of the Amphibious Training Command, Pacific, and on the joint staff of the commander in chief, Far East. He received the Distinguished Service Medal (army) for his work as assistant chief of staff, J-4, Headquarters, Far East and UN Command, from November 1952 to November 1953. In December 1953, well trained to handle the diversity confronting the U.S. Navy in Indochina, he took command of Amphibious Group One. Admiral Sabin received the Distinguished Service Medal for exceptionally meritorious service during Operation

Passage to Freedom, exercising "outstanding initiative, determination and resourcefulness in overcoming the many problems involved in the logistic support of his ships in a remote area, as well as the numerous problems of the refugees in relation to embarkation and debarkation, berthing and feeding, disease control, births and deaths, religion and the language barrier."[4] Admiral Sabin also commanded the amphibious group in the evacuation of the Tachen Islands and served as commandant of the Potomac River Naval Command and superintendent of the Naval Gun Factory. He received his promotion to vice admiral on February 4, 1956, a rank he held until his retirement.

Early in the morning of August 8, 1954, as Admiral Sabin finished his breakfast, he reached over to a box of matches to light a cigarette. As he struck the match against the side of the box, the whole box exploded into flames, causing bad burns on his hands. This was the first of several explosive events on that day and in the days to follow. As he would comment at the end of August, "There have been more headaches in this job than there are aspirin tablets in the world to cure them."[5] Still, the plight of the Vietnamese attempting to escape from the North and his sense of duty inspired him, his staff, and the navy personnel involved as they conducted this passage to freedom. During the operation, Admiral Sabin, his staff, and Task Force 90 personnel were challenged daily with new obstacles; differing people, cultures, and languages; and a rugged climate that tested the skill and ability of all involved. One of the first headaches was the gathering of appropriate navy vessels, many of which were already committed to training exercises with the Republic of Korea.

The timetable for the operation required immediate consultation and action. While Admiral Sabin issued orders for his staff to prepare the operation order that would guide the task force throughout the first phase of the operation, he began a series of meetings to determine the political and military situation in Indochina. He also worked with his superiors to free navy ships and personnel for the operation. In order to facilitate the planned operation and ensure adequate naval participation, the navy cancelled RLT MARLEX 3-55, a training exercise in amphibious landings for U.S. Marines, and promised a quick end to its predecessor, RLT MARLEX 2-55. Admiral Sabin requested from the Pacific Fleet an amphibious command ship (AGC), eight attack transports (APAs), four assault cargo transports (AKAs), four dry-dock landing ships (LSDs), four high-speed transports (APDs), two repair ships (ARLs), eighteen tank landing ships (LSTs), twelve utility landing craft (LCUs), and various other units necessary to embark and disembark personnel and materiel.[6] There was no way to know how many ships would be required for the mission or what contingencies might need to be addressed. The plan called for all the ships Admiral Sabin and his staff thought necessary to finish the job. Of immediate concern was the debarkation of all Republic of Korea personnel aboard ships slated for Indochina and the suspension of shipboard training until the end of the Vietnamese operation. The required ships were released to Admiral Sabin when Admiral Stump promised the return of all Task Force 90 vessels from RLT MARLEX 2-55 earlier than the scheduled August 15 deadline (the exercise officially ended on August 14). Admiral Sabin then requested from the Naval Supply Depot at Yokosuka, Japan, eighty-five thousand life jackets, eighty-five thousand rice mats, seven hundred thousand chopsticks, and seventeen thousand four-quart buckets for the evacuation. The navy arranged with the air force to obtain fifteen hundred tons of rice, more life jackets, and other indigenous Japanese materials after August 14. The admiral and his staff had little intelligence about the refugee situation in Indochina but began the operation in earnest, knowing that they faced a finite timetable.

If planning for the many unknowns of Indochina was not enough, Task Force 90 personnel also had to deal with the realities of limited resources in the Pacific Fleet. Admiral Stump asked Admiral Sabin to organize a plan that would phase out amphibious force ships from the evacuation as soon as possible by substituting Military Sea Transportation Service (MSTS) vessels when practical. The MSTS ships would free navy ships for other duties in the Pacific. On August 14, Admiral Carney informed Admiral Stump that the ultimate plan should use small amphibious craft for shuttle work, in conjunction with the MSTS troop and cargo ships, as they became available and required.[7] It was difficult enough to organize the large-scale humanitarian effort with just Task Force 90 ships. Adding the MSTS, which sometimes followed different regulations, would provide one more set of potential explosions as Operation Passage to Freedom commenced.

When Admiral Sabin met with Ambassador Heath and General O'Daniel the next day, August 10, they agreed with the necessity for full press coverage. This would not only provide a favorable world opinion on the humanitarian effort, but it would also encourage Vietnamese in the North to believe in the operation. Admiral Stump also agreed with this assessment and ordered the assistant public information officer for the Pacific Fleet, three journalists, and a combat camera crew to join Admiral Sabin's staff. Admiral Stump approved press conferences aboard USS *Estes*, Admiral Sabin's flagship, and began setting up procedures to handle movies, photographs, and news stories through navy channels.[8] While concerns about the press and adequate coverage presented challenges, such obstacles seemed like mere distractions to the daily problems emerging as Americans encountered the Vietnamese evacuees. As each obstacle presented itself, American personnel rose to the challenge with creative solutions and common sense.

The installation of sanitation facilities aboard the ships designated for Operation Passage to Freedom was an example of the ingenuity of American personnel. There were too many refugees aboard the ships for existing facilities, and because of security concerns the refugees were restricted from certain areas while aboard, including the crew's compartments.[9] As a result, shipboard sanitary facilities needed to be constructed to accommodate the Vietnamese refugees. Stan Coito, aboard USS *Montague* (AKA-98), remembers the adaptation: "For restrooms we took fifty-five-gallon drums. We cut them in half, split them open, put some boards on top, put a fire hose on one side and let the water run out and just let it go out into the ocean."[10] Ray Bell, a metalsmith second class, was also aboard *Montague* and was directly involved with the installation. Bell and others from the ship fitter department built a privacy shield around the facilities only to discover that the Vietnamese would not use them. After the first trip, *Montague*'s crew took down the shields, with better effect. Also aboard *Montague*, Mel Hone, quartermaster second class, recalled the difficulties involved in getting the Vietnamese to use the facilities correctly. It took time to teach the Vietnamese that the three split fifty-five-gallon oil drums, which were welded together to form one long trough, were not designed for washing the children or clothing, "You'd wash the kids at the front end and the clothes and then things kind of just mitigated down to the serious stuff. They didn't see any problem with that, and it was working just fine for them."[11] Despite the initial cultural disparity, the American sailors showed their passengers the proper usage of this American creation with the same high level of kindness and caring shown throughout the operation.[12] The story of *Montague* was replayed on each ship used to transport refugees during the ten months.

With the question of sanitary facilities resolved, Admiral Sabin was able to divert his attention to other pressing matters, such as medical care and operational organization. He requested that the LSTs receive three helicopters for casualty evacuation and provided mobile surgical teams for four LSTs before they arrived in French Indochina. As Admiral Sabin left for a conference with General O'Daniel in Haiphong, his flagship received elements of the Navy Beach Group One Tactical Air Control Element One, a combat camera crew, and several interpreters. The conference included senior French officer Vice Admiral Philippe Auboyneau, who served as commander of naval facilities at Haiphong; Admiral Querville; army commander of the Haiphong perimeter Major General Franchy; Gerald Strauss; a STEM representative; and the Vietnamese mayor of Haiphong. It was clear from conference discussions that the magnitude of the operation, and its details and organization, had not been given appropriate consideration by the French. Admiral Sabin also worried about the inability of the French and Vietnamese to coordinate their activities and of the French in the North and the South to agree on how they should conduct their end of the operation. Admiral Sabin next flew to Hanoi and had equally frustrating meetings with French commanders, including General Selan, area deputy for General Ely, and Major General René Cogny, commander of the Hanoi perimeter. Admiral Sabin also realized that the task force would be at a further disadvantage by the restrictions of the Geneva Agreement, which prohibited the introduction of foreign military assets north of the seventeenth parallel. This meant that only a limited number of American personnel could be ashore in the embarkation area at any one time and that greater reliance had to be placed on French and Vietnamese personnel.[13] After the meetings, Admiral Sabin announced to the French press that the U.S. Navy would begin assisting in the evacuation process. The public utterance was easier than implementing the actual plan for evacuation. Although the navy may have been eager to proceed, it needed Vietnamese and French officials to coordinate with one another and the United States if the operation were to succeed.

In an update to Admiral Stump, Admiral Sabin observed what he considered to be the primary problems of Task Force 90. These included the transport of personnel and equipment from the North to the South as well as logistics support and security for his ships and personnel. MAAG was principally responsible for getting the Vietnamese to the embarkation center, inspecting them, and getting them to the loading area as well as ensuring that the debarkation area was operating efficiently. MAAG also provided the same services for the equipment and vehicles awaiting transport. Admiral Sabin had full confidence in General O'Daniel and his MAAG staff, but he was worried about the abilities of the French to fulfill their role in the operation. He relayed conflicting conversations he had had with various French officials regarding their responsibility—responses varying from no responsibility at all to complete control of the operation. One telling example of the inability of the French to coordinate was a shipment to a refugee camp in Haiphong of four hundred desperately needed tents, which arrived without the tent poles; the result was a sea of canvas with nothing to hold up the tents except the hands of the refugees.

While in Haiphong, Admiral Sabin also had an opportunity to visit one of the refugee camps. His observations provide another unique perspective on the deplorable state of the Vietnamese awaiting transportation to the South of Vietnam: "There were some 14 thousand people huddled in what to me seemed to be a cesspool. They were dirty, had little food or water and no shelter except a few pieces of cloth between two sticks in the ground. This is the monsoon season and that isn't a very comfortable way to live. They had given up the only things they owned which probably was a little rice paddy and a thatched hut; but they had done it willingly to escape the jaws of Communism."[14]

Because of the isolated nature of the operation in Indochina, it was difficult to refit and replenish the task force. In response to this problem, Admiral Sabin requested the establishment of a logistic support force to assist the ships of Task Force 90. Before traveling with five of his staff to French Indochina as an advance party, Admiral Sabin asked Admiral Roy A. Gano, commander of Task Group 92 and a longtime colleague, for maximum assistance in preparing the ships of Task Force 90. Admiral Gano activated Task Group 92 to fulfill this need on August 23 and then ordered elements of his task group to Tourane Bay, the approximate median point between Haiphong and Saigon. The initial commitment consisted of USS *Ajax* (AR-6), USS *Mispillion* (AO-105), USS *Karin* (AF-33),

USS *Sussex* (AK-213), and USS *Sharps* (AKL-10). The group would provide the necessary support for the operation and the refugees, including providing fuel; frozen, fresh, and dry provisions; rice; paper cups; sleeping mats; chopsticks; and buckets.

Complementing Admiral Gano's task group efforts in Haiphong were the hospital ship USS *Haven* (AH-12) and the repair ship USS *Reclaimer* (ARS-42). *Haven* was to assist the French in evacuating their wounded and sick after their release from Viet Minh prison camps. Most of these soldiers surrendered at the fortress of Dien Bien Phu and were to be evacuated to France. On August 24, Admiral Stump ordered the commander, U.S. Naval forces, Far East (COMNAVFE) to prepare *Haven* to sail for Indochina after Admiral Carney approved the evacuation of French POW patients from Saigon. In planning for the logistical side of the operation, Admiral Gano requested from COMNAVFE the necessary vaccines, biologicals, and antibiotics to meet the requirements of the evacuation. As the operation order foretold, the medical aspects of the operation would prove to be one of the greatest challenges.

Admiral Sabin planned to have a one-day logistics stopover for ships traveling from Saigon to Haiphong when time and weather permitted. Marking the establishment of the Tourane Bay base, Admiral Gano sent the following to Admiral Sabin: "Gano Garage General Store Gas Station Now Going X Grocery Annex Opens Twenty Fifth X Moves and Mail on Demand X Your Patronage Solicited," to which Admiral Sabin replied, "Customers on the Way."[15] Admiral Gano reported to Admiral Sabin that *Ajax* and USS *Caliente* (AO-53) would arrive in Tourane Bay on August 23 and that *Karin* and an assault cargo ship would arrive the following day. He expected USS *Grapple* (ARS-7) on August 25, *Reclaimer* on August 26, and a final assault cargo ship on August 28. All of these ships were bringing rice, indigenous materials, vaccines, recreational supplies, and sea stores from Japan. Admiral Gano expected two water tankers to depart Japan shortly after the completion of tank scaling and requested the use of USS *Derrick* (YO-59) at Tourane Bay after August 22. On August 26, Admiral Gano asked that southbound ships submit their needs when passing Tourane Bay in order for the unit to have the material ready for transfer on their return trip to Haiphong. Tourane Bay became the only link to the United States for the sailors during the operation, as it was the central location for mail, movies, and luxury items.

On August 11, the first American ship, USS *Menard*, capable of transporting a large number of Vietnamese, arrived in Tourane Bay. *Menard* had been headed toward Hong Kong for a scheduled rest and recreation when, about twenty-four hours out from that harbor, it received word that it would participate in Operation Passage to Freedom.[16] Radioman Terry Foley was on duty when *Menard* received the highly classified message by Morse code. When the message was decoded, the crew learned that they would not be going to Hong Kong but were instead being diverted to French Indochina. Unfortunately, *Menard* had arrived before the embarkation area in Haiphong became operational for U.S. ships, so it steamed in a ten-mile-by-ten-mile square off Tourane Bay as other U.S. assets became available for the operation.[17]

At the time other ships were en route, including USS *Estes*, USS *Montague*, USS *Comstock* (LSD-19) with three LCUs aboard, USS *Montrose*, USS *Telfair* (APA-210), and six LSTs. With the operation beginning in earnest, Admiral Sabin ordered the commander of Transportation Unit Baker, of Transportation Division 14, Captain B. N. Rittenhouse, in USS *Begor* (APD 127), to Haiphong to take over initial command of loading in that port. Aboard *Begor*, Captain Rittenhouse planned to rendezvous with three attack transports (APAs), two attack cargo ships (AKAs), and one high-speed transport (APD) at Tourane Bay and then proceed in company to the Do Son anchorage near Haiphong. The commander of Naval Beach Group One, Captain C. E. Coffin, Jr., reported that he had a beachmaster unit en route to Indochina capable of embarking personnel along the one thousand yards of dock space at Haiphong and the two beach sites on the Do Son Peninsula on a twenty-four-hour basis. Along with the beachmaster unit, Captain Coffin had eight pontoon causeway sections, three bulldozers, three amphibious utility vehicles (DUKWs), and two LCM salvage boats on the way to assist with the embarkation.

One of the restrictions of the 1954 Geneva Conference was the introduction of military personnel beyond the recognized ceiling established on July 21. The requirement for U.S. military personnel in Haiphong, whether they were seamen or marines, was paramount if the evacuation were to proceed in a timely and efficient manner. On August 12, Admiral Sabin met with Ambassador Heath and General O'Daniel to discuss the use of shore parties for communications, liaison, technical advice, and beach supervision.[18] After negotiations with the French, who seemed reluctant to test the cease-fire while they were in a vulnerable position in the North, both parties agreed to a contingent of fifteen to twenty unarmed personnel at Haiphong to oversee the land operation. Admiral Stump agreed with the proposal, after which Admiral Sabin ordered his staff to add this component to the operation order.

The French expected a potential one hundred thousand evacuees per month at the beginning of the operation. The French military in Haiphong guaranteed Admiral Sabin that they would search all refugees and their baggage before allowing them to board ships for transport south. The French set a baggage weight limit of sixty pounds per person and offered to provide five interpreters for each APA and one for each LST, as provided for in the operation order. They also informed Admiral Sabin that they would provide rice, fish, water cans, and other rations necessary for the civilian population and give smallpox vaccinations and cholera inoculations. In Saigon the French offered Vietnamese laborers and disinfectants to clean the ships after debarkation. Despite these French promises, Admiral Sabin requested four additional MSTS troop ships as soon as possible to bring amphibious transport capacity up from fifty-five thousand to the one hundred thousand requirement. On August 13, Admiral Stump then ordered Admiral Sabin to release one APA and four LSTs to COMNAVFE to transport Japanese Self-Defense Force units from Kyushu and Honshu to Hokkaido, an operation that had been scheduled earlier. The release did not seriously affect the Indochina operation, as elements were not in place in Haiphong to begin full-scale operations, and the Japanese transport would end before the APA and LSTs were required, but this event demonstrated the necessity of juggling resources by the Task Force 90 staff while continuing to provide for the evacuation.

With the arrival of the ships and basic agreements with the French and Vietnamese in place, the operation was ready to commence. The weather was not cooperative; typhoons Grace and Helen made their appearances. Because of them Admiral Sabin was not able to fly to Okinawa to embark on USS *Estes*; instead, he met the ship at Sangley Point in the Phillipines. Pacific Fleet Command warned all ships of the approach of the typhoons, both of which would cause delays in all aspects of this first stage of the operation, though nothing serious occurred that the navy could not handle.

Security was always on the minds of those involved in the operation, but General O'Daniel provided some relief when he informed those involved that he anticipated no interference in the use of U.S. ships during the period in which French Union forces remained in the DRV. To facilitate the operation and provide security in an indirect manner, the navy did arrange for hunter-killer submarine exercises to be held in the sea lanes used during the Indochina operation as well as at points between known PRC areas and ships inbound and outbound from Indochina. This provided the extra sea power necessary to deal with any overt threat from those nations that might oppose American involvement in Indochina.

With initial security established on the seas, the United States turned to the myriad problems on land. On August 15, Admiral Sabin, under the orders of Admiral Stump, refused a French request to transport 18,000 Vietnamese POWs to the North. Though Viet Minh remaining in the South were a potential problem to the stability of the republic, Admiral Stump ordered Admiral Sabin to refuse further requests involving Vietnamese POWs and Viet Minh regular forces, arguing that the PRC would provide the shipping if the French were not able to or were unwilling.[19] At the same time, Admiral Carney ordered Admiral Stump to hold the hospital ship *Haven* at Yokosuka, Japan, until after Admiral Stump visited Saigon and assessed the need for the ship. There was still a question whether French POWs, those captured during the battle for Dien Bien Phu, would be released in time for the United States to transport them to France and whether the French required American assistance in the endeavor. On August 26, the commander of the Service Fleet for the Pacific (COMSERVPAC) proposed that USS *Haven* depart from Saigon with approximately 725 French POW patients for Marseilles, France, then return to Long Beach, California, which it finally did on September 10. While *Haven*'s mission orders were considered, Task Force 90 began to collect in Indochinese waters.

Earlier, on August 14, USS *Wantuck* (APD-125) joined *Menard* and *Montague*, which had arrived earlier, at Tourane Bay. Another APA, an LSD, and four LSTs were en route, evading Typhoon Grace. These ships were in addition to USS *Estes*, six APAs, two AKAs, four LSDs, three APDs, and nine LSTs on their way to the objective area. These ships were redirected to Haiphong to commence embarkation of Vietnamese and French nationals. As the ships involved in Operation Passage to Free-

Fig. 4.1. Vietnamese refugees aboard USS *Menard.*
Photograph courtesy of Douglas Fraser, USS *Menard* (APA-201).

dom converged on Indochina, the first to arrive was ready to begin the process.

On August 15, USS *Menard* arrived in Haiphong to begin embarkation, and on the same day two APAs, two AKAs, and one APD joined Captain Rittenhouse, who was aboard *Begor* at Tourane Bay. On August 15, Admiral Sabin held a press conference in Manila at the American embassy to outline the purpose of the U.S. Navy's presence in Indochina and provide background information on the United States' participation in the evacuation. After the conference, Admiral Sabin embarked on *Estes* at Subic Bay and left for Haiphong to oversee the naval operations. There were still some twenty-four ships of varying classes en route to the objective area. On August 16, *Menard* began loading refugees at Haiphong, using two French LCTs, which carried approximately 1,000 passengers each. *Menard* loaded 1,924 refugees and sailed for Saigon, becoming the first U.S. Navy ship to participate in the Indochina evacuation.

Menard could carry, in addition to its crew, approximately 1,200 marines with their equipment. During the operation, *Menard* made three

Fig. 4.2. "A helping hand" during Operation Passage to Freedom.
Photograph courtesy of the Douglas Pike Photograph
Collection, Vietnam Archive (VA000879).

round-trips between Haiphong and Saigon, carrying 6,341 refugees, according to the official record. Ensign Carl Benning remembers, however, that the total number was probably much more. Benning, using a counter, was given the task of counting the Vietnamese when they boarded. "As the refugees came aboard, some of the women would have babies and small children hanging all over them. As they came aboard I was pushing the counter button fast and furious to keep up with the number coming aboard. I am reasonably sure I probably didn't get them all counted."[20] Jack Majesky, first lieutenant on *Menard*, remembers the Vietnamese who came aboard that first journey: "The thing that sticks out in my mind more than anything else is that they came aboard with every possession in the world that they still owned, which was essentially nothing. If they had some kind of a container with them that was the size of a gym bag, that might have been a lot. In fact, I recall most came aboard without anything."[21] Majesky was so moved by the spectacle that he wrote a letter to his parents about the experience, describing the Vietnamese who had left their homes and country with little more than the clothes on their back.

For those aboard *Menard*, the loading process was organized chaos. Differences in language and culture added to the anxiety felt by many of the Vietnamese, who had never seen such a large ship nor, most likely, the sea or Americans. Despite the immediate obstacles, the loading proceeded with only one incident. Ensign Carl Benning recalled:

> The French brought them out in landing craft type boats. I believe they were LCI boats. There were about 100 refugees packed in the well-deck of the boat. We lowered a steel ladder (weighed about two tons) into the well-deck and the refugees climbed up the ladder to get aboard the *Menard*. There were about thirty steps in the ladder. The ladder had a roller at the bottom that allowed it to roll in the well-deck of the refugee boat when it moved up and down as sea swells moved by. One old Vietnamese man got his foot crushed when the ladder rolled over his foot as a swell moved by.[22]

The man was treated by the ship's doctor and released for his passage to freedom. The crew of the *Menard* learned from this first experience and moved away from the rough waters at the mouth of Henriette Pass to calmer areas. With the first group loaded and ready to go, Operation Passage to Freedom had officially begun.[23]

After a fifty-nine-hour trip, *Menard* arrived in Saigon on August 19 to be greeted by a band, an honor guard, and French, American, and Vietnamese officials. In the midst of a downpour, the refugees debarked from the ship with remarkable order and dispatch. As the refugees debarked, they were handed bread, bananas, and soft drinks by the Vietnamese Red Cross and the American Women's Group, which was made

Fig. 4.3. View from USS *Menard* during the first debarkation of Vietnamese refugees in Saigon. Photograph courtesy of Dean Hewitt, USS *Menard* (APA-201).

up mainly of wives of American personnel in Vietnam. *Menard* reported a smooth debarkation and again praised the organizational efforts of the priests during the process. The Catholic priests aboard *Menard*, as well as those involved with the other ships that were beginning their participation in the operation, played an important role in maintaining order during the passage. John Ruotsala, aboard USS *Montrose*, recalled the value of the priests during the ship's first journey south. The evacuees had trouble understanding how to use the sanitary facilities and refused to eat the rice. The priest translated instructions between the Vietnamese and Americans to solve the immediate problems.[24] "The main cohesiveness that we saw," recalled Lieutenant (junior grade) Forrest Lockwood, who served aboard USS *Telfair* as assistant navigator, "was the Roman Catholic Priests, and they were the ones that really shepherded their flocks."[25]

The evacuees turned refugees also found that there was assistance waiting for them in Saigon. As they debarked, the Red Cross provided packets of food for them before they boarded transportation to relocation centers and their final camps in South Vietnam. Because the priests

Fig. 4.4. Vietnamese Catholic priests overseeing the preparation of rice.
Photograph courtesy of Douglas Fraser, USS *Menard* (APA-201).

proved so valuable, *Menard*'s captain, L. E. Ruff, suggested that priests
be carried on each ship.

One worry raised during preoperation planning was the physical transport of Vietnamese from landing craft to the ships. *Menard* reported that
the accommodation ladders to the LCTs worked effectively as a means of
embarkation. Captain Ruff also reported that two meals of rice daily were
sufficient, although Vietnamese should be used to supervise the preparation of the meals in order to satisfy Vietnamese tastes. Ruff also reported
widespread malnutrition among *Menard*'s passengers and, regrettably,
the deaths of a child en route to the ship and an undernourished infant
soon after departure.[26]

One major problem during the early part of the operation was the
need to clean the ships after debarkation. The majority of the Vietnamese were not used to the high seas, and, combined with their generally
poor health and the first full meals they had had in some time, they often
succumbed to seasickness. The French had pledged enough laborers
and disinfectants at the dock to clean *Menard*, but they failed to fulfill the
promise. This placed an additional burden on the ship's crew. Despite

Fig. 4.5. Vietnamese refugees being served food aboard USS *Bayfield* (APA-33), August 1954. Photograph courtesy of the Douglas Pike Photograph Collection, Vietnam Archive (VA000854).

the ineffectiveness of the French, *Menard* left Saigon on August 20 for its return trip to Haiphong.

In retrospect, the clash of cultures once again emerged with the feeding of the Vietnamese aboard the American ships. The feeding of two thousand Vietnamese aboard the APAs and AKAs, while still maintaining some semblance of security and order, was a challenge. Once again, navy personnel improvised a workable process. Clean garbage cans were filled with steamed rice, while others were filled with tea to serve out on the decks of the ships. Often, the heads of families or leaders of communities would make their way down the food line filling vats with rice and bottles with tea and collecting cans of sardines to bring back to their charges.[27] Once the food was distributed, sailors helped the Vietnamese open the cans of sardines and ensured that everyone received their fair share. The distribution of food was quite an accomplishment, but it did not mean that the problems of feeding the evacuees had ended.

During many of the early voyages, the Vietnamese refused to eat the first meal. They had been told by the Viet Minh that the United States would poison their food or feed them spoiled meat. Even when the sailors overcame these initial obstacles, the Vietnamese would not eat. It was only after some time and communication that the sailors learned the reasons. "We had a lot of fish we were going to feed them because we thought everybody in Asia ate fish. They hated the fish, they wouldn't eat the fish, and we had these huge vats and we cooked up this rice for the refugees, and they wouldn't eat the rice," Lieutenant (junior grade) Leo Andrade, who served on *Menard*, recalled. "We finally learned that it was sort of like a rebellion; they just wouldn't eat it. They didn't like the way we cooked it, and so we had to get some Vietnamese down there to help the cooks. They like their rice more steamed, and normally we cooked rice loose."[28] While the process did improve with time, the first experiences were often the same. Aboard *Montague*, the third ship to embark on Passage to Freedom, the situation was similar to on *Menard*. Rice and sardines were the main food for the Vietnamese, and, once the cooking process was handed over to them, they accepted it with smiles and thanks. The sailors quickly learned that, although the food was appreciated, the ship's stores offered items of greater demand. Jim Daniels, who served on USS *Calvert*, discovered that candy was an immediate favorite of the children aboard. "They had never had nothing like that," Daniels remembered. "They were kind of leery of it at first until we unwrapped a candy bar and showed the one girl, we ate a bite, and so she seen us do it so she unwrapped it and once she got to eating that candy bar it didn't take her long to finish it!"[29]

Fig. 4.6. Instant friends. Photograph courtesy of
Dean Hewitt, USS *Menard* (APA-201).

With the loading of the first refugees on *Menard*, Admiral Sabin ordered Captain Rittenhouse to assume command of the Haiphong embarkation. The admiral also instructed Rittenhouse to maintain close
contact with French and Vietnamese officials in Haiphong as well as the
representatives of CTF 90 who were organizing the embarkation point.
All ships arriving at Haiphong were then ordered to report to the commander of the Evacuation Group (CTG 90.8), Captain Nicholas J. Frank,
Jr. Upon the recommendation of Admiral Stump, Admiral Sabin ordered
Captain Winn, in charge of embarkation, not to load equipment and passengers together or to load equipment in APAs. The troop ships were
not designed to carry a large amount of cargo, and the combination of
cargo and passengers increased the risks of injury and sabotage. The
admiral also ordered AKAs to transport passengers when equipment was
not ready for loading. At the request of Admiral Sabin, Admiral Carney
ordered the activation of the water distilling ship USS *Pasig* (AW-3) and
requested that it sail to Haiphong in support of the operation. *Pasig* was

responsible for replenishing fresh water supplies of other ships involved in the operation.

By August 16, all ships assigned to Task Force 90 had left Japan and were en route to Haiphong or Tourane Bay except four LSTs loaded with pontoon causeways. Three of those ships were delayed because of high seas, and one was still undergoing repairs. Because of Typhoon Grace, four APAs, one AKA, four LSDs, two APDs, and nine LSTs were delayed in arriving at Haiphong. Typhoon Helen detained four LSTs in Yokosuka, but the ships that had encountered Typhoon Grace were making progress toward their goal. On August 21, USS *Andromeda* (AKA-15) diverted to Tourane Bay to await USS *Ajax* and receive repairs to the damage it had suffered from the typhoon. Anticipating the anchorage at Do Son, Captain Rittenhouse ordered USS *Wantuck* to assume the duties of station ship in that area. By August 18, the four LSTs were proceeding to the objective area as scheduled, and all other ships caught in the typhoons were clear and had posted firm ETAs to Haiphong. As firm dates for ship arrival in Haiphong materialized, Admiral Sabin ordered a survey of the Do Son Peninsula beaches for possible use as an evacuation point, as outlined in the operation order. Although the area had real promise, a single major obstacle was that there were no vehicles available to transport evacuees to Do Son.

Admiral Sabin asked Admiral Stump to make East Coast and Mediterranean T-APs ready for sail to Haiphong as soon as possible. These Military Sea Transportation Service (MSTS) ships had a transport capacity of thirty-five hundred passengers. With MSTS ships, Admiral Sabin could phase out the amphibious ships that had been engaged in the operation during their scheduled sailing dates to the United States. He believed the requirement of ten T-APs during October 1954 would bring the total capacity of Task Force 90 ships to fifty thousand persons and forty thousand tons of equipment per month. Twelve additional T-AKs would double the personnel load and increase the cargo load to seventy-two thousand tons per month. If required, five additional T-APs would increase the passenger load to one hundred fifty thousand people per month. In order to meet the preoperation levels of five hundred thousand passengers by December 18 and two hundred thousand tons by November 17, Admiral Sabin reasoned that ten T-APs and sixteen T-AKs

Fig. 4.7. Refugee groups at Phom Xa railway station, Haiphong, 1954. Photograph courtesy of the Douglas Pike Photograph Collection, Vietnam Archive (VA000877).

were required along with the amphibious ships engaged in the operation. Admiral Sabin also recommended that an MSTS officer assume command of sea operations when the phasing out of the Amphibious Force ships was completed. On August 21, the first MSTS ship was ordered to Haiphong; others were to follow.

The U.S. Navy was fully engaged in the evacuation, but there was still some concern regarding the lack of action of Vietnamese and French personnel. In a letter to the chief of staff for the commander in chief of the U.S. Pacific Fleet, Rear Admiral H. G. Hopwood, Admiral Sabin remarked on the lack of organization and preparation of the French and Vietnamese personnel in Haiphong. Admiral Sabin recounted one visit to the embarkation center in Haiphong, where he expected to see a "beehive of activity" only to find the organizers taking a siesta and almost complete inactivity.[30]

Admiral Sabin arrived in Indochina on August 18. When he moved his flagship from Henriette Passe to an anchorage off the Do Son Peninsula, he received the following from General O'Daniel: "All around Saigon tent camps are being constructed. STEM has 2,500 tents on hand, 5,000 ordered. However, sanitary utilities, mass feeding, and truck transportation are still major problems. In Northern Indo China, camp organization is as yet non-existent, since neither French nor Vietnamese have assumed responsibility. No registration or inoculations in the makeshift camps. MAAG with the cooperation of the Catholic Church and Vietnamese Government is attempting to allay fears and to educate refugees for inevitable discomforts that Communists might try to turn to their advantage."[31] General O'Daniel also informed Admiral Sabin that an embarkation center was to be installed at Haiphong. While the existing center was workable, the arrival of the five hundred tents expected would improve conditions and allow for a more organized center.

On the same day, USS *Montrose* became the second ship to load Vietnamese, 2,109 refugees, and set sail for Saigon. When the Vietnamese boarded *Montrose*, the consensus aboard ship was that the Americans were receiving a people who had suffered much to get to the embarkation point but who were still wary of U.S. motives. As one sailor remembered, "They were serious faced, and most of them had very little. . . . I think some of them were really . . . how do you say it, puzzled, really didn't question just what was going to happen to them."[32] The loading of the evacuees aboard *Montrose* proceeded smoothly even though the lessons of *Menard* and *Montague* had yet to be shared. French LCMs and LCUs brought the Vietnamese to the ship and transferred them by ladder to the gangway of *Montrose*.

Once aboard, the American medical staff, with the help of the sailors, sprayed DDT in powdered form to kill the lice and other pestilent hitchhikers that had attached themselves to the evacuees. The process was traumatic for many of the Vietnamese, but the friendly nature of the sailors soon overcame the initial fear. As John Ruotsala remembered, "After the first day out, and they realized that we were not going to throw them overboard, then suddenly the smiles broke out and the sadness disappeared."[33] The goodwill aboard *Montrose* continued as the Vietnamese debarked. The sailors had made their own care packages with supplies from the cargo ship USS *Uvalde* (AKA-88). The packages included two packs of cigarettes for adults, rice, and chopsticks. As the new refugees left the ship, *Montrose* sailors stood at the bottom of the gangway to hand

Fig. 4.8. A ladder is lowered to a French LSM alongside USS *Montague* (APA-98) to take aboard refugees, August 1954. Photograph courtesy of the Douglas Pike Photograph Collection, Vietnam Archive (VA000886).

out the packages, which often included candy bars and chewing gum they had purchased from the ship's stores.[34]

Feeding and taking care of the initial medical needs of the Vietnamese often was enough to break the barriers created by the clash of cultures and communist propaganda. Often, events would occur that endeared

Fig. 4.9. Reception committee passing out welcome packages. Photograph courtesy of Douglas Fraser, USS *Menard* (APA-201).

the Americans to the Vietnamese. On the first full day at sea, one of the *Montague* corpsmen tracked down the ship's doctor, Eugene Mauch, to investigate one of the Vietnamese women, who appeared to be in pain and acting strangely. Dr. Mauch followed the corpsman and, once on the scene, helped to deliver the first new passenger on the ship. The event became the talk of the ship for the sailors and most likely reaffirmed the growing trust the Vietnamese felt for the Americans.[35]

Dr. Mauch was also vital in organizing the sanitary facilities for the Vietnamese aboard *Montrose*. Here, the lessons of *Menard* and *Montague* were carried over, and the crew constructed deck-level bathrooms that were easily accessible and effective. *Montrose*'s engineers cut a number of empty fifty-five-gallon drums with acetylene torches and welded them together across the fantail of the ship. They then placed six- to eight-foot-long, one-inch planks across the drums to stand on and connected hoses to continuously pump sea water through the troughs. Like the other ships before, it took some explanation to get the Vietnamese to use the system. "It wasn't probably an hour once this thing was put into operation when we were out on the deck on the fantail trying to see what was going on, and the ladies had begun to wash their clothes in this thing."[36] American ingenuity met Vietnamese ingenuity aboard *Montrose* that day, but in the end the Vietnamese came to understand the facilities and the American sailors had overcome yet one more obstacle.[37]

Even while *Montrose* conducted its first Passage to Freedom, Admiral Sabin advised Admiral Stump that the restrictions placed upon the use of American personnel and equipment at Haiphong would hamper embarkation efforts despite French optimism and attempts at cooperation. In order to resolve this obstacle, Admiral Sabin planned to renew discussions on these restrictions at the next conference between American and French officials.[38] Only one hundred forty-five thousand Vietnamese had signed up for evacuation, but Admiral Sabin believed that with the establishment of the evacuation center and constant pressure on the French and Vietnamese officials, more refugees would register and greater efficiency would result. Through Captain Dickey, his chief of staff, he arranged a conference with Mr. Compaigne, the French civilian in charge of moving nonmilitary evacuees, to address his concerns and push for an increased pace to accommodate the Vietnamese ashore. On August 31, MAAG Haiphong learned that the Viet Minh had infiltrated the embarkation center to offer prepared land titles to Vietnamese who agreed to stay in the North. Viet Minh interference with the evacuation process proved to be one of the main obstacles for both the Vietnamese and the Americans for the duration of the operation. Despite these concerns, the movement of refugees proceeded.

On August 19, USS *Telfair* became the fourth ship to load Vietnamese, 2,080 evacuees, in Haiphong and to depart for Saigon. *Telfair* reported that there were two births and two deaths during the trip to Saigon. The deaths were caused by malaria and general weakness. "There were some people, it was pretty hard to tell their age, they looked pretty old, but with the conditions and so forth they were all pretty shabbily dressed," recalled Lieutenant Lockwood.[39] The physical condition of the Vietnamese as they boarded the American ships was often observed as desperate. Many of the Vietnamese had traveled great distances to reach the embarkation center, often at peril to themselves and seldom without hardship.

USS *Algol* (AKA-54) loaded the next group of Vietnamese, 2,140 evacuees, and departed Haiphong for Saigon on August 20. Based on the embarkation experiences for that day, the ship's captain, David D. Hawkins, recommended to Admiral Sabin that there was special need for jury-rigged ladders to accommodate the small children and older passengers. Admiral Sabin responded immediately by ordering USS *Reclaimer*, docked at Subic Bay, Philippines, to load lumber to construct the ladders in Tourane for distribution to all ships that required them. Captain Hawkins also noted the problems of ventilation on the AKA ships and suggested the possible solution of using wind sails on all the hatches to direct breezes below decks. He also suggested the addition of sleeping mats for those refugees who embarked without anything on which to sleep.

As more ships and navy personnel actively participated in the evacuation operation, more recommendations for improved operations surfaced. The officers of *Montrose* recommended to Admiral Sabin that after debarkation of the Vietnamese at Saigon, all passengers should be deloused ashore and numerically accounted for during embarkation and debarkation. Captain Andrews of *Montrose* also recommended the use of cargo nets to lift heavy baggage to and from the holds to reduce docking time and that ration cards be issued for meals, with special cards for infants, the sick, and the aged who required milk, which was a limited commodity. To ease navigation to Haiphong, Captain Andrews also recommended the installation of temporary navigation lights at Henriette Passe. Based on earlier recommendations from APAs and AKAs also involved in the operation, the navy ordered wind sails, ladders, and cooking facilities installed on MSTS ships at Subic Bay, if requested. Captain Andrews also reported that members of his crew had found evidence of the hoarding and selling of food among their passengers, noting that the strong ate while the weak went hungry. As a result, he recommended that the Vietnamese receive their meals on deck rather than in the holds. That method would be more efficient, cleaner, and equitable to all passengers.

Captain J. G. Spangler of *Telfair* informed Admiral Sabin that his ship's second trip went more smoothly than the first. The passengers seemed better prepared and more comfortable with life aboard the ship. He did recommend that each passenger receive a cake of soap, because many had not bathed for weeks and expressed a great interest in becoming clean. Captain Andrews also reported experience similar to that of *Telfair*: that his last load of passengers on *Montrose* seemed cleaner than their predecessors but demonstrated poor sanitary habits and were harder to control. For example, cigarettes distributed among the Vietnamese

Fig. 4.10. Delousing of Vietnamese refugees before they board USS *Montrose*. Photograph courtesy of Jim Ruotsala, USS *Montrose* (APA-212).

started a black market trade. In response to this last point, Admiral Sabin ordered that cigarettes distributed to the Vietnamese have the seal cut to impede the burgeoning trade, as the cut seal might discourage individuals from buying the packages. Captain R. Cox of *Montague* recommended carrying only eighteen hundred passengers because of the poor hygienic habits and physical condition of the refugees and inadequate ventilation systems. To resolve the shortages of Vietnamese control teams and cooks, Admiral Sabin decided to retain those with these special skills, after their initial transportation to the South, in return for giving their families housing and care in Saigon. For many in the navy, the transportation of civilians was something new; the lessons learned often revised the operation order as American personnel discovered the complexities of the Indochina dilemma.

Even as naval operations progressed without serious incident, there were still improvements to be made. On August 21, USS *Montague* loaded 2,127 Vietnamese and encountered a number of problems in the process. The Vietnamese came from five different camps, which confused French drivers, who got lost. The Vietnamese arrived at the embarkation point in vehicles they had acquired themselves, without French assistance. Once the Vietnamese assembled at the embarkation point, after the disorganized start, a navy doctor ordered the removal of one Vietnamese woman with advanced dysentery from an LSM, while another woman on the same ship gave birth. When the first boatload of Vietnamese approached *Montague*, the crew was not ready for the arrival. Then high seas and swells produced much movement between *Montague* and the LSM, making for a difficult transfer from the French vessels to the American ship. Mel Hone, a quartermaster who worked on the bridge of *Montague*, watched the process unfold as the Vietnamese were eventually transferred and then sprayed with DDT in an attempt to delouse them. "The thing that struck me was just the pathetic appearance of these people and the lack of worldly goods that they were bringing with them. You literally were limited to what you could carry on your back," Hone recalled.

> One scene that stuck with me over the years was of this little young girl about eight, nine years old and she was caring for what I felt to be her little brother, who was probably three or four. [W]hen they dusted him, they were basically delousing their head, getting rid of the lice, and when they dusted him he got some of that in his eye and he was crying and trying to clear it out of his eye. It was such a touching moment that she bent down and very calmly cleaned his eye out for him and hugged him, and then the two of them came up the ladder on board ship.[40]

Cases such as this reinforced the humanitarian nature of the mission and proved inspirational for the young sailors involved in the operation.

The Vietnamese determination to leave North Vietnam and flee Viet Minh rule was a powerful reminder to the sailors in Task Force 90 that their mission involved more than simply fulfilling orders. The daily contact with the Vietnamese was a reward in itself, but it was not the only one the navy received.

On August 21, the members of Task Force 90 received the encouraging word from Admiral Stump that their efforts in Indochina had not gone unnoticed:

> Both from reports received and from my own personal observation in Indochina, I have been much impressed with the efficient and enthusiastic manner in which all hands of Task Force 90 are conducting the current operations designed to save the freedom loving people of the Tonkin Delta from Communist slavery. You are embarked on an historic task of great importance to all the Free World. Your present tasks are foreign to your normal operations, involve great discomfort, patience and hard work. To perform such humanitarian tasks to aid civilians in distress is traditional in our Navy. As American citizens and free men you can be justly proud of what you are doing, as I am proud of your response to this assignment.[41]

Accolades aside, the seriousness of the operation and importance of conviction never waned, as Task Force 90 members were constantly reminded of what was at stake for those Vietnamese who chose to flee. On August 21 the mayor of Haiphong informed Captain Dickey that a group of refugees had fought their way to the embarkation point past a knife-wielding Viet Minh patrol. Other refugees seemed reluctant to leave because of the threat as well as the loss of family possessions. The navy engaged in its own form of propaganda by welcoming, as best they could, those who arrived at the embarkation points. Admiral Sabin ordered banners at the embarkation ship and aboard transporting ships that read, "Your Passage to Freedom." He also directed that, as each refugee left the transports in the South, he receive two pounds of rice, two packs of cigarettes, and chopsticks. USS *Uvalde* brought these supplies with it when it arrived in Tourane Bay on August 28, as well as "Passage to Freedom" stickers, which were available for each ship as it passed through the logistics area. The propaganda war would continue throughout the operation.

The operation continued to progress and intensify as more American ships and personnel arrived at Haiphong. While the mission objective became clearer, Task Force 90 still encountered unforeseen challenges. On August 23, the French informed Admiral Sabin that they planned to load a battalion, with their equipment, aboard USS *Comstock* and USS *Whetstone* (LSD-27). The original agreement between the United States and France did not include the removal of military personnel, so Admiral Sabin referred the matter to Admiral Stump. Responding to an earlier request from Admiral Sabin regarding ammunition transport, Admiral Stump limited the movement of small-arms and fixed ammunition. He then clarified navy policy regarding the evacuation of military units, suggesting that it was at the discretion of Admiral Sabin and General O'Daniel as long as the movement of civilians and MDAP equipment took precedence. The issue of military unit transport arose, according to Admiral Stump, when he stated in a Saigon conference that a greater use of LSTs would be to move equipment rather than personnel, though it was acceptable for personnel to accompany the equipment. While Admiral Stump referred to truck drivers, the French interpreted the statement to mean military units and assumed that U.S. Navy ships carrying military equipment would necessarily carry troops as well. This type of misunderstanding would continue to plague American-French relations in Indochina whether by design or happenstance.

Putting aside the question of French support or intransigence in the movement of Vietnamese, the real test of the operation's success was determined by the ability of the American servicemen to accomplish their mission as well as to serve as the first contact for the Vietnamese people. Aboard USS *Bayfield* (APA-33), U.S. personnel were successful on both counts. On August 23, the chaplain aboard *Bayfield* suggested that Vietnamese priests be allowed six complete vestments in order to hold Mass aboard ships in transport from Haiphong to Saigon. As the majority of the evacuees were Catholic, this concession seemed a small price to pay for the priests' valuable assistance. On August 25, *Bayfield* arrived in Saigon with 2,144 Vietnamese. From the ship, the following AP story was retold based on the events of its trip from Haiphong. Although the story provides a good account of the level of propaganda desired from the U.S. participation, it also gives insight into the role of the American sailors as ambassadors to the Vietnamese people:

The three hundred and twenty bluejackets in this ship have been accepted as full-fledged priests. None of them has even been to Divinity School, and none of them, as yet, has turned his collar backwards or worn a cassock. Nevertheless, these sailors are practicing like ministers. They have an enthusiastic congregation of over two thousand Catholic Vietnamese refugees. It is the members of this congregation who, in their own way, have ordained the three hundred and twenty enlisted men of USS *Bayfield*.

The refugees recently fled from the hills and rice paddies of Tonkin. Running from the Communists, several hundred thousand Vietnamese sought refuge and freedom of worship in South Vietnam. Transporting them is the U.S. Navy's "Operation Passage to Freedom."

The two thousand refugees in this ship are mostly old and sick or are young children. They arrived here in pitiable condition following a torturous journey by crowded truck and on the hot deck of a French landing ship. They had little to eat or drink for twelve hours. The temperature today has been one hundred and one degrees. Some of the refugees had to be carried aboard; the others staggered across the gangway carrying all their possessions on their backs. Rolling their eyes and biting their lips, they came with obvious fear in their hearts. The Communists had spread propaganda that the Americans would beat them and throw them overboard.

One of the first to reach the deck was an eight year old girl with her three year old brother strapped to her back. Mud had caked on her legs and arms; the only clean part of her was the path made by tears rolling down her cheeks. As she reached the quarterdeck, she was met by the biggest man on the *Bayfield*, engineman first class David Bollingham of New Orleans. Bollingham was head of the enlisted men's reception committee. "Why, bless my soul," said the two hundred and fifty pounder, "if you aren't the dirtiest little gal I've ever seen."

The girl, tense and frightened, turned to a Vietnamese priest who acted as interpreter. She asked, "Have I done something wrong?" The priest, who understands only a little English, said, "No, my child. He is blessing you."

The big sailor took the girl's small hand and led her to the shower. He gave her a piece of soap but she did not know what to do with it. Smiling gently, Bollingham set the example by washing his own hands and arms and face. Then he undressed the frightened children and bathed them. When this was over he brought them back to their family. Laughing happily, the girl ran to her mother. She related what the big "American priest" had done for her. The mother did not quite understand and proudly spread the tale that her children had been "baptized in the American way." Other children requested American baptism. And there were many willing assistants among the *Bayfield* sailors. The older refugees joined. Between the salt water hoses topside and the showers below, the 2,000 Vietnamese were "immersed" in the cleansing waters.

When that was over it was time for dinner. Navy cooks laid rice out in large pots. The refugees didn't touch it. They were waiting for permission to eat. "What the heck is the matter," muttered the master at arms. "These guys are starving, yet they won't eat." Someone said, "Perhaps they are waiting to say grace." One of the sailors said the grace in French, picked up a handful of rice, and stuffed it into his mouth. A murmur of understanding rose from the refugees. They rushed for the rice. They filled their hats with it and took it back to their families. Laughter and eating noises echoed through the compartment.

After dinner the sailors played games with the children. Parents watched contentedly. One old Vietnamese lady said, "The Communists told us lies. They said the Americans would send soldiers to take us away and beat us. Instead, the Americans came with a ship full of kindly young priests. Already, even in a few hours, they have blessed us and our food, baptized us in the American way, given us supper, and made friends with us." Now, when the refugees in USS *Bayfield* speak to an American Sailor, they address him as "padre" and when that name is mentioned, 320 bluejackets jump to give assistance. A few are getting into the habit of answering with, "Yes, my child." Some of the refugees asked why the American priests do not wear black cassocks. The sailors tried to explain that they were not real ministers but only laymen trying to treat their friends by the golden rule. But that did not convince the grateful Vietnamese. They still speak of the sailors as "padres." That is, all except Dave Bollingham. They call him "the Bishop."[42]

On August 26, Commander Lederer of the Pacific Fleet Public Information Office, after completing a trip from Haiphong to Saigon on *Bayfield*, recommended that three public information officers could cover the operation effectively. He also suggested using television and popular magazines for future publicity.

Issues revolving around publicity remained a priority for the U.S. Navy, but there were greater areas of concerns for those directly involved in the operation. While threats of sabotage and inattentiveness of the French and Vietnamese personnel on the ground in Hanoi and Haiphong challenged the American personnel conducting the operation, the realities of disease and epidemic always loomed. Captain Rittenhouse reported that the embarkation area at Haiphong continued to have a serious sanitation problem. At American insistence, French army personnel conducted daily clean-ups of the area, and it was expected that the problem would lessen with the installation of a delousing station, set to become operational on August 30. On August 27, *Bayfield* reported eight serious and fifty simple cases of diarrhea among the ship's enlisted personnel. The next day, USS *Algol* emphasized the real crisis of the health risks brought aboard by the Vietnamese, reporting two cases of measles, two cases of typhoid, thirty-one cases of dysentery, fifty-seven cases of conjunctivitis, six cases of pneumonia, five cases of impetigo, ten cases of tuberculosis, and twelve cases of influenza. During a trip to assess the medical and sanitation conditions at the embarkation area in and around Haiphong, Admiral Sabin noted the deplorable conditions ashore and understood the need for a better organizational structure. He then established the Preventive and Sanitation Unit, under Dr. Julius M. Amberson, to coordinate with French and Vietnamese officials through MAAG all medical matters arising from embarkation and provide medical and sanitation assistance to the Vietnamese in Hanoi and Haiphong. Earlier, on August 20, the navy assigned additional medical personnel to transports conducting the evacuation to bring the total medical staff to two officers and fifteen enlisted men per ship. Admiral Sabin then ordered all ships to take special care in eliminating insects and rodents before their release from Indochina, to include disinfecting all passenger spaces.

By the end of August, Admiral Sabin also became concerned about the morale of the men and officers involved in the operation, as many had been forced to extend their time in service to accommodate the needs of the operation. He granted liberty for ships in Saigon with the restrictions that only one-third of the sailors of each ship would receive it and that a midnight curfew be imposed. There would be no liberty in the DRV, based in part on security concerns but also as a result of the Geneva Conference agreements. The same restrictions applied to MSTS personnel. Liberty in Saigon was a unique event for those who had the opportunity, even if the time ashore was limited because of the quick turnaround time for the American ships. Saigon, considered by many to be the Paris of the Orient, was filled with outdoor cafes, French Union soldiers, and a different culture. Across the street from the two wharfs the Americans used in Saigon was the Majestic Hotel.[43] For many of the American sailors, the hotel bar served as a prime spot for their time off. The city had much to offer. Few experienced or witnessed any violence while on liberty, because numerous French Union troops policed the area and were not groups one tried to outsmart or confront. The U.S. Navy shore patrol did police the debarkation area without incident. The worst that happened to those who had liberty was the loss of the white caps they wore when they went ashore.[44]

Although there were no real incidents in Saigon, young eighteen- and nineteen-year-old sailors in a foreign city for the first time did have a certain amount of fun. On August 28, Admiral Sabin had to warn all U.S. Navy personnel that he would cancel liberty if they did not correct their unsatisfactory behavior. Although there is little record of what transpired during those few days, it is not difficult to imagine the opportunities for mischief in the city coined the Paris of the Orient. Because Hanoi and Haiphong were off limits and the turnaround time in Saigon was so quick, the layover at Tourane was better suited for rest and recreation.

Although questions of liberty and rest and relaxation occupied the thoughts of the sailors, the immediate concern of the mission always took priority. On August 24, USS *Menard* and USS *Skagit* (AKA-105) loaded a total 4,277 Vietnamese civilians for their passage to freedom. Including the people in those two ships, more than 150,000 people had been evacuated from North Vietnam. The United States had transported 21,085 Vietnamese civilians by sea, and the French had transported approximately 133,000 individuals by air and sea. USS *Calvert* reported that for its August 25–28 trip to Saigon approximately sixty Hanoi university students, well-dressed and healthy, had boarded the ship without eating utensils and with few personal belongings. When the crew held a party for the children on the second day at sea, several of the students told the parents and their children not to accept gifts from the Americans, because it was nothing more than pure propaganda. No further demonstrations occurred during the voyage, and the culprits were not identified, even though their association with the Viet Minh was obvious.

James Chapman, boatswain's mate aboard USS *Calvert*, remembered vividly the loading of the Vietnamese aboard the ship. What to do with the Vietnamese for the three-day trip often presented a problem. "The captain came up with the idea of showing them a movie. The movie was shown on the deck, and that's the area where they would have enough room for all of the refugees, and some of the ship's crew could watch the movie if they wanted to," Chapman recalled. "Well, when it got dark and they turned the movie on, those people were running like there had just been a war started next to them. They didn't even know what the movie was. So, that gave you the idea that they weren't very much aware of what was going on in the human world. It was kind of disheartening to see people that were in so much poverty."[45] The crew of *Calvert*, like those of earlier transports, broke down the language and cultural barriers by acts of charity and care.[46] At one point during the first loading, the line of Vietnamese ready to board stopped. Willy Carrillo, a seaman who served on the deck force, went to investigate and get the line moving again. He discovered an older lady stalled at the base of the ladder. Carrillo planned to carry her up only to discover that she was carrying her husband. It was at that moment that Carrillo understood the plight of the Vietnamese; he made sure both reached the safety of the ship. [47]

By the end of August, the evacuee situation had become clearer. Even though the number of Vietnamese intent on moving to the South could no longer be counted in the tens of thousands, the navy was prepared to handle the situation. Admiral Sabin received word from the French on August 26 that they wanted help in evacuating forty thousand Chinese from North Vietnam despite earlier statements that no assistance was necessary.[48] Admiral Stump approved the use of American ships for this purpose, and Admiral Sabin ordered Captain Rittenhouse to begin loading Chinese in an APA on September 2, the first load accounting for nearly twenty-five hundred of the forty thousand awaiting evacuation. To ensure security, MAAG Haiphong recommended separate staging areas and control teams. There were no other changes in the procedures.

The additional needs of the French were well within the capacity of available U.S. resources in Indochina. As Admiral Sabin handled the personnel problem, another one related to materiel arose. The transfer of MDAP equipment to the South was not moving as expected because the French in Hanoi and Haiphong had no instructions on the final destination of the equipment, nor were they able to distinguish between MDAP equipment and some French equipment. Admiral Sabin therefore decided to move any equipment recommended by MAAG. There was a constant shortage of stevedores and winchmen during the operation, which hampered the loading and unloading of cargo. To satisfy the requirement, the admiral sought stevedore gangs in the Philippines as the likely replacements; Japanese gangs were not available because of immigration rules.

By the last week of August, the patterns of evacuation took shape with the full commitment of U.S. resources. USS *Mountrail* (APA-213) loaded between 2,100 and 2,200 Vietnamese in Haiphong and arrived in Saigon/ Cap St. Jacques on August 26. USS *Magoffin* (APA-199) loaded approximately 2,029 to 2,046 Vietnamese in Haiphong and arrived in Saigon on the same day. On August 27, the Vietnamese 18th Infantry Battalion, consisting of 698 soldiers with 1,495 dependents, thirty-three vehicles, and accompanying baggage, left in two LSDs for Nha Trang. The battalion had received two decorations for gallantry in action during nearly three years of continuous fighting against the Viet Minh. On August 29, two LSTs loaded elements of the 14th Vietnamese Infantry Battalion before the suspension of operations caused by Typhoon Ida.

As the flow of refugees increased, General O'Daniel pushed the construction of an alternative debarkation site at Cap St. Jacques (Vung Tau) at the mouth of the Saigon River. The commander of the Debarkation Group (CTG 90.9), Captain Rittenhouse, estimated that it would take approximately one week by Beach Group personnel to clear undergrowth and trees and lay out the tents and latrines. Admiral Sabin, responding to General O'Daniel and Captain Rittenhouse, ordered USS *Epping Forest* (LSD-4) to deposit one LCU at the new debarkation point and survey the proposed area before commencing operations. The next day, *Epping Forest* arrived at Cap St. Jacques. It reported the capacity of the camp at thirty-five hundred, with room for expansion to fifteen thousand by September 11, provided a bulldozer became available to clear trees and undergrowth at the tent site. Although there were no LST beach sites available, the pier and LCU ramp were satisfactory, as were the water supply and sanitary facilities. Mr. Kearny, the STEM representative in Saigon, requested from Captain Rittenhouse the loan of one LCU to transport supplies from Saigon to Cap St. Jacques to establish the debarkation center, and he told Admiral Sabin that the French had three available bulldozers in Saigon that they refused to provide for the emerging center at Cap St. Jacques. On August 29, USS *Whetstone* left two LCUs at Cap St. Jacques to assist in the establishment of the site. While the pattern of U.S. operations emerged, so did the difficulties of U.S.–French interaction regarding procedures necessary for the completion of the mission.

Admiral Querville informed Captain Winn that the French LSMs at Haiphong would move south with the last French POWs. Accordingly, Captain Winn decided to use an LST and a French LCT to ferry evacuees from the shore to the transport ships. On August 29, Captain Rittenhouse told Admiral Sabin that U.S. ships entering the mouth of Saigon River had been taking aboard a French pilot to navigate the river. Upon arriving in Saigon, the ship captains then signed a certificate for pilotage fees. The round-trip costs were approximately $750. Admiral Sabin did not know if the French intended to collect the fees, given the significant humanitarian effort provided by the United States without cost, and asked the MAAG office in Saigon to investigate the matter. It is telling that the French would require the United States to pay the pilot fees when the Americans had already committed more than one hundred ships to the operation as well as millions of dollars. The total fee was not insignificant, though it paled in the overall American contribution, but the principle of the matter seemed insulting to the Americans involved in the operation.

Weather once again played a factor in the evacuation process when, on August 28, Typhoon Ida took a direct path for Hong Kong and became a real threat to impede the evacuation process in Hanoi and Haiphong. Admiral Sabin placed Captain Winn on Typhoon Condition One the following day. To make up for the delay because of the inclement weather, Captain Winn planned to load two LSTs and three APAs, some 6,000 Vietnamese plus vehicles, for Saigon the next day. On August 31, despite high winds and torrential downpours, two APAs loaded 4,152 refugees and one

APA loaded 2,118 Vietnamese military personnel and their dependents, while one LST loaded fifty-six vehicles and forty tons of equipment.

Typhoon Ida destroyed nearly half of the staging area in Haiphong, although the personnel were able to save almost all of the tents. The approach to the area had been inundated during the rains, but the French provided crushed rock and a more acceptable road to the staging area. MAAG Haiphong reported that they had enough tents to restore those that had been damaged and increased the capacity of the embarkation center from six to ten thousand people. The end of August ended much as it had begun for Admiral Sabin. August departed with a typhoon instead of a matchbox bursting, but while it might have soaked those exposed to the elements, it did not dampen the spirit of those involved in the operation.

CHAPTER 5

Challenges by Land
August 1954

One immediate, and continual, concern following the Geneva Agreements was the coordination of French, Vietnamese, and American programs. Each nation had a different vision of how to accomplish its objectives in South Vietnam. The Vietnamese took a more decentralized approach at the start of the operation, and the French appeared standoffish. It was the objective of the American officials in August 1954 to bring the French and Vietnamese together while trying to maximize the limited U.S. resources available. Without a coordinated approach there could be too much duplication of effort and resources. As the evacuation gained momentum, these redundancies would prove detrimental to the overall operation.

Duplication of effort was a particular problem with Vietnamese coordination in the evacuation process. Each Vietnamese ministry formed its own committee on refugees with the objective of moving its counterparts from North Vietnam. Although the United States discouraged this decentralized approach in evacuating, it did not resist the effort and worked with the ministries to ensure optimal results. One example of this counterproductive Vietnamese approach and the American response to it occurred when the Vietnamese Ministry of the Interior approached the American public administration adviser, Joseph R. Starr, to request aid in the construction of a reception area and temporary shelters in the Tonkin Delta for three to four thousand civil servants of the Ministry of the Interior.[1] It would have been more appropriate to integrate the movement of this population into the overall structure of the operation, but the United States acquiesced in order to ensure further assistance from the Ministry of the Interior. The ministry was the largest agency in the Vietnamese government and perhaps the most important in terms of the internal obstacles it could have created regarding the evacuees if provoked. By assisting the Ministry of the Interior, STEM would be able to assess the abilities of the civil servants entering South Vietnam as well as introduce the principles of scientific personnel management to their counterparts in the South.

By August 12, nearly one hundred thousand refugees had left North Vietnam by various means from Haiphong, Dong Hoi, and Qui Nhon, and five thousand tons of equipment and 161 vehicles had been transferred to the South.[2] As the number of evacuees waiting for transportation continued to grow, the Vietnamese finalized arrangements for their evacuation. President Ngo Dinh Diem had named Nguyen Van Thoai RVN secretary of state for economic affairs as the high commissioner for refugees, an appointment that the French high commissioner, General Ely, approved. The chief of staff for French forces, General Jean Gambiez, became Thoai's adviser and coordinator of French military and civilian efforts in the evacuation. With this management structure in place, U.S. officers also agreed upon an organizational structure to maximize American efforts. General O'Daniel and Admiral Sabin agreed to coordinate, through the MAAG offices, navy and STEM activities, and General O'Daniel appointed Colonel Rolland Hamelin, USMC, as his representative in the North to work with the navy personnel.

A meeting of the French, Secretary Thoai, and D. C. Lavergne, acting special deputy for refugee affairs, on August 17, marked a significant step in the coordination of aid for the evacuees.[3] Because of the United States' deep involvement in the operation, it was able to help broker agreements between the French and the Vietnamese as well as ease pressure on the overburdened French and Vietnamese resources obligated to the operation. During the meeting, the group arranged for transportation of civilian refugees from reception centers in Saigon to the resettlement area. The French provided thirty trucks for small groups, and the Vietnamese Bureau of Public Works provided one hundred for large groups. The coordinating group also established a method of communicating the

Table 5.1. Estimated Space Available for Evacuees
in South Vietnam

Resettlement Area	Potential Number of Evacuees
Hoa Kanh	600
My Tho	2,000
Bien Hoa	100,000
Xuan Loc	200,000
Hue	9,000
Da Lat	4,000
Nha Trang	2,000
Tourane	16,000
Quang Tri	25,500
Quang Binh	36,000
Total	395,100

number of refugees arriving each day and a procedure to identify the approximate times of ship arrivals. A large number of Vietnamese civilian refugees in the first stage were dependents of the military, making them the responsibility of the Vietnamese rather than the French. At the request of Thoai, Lavergne agreed to treat the refugees as civilians and provide American aid. French acting high commissioner Michel Wintrebert, second counselor of the French embassy in Vietnam, informed the group that General Gambiez would take care of sanitary needs in Haiphong and organize medical aid for those planning to board the ships. The group also discussed shelter and food requirements as well as how the refugees would be distributed throughout South Vietnam, although at that time they could provide only a best guess. The area they allocated would be sufficient for four hundred thousand individuals. Because the number of evacuees in need of resettlement remained below this number, space would not be a problem.

After coordination of the three principal relief providers, the United States faced the challenge of providing a positive first impression to the refugees and ensuring efficient integration of the new inhabitants of the South. In the spirit of goodwill, STEM organized the distribution of welcome kits for Vietnamese refugees as they debarked in Saigon. The kits, placed in a plastic drawstring bag and provided by the Cooperative for American Remittances to Everywhere, Inc. (CARE) for $1.69 each, consisted of a bar of Ivory soap, a bottle of Vaseline hair oil, a toothbrush and case, a tube of Colgate toothpaste and tube of Colgate shampoo, a comb, and a Turkish face cloth. CARE provided STEM ten thousand kits at a cost of approximately $50,000 after air freight charges were included. The kits, however, were well worth the cost in providing goodwill and basic care for the refugees as they first entered Saigon. Unfortunately, the kits arrived in late September—too late to be used for propaganda, as many refugees had already passed through the debarkation area, and the navy's public information officers had departed. STEM also authorized 3,000 piasters to the American Women's Group, under the leadership of Mrs. Frank O. Blake, for the purchase of bananas. The women's group planned to distribute the fruit to the refugees at the debarkation area.[4] An American presence at the debarkation point providing some kind of additional relief, regardless of quantity, was important to the overall mission of the United States to assist in the development of the Republic of Vietnam.

The RVN Ministry of Health requested assistance from the USOM Nursing Section in their effort to distribute powdered milk donated by Catholic Charities of America, CARE, and the United Nations International Children's Emergency Fund (UNICEF).[5] The Vietnamese required instructions on reconstituting the milk and estimates on the number of personnel needed to complete the operation. Cognizant that this kind of American assistance benefited not only the refugees but also the Vietnamese officials who would oversee the operation, the USOM was quick to respond. On August 9, CARE signed an agreement with the government of Vietnam to assist in the welfare and care of the Vietnamese people. The addition of CARE personnel, who brought with them an established infrastructure, experts, and assets, would be of great advantage to the U.S. effort to aid the South Vietnamese people. UNICEF and the Catholic World Service also committed themselves to the care of the children of the refugees. Ambassador Heath learned on the same day that UNICEF had two shipments of 250 tons of milk for South Vietnam, another 250 tons for refugee children, and 100 tons for nonevacuee children.[6] The supply of milk not only provided legitimate humanitarian assistance to the Vietnamese but also was an important symbolic gesture for those helping the refugees. The notion of helping children who were helpless, save for the assistance of the U.S. and South Vietnamese officials, was a powerful message to the Vietnamese leaving North Vietnam as well as representatives of the international community who observed the exodus.

Fig. 5.1. View of the debarkation point in Saigon from USS *Calvert* (APA-32). Photograph courtesy of Joel C. Snider.

Once the first evacuees arrived in Saigon, they were transferred to the reception center at Go Vap. They had the advantage of experiencing evacuation before the number of refugees increased dramatically. The camp at Go Vap, well organized and expandable, if needed, contained approximately eleven hundred inhabitants by August 18. The camp had a dozen large huts for shelter and several others near completion, a dispensary, and drainage ditches in process of being completed. The reception center, with a capacity of two thousand, had eight wells five meters deep. When John P. Thelen, a relief and rehabilitation specialist, visited the camp on August 17, he noted its remarkable cleanliness.[7] The real test would be whether the camp remained clean and sanitary as it was expanded and more refugees arrived in the South. The population of all the reception centers in Saigon was 19,125 on August 18.

Another reception center was established at the Hippodrome, located in an open field next to the race course. By August 19, it had ninety-five tents constructed and another two hundred anticipated, even though some of them lacked wooden poles. The camp, with sixty workers preparing the tents, digging privies, and organizing water tanks and the kitchen, would be the home of 2,000 Vietnamese who had successfully completed their passage to freedom. Thelen visited the camp on August 20 and found 999 civilian refugees who had been airlifted from North Vietnam. The refugees aboard USS *Menard*, who had been scheduled to occupy the camp, were diverted instead to the Hospital Populaire, even though it was equipped to handle only 600 people. Thelen discovered that only one additional tent had been erected and that the pit privies were useless. The Hippodrome camp suffered from a recent rain, and litter was strewn everywhere. Thelen also learned that no refugee had received the twelve-piaster-per-day allowance and that no wells had been dug, nor had water tanks arrived to relieve the suffering. Thelen found it difficult to get a definitive answer from any of the South Vietnamese minor administrators in the camp and recommended to Herman Holiday, chief of the Community Development Division, USOM, that he replace the camp coordinator with a competent official, establish a first aid tent, and distribute educational posters on sanitary responsibility as soon as possible.[8]

When Thelen revisited the Hippodrome Receiving Center the next day, 126 tents had been constructed for more than a thousand refugees.[9] The pit privies had been dug, but the water supply was still limited. The camp officials had planned to transfer the refugees in the camp to Hoa Khanh (Cholon) in order to make room for the refugees arriving by ship that day. The camp still did not have a first aid tent, but medical care was improved by the arrival of disinfectants from the Vietnamese Red Cross the night before. A separate camp of 100 tents was in the process of being constructed behind the Hippodrome, but it would not become operational until after the installation of pit privies, water wells, and a first aid tent. Thelen again commented on the ineffectiveness of the camp officials and called upon the mission to provide resources to install water wells, construct a first aid tent, and supply mosquito netting for the comfort of the temporary inhabitants.

When Thelen went back to the Hippodrome on August 23 to check on the situation, he found that 130 tents had been erected, though only 80 were in use. A strong storm had passed through the area the night before, collapsing 40 tents in the camp being constructed behind the Hippodrome, although that caused only a minimal delay in their occupation. The Hippodrome had adopted a new policy of becoming a one-night transit camp for refugees as they arrived in Saigon. This type of camp was urgently needed, as the flow of refugees to Saigon steadied with the arrival of U.S. Navy ships. Thelen noted that the camp still lacked proper sanitary measures, adequate water wells, and a first aid tent.[10] During his last inspection of the camp that month, on August 24, Thelen found approximately twenty-two hundred refugees, with another four thousand expected that evening. The overflow would be housed in the additional camp behind the Hippodrome. He was pleased to learn that a first aid tent, operated by the Vietnamese Red Cross, had been installed. He also witnessed refugees receiving rice, bread, salt, tea, and fish or meat. With water always a concern for those in the refugee camps, Dr. Paul Q. Peterson, chief of the Health and Sanitation Division of USOM, requested two U.S. Army field kits for water quality control. These kits were urgently needed to fulfill the basic requirement of a safe water supply in the refugee camps and the resettlement areas.[11] At that time water was available only from tank cars. Thelen remarked that the camp had shown major improvements, in part because of the addition of three American army personnel who helped coordinate and prioritize the needed work. Thelen's experiences during the month of August resulted in many lessons learned. First, the handling and coordination of refugees from the North were a major undertaking. Second, the United States needed to take the initiative in the process to ensure successful completion of requirements. Finally, the United States had to monitor the new South Vietnamese government's handling of the situation to ensure that it met its responsibilities.

It was extremely important for the United States to oversee efficient reception camps in Saigon if the propaganda value of the operation were to be achieved. Vietnamese refugees had fled the North in order to make a better life for themselves. It was expected that this population would also serve as the foundation for the Ngo Dinh Diem government. Proper treatment of the evacuees would further strengthen both objectives, while mistreatment, however innocent, would negate the goodwill generated by Operation Passage to Freedom.

As the flow of refugees into Saigon increased, U.S., French, and Vietnamese officials looked to other areas in South Vietnam to house the new population temporarily until they could construct new permanent villages. The South Vietnamese government and the provincial chiefs were not prepared for the large influx of refugees, and, because of the

Fig. 5.2. Refugee camp in South Vietnam. Photograph courtesy of the
Douglas Pike Photograph Collection, Vietnam Archive (VA000888).

nature of French colonial rule, they did not have the infrastructure to
handle the situation. At a meeting of various offices coordinating the
evacuation effort, Vietnamese officials announced that church dignitar-
ies and the province chief of Bien Hoa had offered fifty thousand acres
around Bien Hoa to accommodate one hundred thousand refugees from
the North.[12] They agreed to provide ten villages of one hundred tents per
village as temporary shelters until the families built their own homes.
Because of the lack of available large tents, the French army offered to
make available eighty thousand individual tents for families until other
supplies could be procured. The French army also pledged assistance in
constructing the villages and in aiding the Vietnamese in other evacuation activities in and around Saigon.

On August 28, E. V. Earle of the Transportation, Communication, and
Power Division; Bishop Chi; and Monsignor Harnett went to Bien Hoa to
investigate housing sites for refugees.[13] Bishop Chi was the former bishop of Bui Chu, North Vietnam, and had been appointed by Monsignor

Deeley, the apostolic delegate in Hanoi, to head Catholic resettlement in South Vietnam. Monsignor Harnett represented Catholic War Relief Services from the United States. The group visited two proposed sites, one for six hundred families and the other for twenty-five thousand families. The larger site was twenty kilometers northeast of Bien Hoa, near the French fort at Lac An and situated near a large river and wood and bamboo forests. The area had been a former Viet Minh stronghold and was chosen in part to fill the vacuum left after the removal of its pro–Viet Minh inhabitants.

Bien Hoa was not the only site examined for possible settlement of the evacuees. Earlier, on August 8, several members of the USOM traveled to Cap St. Jacques and Nha Trang to examine existing refugee camps and explore the possibility of additional resettlement areas for the evacuees from the North.[14] They concluded that the area of the village of Thaung Nhut near Cap St. Jacques, built using USOM project funds in 1952–1953, could accommodate fifty thousand refugees, and they examined another smaller area near the city limits of Cap St. Jacques that, with some earth-moving equipment, could be transformed into a refugee resettlement area. The last stop, Ponte de Rach-Dua, had been used as a Japanese prisoner-of-war camp and was suitable to accommodate the resettlement of twenty to thirty thousand refugees; it was also used as a reception center to take the pressure off of Saigon.

Although Cap St. Jacques appeared well suited to the needs of the initial resettlement effort, Nha Trang proved otherwise. In Nha Trang the group visited three sites, all of which had unlimited space and fresh water. One of the sites proved to be a graveyard. The French delegate in Nha Trang informed the group that the headquarters for the Third Military region would be in that city. In addition, the French expected twenty-five thousand French Union troops, with twelve thousand vehicles and forty thousand Chinese Nung militia to be resettled in the area—as well as an estimated thirty-five thousand of their dependents. USOM recommended that Nha Trang not receive civilian evacuees or become a reception center.

Although Cap St. Jacques possessed all of the physical attributes a reception center required, it still had problems. Dr. Emil Kotcher, Public Health Laboratory consultant to STEM, warned of the potential medical problems associated with the sandy terrain around Nha Trang and Cap

St. Jacques. Sandy soil was most favorable for the development of hook-worm larvae, and, with the probability that many of the refugees would be infected with the parasites when they arrived at the reception centers, the possibility of epidemic seemed high. Dr. Kotcher warned the officials responsible for the refugee program about the dangers of that disease should it not be contained, and to combat it in Cap St. Jacques and Nha Trang Kotcher recommended the development of adequate sanitation systems and education to prevent promiscuous defecation. Kotcher's warning, repeated by others in unrelated inspections, was strongly ex-pressed and wisely accepted during the relocation and resettlement op-eration, though the problem was greater than any medical doctor had expected.[15]

The coordination among U.S., Vietnamese, and French officials to de-velop refugee camps in the Cap St. Jacques area progressed well despite the urgent need for tents to complete the camps. The tents provided by American Economic Aid had been transferred to the South Vietnamese government, and all requests for immediate need had to go through the RVN representative. The officials were also especially concerned about the availability of food, cooking utensils, mats, and other supplies ex-pected from the Vietnamese. The need for completion heightened as the camp coordinators anticipated the first wave of refugees in a matter of days.

The camp at Cap St. Jacques began to take shape by the end of August, although Vietnamese personnel were desperately needed to support the project, as was food for those debarked in the area. On August 30, the camp held 6,600, with more expected, and a 150-bed hospital had been set up to provide medical care. Before the hospital became operational, however, it required nurses, laboratory technicians, and supporting staff. STEM member Laura Yergan traveled to the camp on August 31 to sur-vey the health facilities and found them in remarkable condition.[16] Dr. Poindexter asked her to take control of the Vietnamese nurses at the hos-pital once it became functional, a request she agreed to fulfill for a period of one or two months if Dr. Peterson agreed. She would work with Dr. Rougelet, the French doctor, and his five French nurses while helping to train the Vietnamese nurses. Yergan found only one case of typhoid and a little dysentery. Poindexter and Yergan discussed the commencement of health education to maintain sanitary conditions, and they organized the distribution of powdered milk for the refugees as well as equipment for mixing the milk.

The camp had a capacity of nine thousand in overcrowded conditions, although bulldozers were to clear additional land for additional shelters to satisfy housing needs. The refugee camp would not be able to accommodate more than nine thousand until additional building materials were released from the French, Vietnamese, or Americans. The size of the camp fit well with the organizational schedule established for the arrival of U.S. Navy ships. With one ship arriving every other day, the camp officials could maintain an organized camp. Vacillating ship schedules, however, would turn an efficient tent camp into an area saturated with tents that provided shelter but little in the way of everyday comforts. The first camp at Cap St. Jacques was well planned and laid out with electricity, pit privies, and an area for medical facilities. As long as the camp remained small, there would be no problem. Unfortunately, these optimal conditions would not last.

As refugees began to flow into the South, the Community Development Division of STEM turned its attention to how those relocated would fit into the South Vietnamese economy.[17] There was no accurate count of the number of refugees who would be completely dependent upon public assistance until their resettlement process was complete, though an estimate of one hundred thousand was considered reasonable. It was also likely that many refugees would remain in southern reception centers for a year or more waiting for the completion of resettlement projects in the South. To ease the burden on the economy, the Community Development Division devised work relief employment instead of public assistance. That was of immediate psychological benefit to the program. If refugees who were capable of working were given opportunities, it would lessen the possibility of demoralization and possible unrest within the reception camps. The cost of work relief employment would not be any more than that of public assistance, and the economic benefits of thousands of man-hours of labor were tremendous, compared to a social welfare system that would yield no positive economic benefits. The type and number of projects possible for this program were limitless. It could accomplish the completion and maintenance of reception camps as well as resettlement camps. The number of public works projects available in Vietnam were comparable to those in the United States in the 1930s, and the populations of the two countries, though separated by time and short-term circumstance, shared similar characteristics of ability and need.

The importance of stabilizing the South Vietnamese economy depended upon a quick and efficient transition of evacuees from refugees to contributing citizens. On August 12, Herman Holiday outlined a plan to disperse evacuees from reception centers to permanent resettlement areas.[18] Holiday divided the transition plan into five sections and focused on the coordination and administration of resettlement aid and advice. He recommended that transportation be provided for all refugees and their baggage from the reception centers to the final area of resettlement. This would allow for quick turnaround in the reception camps and assurance that the evacuees arrived in the correct location. These locations would be preselected and established in advance of their new inhabitants. Holiday stressed the need to ensure that the refugees received all services that might provide for a better transition and recommended the establishment of Community Development welfare teams consisting of information, agriculture, education, public administration, health and sanitation, and public works officers.

Holiday met with Vietnamese officials to discuss resettlement issues resulting from the evacuation and learned from the discussions that the Vietnamese were well aware of the necessity of a quick, organized plan for moving refugees out of the reception centers.[19] There was also a real understanding that these areas had to have potential for agricultural development and public works projects as well as be secure from roving Viet Minh agents. The South Vietnamese government's resettlement plan provided for housing, care, and maintenance for ninety days as well as medical care and other public welfare services as required. Holiday promised that his division would assist the government in the resettlement program, making available the financial resources and expertise to ensure a smooth transition. Even as the trauma of evacuation and resettlement made the operation that much more difficult, one strong element of cohesion within the Vietnamese refugee community allowed greater organization and efficiency throughout the period of evacuation: the Catholic Church.

The Church and its priests in Vietnam provided much-needed administrative capabilities when the South Vietnamese government failed to step forward. One example of this dedication was the work of Father Marquis, who had registered five hundred families, more than three thousand refugees, and had personally arranged for their transportation and resettlement on land he had in Cu Chi, northwest of Saigon. U.S. officials worked with individuals like Father Marquis to ensure that his people received the same benefits as those transferred through the government evacuation. On August 23, D. C. Lavergne suggested providing one hundred tents for temporary shelter, while Father Marquis constructed more permanent housing for his people, as well as tools to aid in the construction of the permanent resettlement villages. Father Marquis also was involved in another project to resettle one thousand refugees from Blau to Dalat, where five thousand refugees had been airlifted by the French earlier. Lavergne recommended that STEM provide construction material for housing and food for the refugees in Dalat, where food was in short supply and no assistance had been made available for the new population.[20]

Ambassador Heath reported to Secretary of State John Foster Dulles on the refugee situation on August 25.[21] Heath informed Dulles that it was still too early to judge whether the Vietnamese government could achieve its objective. Heath did note that early Vietnamese efforts were hampered by protracted indecision, vacillation, change of personnel, and a lack of vehicles to transport the evacuees. He assured Dulles that the Vietnamese government had been given every opportunity to succeed with the full cooperation of the American agencies and French officials. The Vietnamese, in turn, made a real effort to centralize their refugee operation. President Diem named Ngo Ngoc Doi as commissioner general for evacuation with cabinet rank. Diem also instructed his chief of staff for the Vietnamese armed forces, General Duong Van Minh, to cooperate with Doi and provide all requested materials and services. Doi also set up a headquarters in Saigon with desks for STEM and MAAG. The improvements, however, did not offset the potential for disaster in the minds of STEM officials, who worried that the arrival rate of the evacuees exceeded the Vietnamese ability to register them and reassign them to permanent resettlement areas. Secretary General of the Vietnamese Public Works Ministry Nguyen Van Ho outlined future Vietnamese preparations the day before STEM's warning.[22] Ho argued that the South Vietnamese government had an obligation first to evacuate all northern

Vietnamese who did not want to "endure the yoke of communism" and then to resettle that population with appropriate living facilities and renewed hope. Ho emphasized the time restrictions, arguing that "each day that passes by is one day less on the relentless time table inflicted by the Geneva treaty, which was concluded without our knowledge and against our will." While STEM and the Vietnamese were in accord concerning the goals and objectives of evacuation and resettlement, there was still a great difference between this theory and the realities the Vietnamese faced in reorganizing the new population.

Just as conditions for the refugees differed from the North to the South, so did the organization of the land operation take on different characteristics by region. For the United States in North Vietnam, Operation Passage to Freedom began in the reception centers around Hanoi and Haiphong. Because these areas were the point of first contact between the Vietnamese and Americans, it was important for the centers to be organized, clean, and efficient for those who would begin their journey south. On August 14 and 15, STEM representatives visited Hanoi and Haiphong to inspect the camps, and what they found disturbed them and caused some anxiety for the Vietnamese scheduled to pass through those areas on their way to the South. These camps were supposed to have been maintained by the Vietnamese, but physical conditions in them were miserable. "Never in the experience of either of us," wrote Richard R. Brown and James Campbell, "have we seen such unsanitary, unhealthful, and disagreeable living conditions."[23] Brown and Campbell, along with Herman Holiday, found inadequate sanitary facilities, water quality, and shelter, with the possibility of real epidemic widespread. They discovered confusion among the Vietnamese officials, no organizational authority, and few willing to accept responsibility.

In neither city was there a scheme for registering refugees, nor did anyone have a real estimate of the number of individuals who wished evacuation. In Haiphong the only registration list they found for a group living in a rice paddy was in the pocket of a village priest. The medical records for the camps they visited were also nonexistent. There was no medical control and no real knowledge of who had been vaccinated and inoculated. Although the United States could help plan and organize the camps, it was restricted in the number of personnel it could place ashore. This restriction, and the conditions of the camps, gave the Viet Minh, according to the STEM group, their best propaganda as agents moved among the refugees and pointed out the obvious problems in the camps with the observation that things would only get worse as they traveled south.

The group made several recommendations, including a change in the French government's policy toward the evacuation. The French had made the military evacuation a priority and had refused Vietnamese civilians rail transportation into Haiphong, forcing them to walk five to six kilometers into the city. The United States had to intervene in some capacity if it had any real desire to succeed in protecting the civilians. The group also recommended a high-level group, with U.S., Vietnamese, and French representation, to coordinate the camps and transportation and a better line of communication between North and South Vietnam. They pressed American officials to reach an agreement with the French for better shelter in Hanoi, Haiduong, and Haiphong and an agreement with the Vietnamese for more trained officials to aid in the process. The remainder of their recommendations dealt with the day-to-day concerns of the civilians in the camps, including health, welfare, and security. Nothing in the report surprised any of the officials involved in the operation, though it had been hoped that the French and Vietnamese would have coordinated better as the push to evacuate the North gained steam. With the United States formally involved, the real challenge was the organization of the camps and the orderly and efficient transportation of those wanting and deserving to go south. In a separate report, Holiday noted that the chiefs of the provinces around Haiphong were not serving their people, nor had those leaders made an effort to understand conditions or made available relief supplies assigned to them for the purpose of relieving the horrible conditions. Holiday urged the immediate transportation of refugees to the South to relieve the conditions around Haiphong.

By August 17, one hundred thirty-two thousand refugees had registered to travel from North to South Vietnam. There were no data on the refugees despite earlier French efforts to assign each person an identification card. This became critical as the refugees arrived in the South. Without this information, it was difficult to determine the best resettlement area without conducting interviews with each individual. This would not be a problem as long as the southern reception areas were not inundated with refugees, but unfortunately, those times were few and far between, and refugees were often resettled in areas ill-suited for their talents. For the refugee who had worked all of his life as a fisherman, the logical resettlement area would have been near the coast. Without prior knowledge of the refugees' occupation, more often than not, the fisherman turned evacuee would be placed inland away from his traditional occupation and faced with the daunting prospects of learning a new livelihood at the same time he had to learn a new region. Organization and coordination would have limited these problems, but these talents were often pushed aside in order to deal with the large number of refugees arriving in the South and the need to move them out of the reception centers quickly in order to prepare for the next group.

There is no question that the rapid influx of refugees into and around the Haiphong area during the month of August created an atmosphere best characterized as disorganized and confused. The loss of equipment through pilfering or misplacement hampered the process greatly, especially in the area of radio equipment, which was used to spread propaganda. Radio Hanoi provided a great deal of information and coordination for the evacuation operation. It had planned to go off the air on September 1; its equipment was to be dismantled beginning on August 25 and then reassembled in Haiphong and Saigon. Le Quang Luit, South Vietnamese government delegate in North Vietnam, insisted on having one of the Hanoi transmitters for Radio Haiphong so the Ministry of Information could be on air until the end of the operation in May 1955. STEM advisers, however, did not believe that Radio Haiphong would become operational for several weeks, as those in charge would find it difficult to overcome the administrative and technical obstacles associated with a new station.[24] Radio Hanoi had always been considered a disorganized unit and had only one technician to assist in the reassembly of the equipment. There was also little likelihood that those running Radio Hanoi would follow the station to Haiphong. The chief editor at Radio Hanoi, Pham Manh Phan, had refused to assume responsibility for evacuating the station's equipment, and the director, Tham Oanh, had been threatened by the Viet Minh and had requested immediate evacuation to Saigon. STEM officials recommended that a STEM contract engineer be assigned to assist in the assembly of Radio Haiphong, and they urged the withdrawal of all other equipment to South Vietnam as quickly as possible. Although the radio station's administration was nearly nonexistent, the broadcasting equipment became increasingly prone to disappear. Approximately 20 percent of the equipment vanished. This was considered a low number, although a very high percentage of the remaining equipment was not operable. The mobile units used by the station were removed to Haiphong with the loss of one truck, which had deserted to the Viet Minh–held territory around Son Tay. Eventually the station became inoperable as its parts moved to the South.

As for the print media, the South Vietnamese ministry was able to dismantle and transport the Hanoi government printing plant to Saigon at the cost of 1 million piasters. The Viet Minh, however, were effective in keeping other print media sources intact in the North. In Hanoi the French newspaper *L'Entente* had sold its press to "unknown persons" for 780,000 piasters, and the former minister of information, Le Thanh, sold the Imprimerie Bac Thanh to persons remaining in the North for 200,000 piasters. The print media played an important role in the propaganda war during the evacuation period. Villagers from Viet Minh–controlled areas would sweep the cities of Hanoi and Haiphong on a daily basis to pass out flyers warning the refugees of their fate aboard the American ships and in South Vietnam. Additionally, many of the remaining Vietnamese newspapers in the North adopted a pro–Viet Minh stance in reporting on and publicizing events in the area.

On August 24, a Mr. Thanh, chairman of the Vietnamese Evacuation Committee, informed Captain Dickey that Viet Minh propaganda was working on Vietnamese interested in leaving the North. The Viet Minh were telling the Vietnamese that U.S. Navy personnel were throwing the sick overboard and mistreating the evacuees. Mr. Thanh complained that American propaganda was ineffective and was nonexistent in areas as close as thirty-five miles from Hanoi. Despite this observation, the number of evacuees increased daily, creating problems ashore for U.S. personnel assigned to screen people who were unfit for travel.[25] The American sailors did many things to counter the Viet Minh propaganda. Besides a friendly smile, many provided ice cream and food from the ship's stores, and others offered cigarettes. To overcome negative stories it was often simply a matter of trying to make the Vietnamese as comfortable as possible.

USS *Montrose* CIC officer Lieutenant (junior grade) George Dowd remembered "the terrified civilians coming on deck to be de-loused by a spray gun that shot powder into their hair. The refugees had been told by the Communists that we would take them out to sea and dump them over the side. Our ship's store soon exhausted its inventory of candy bars as the crew bought them to give to the frightened children. The fright had disappeared by the time we docked in Saigon to deliver them to their new homes."[26] One story from Boatswain's Mate James Chapman, who was aboard USS *Calvert*, serves as a good example of how the Americans effectively countered Viet Minh propaganda. Chapman and the men of his division took charge of a young Vietnamese boy who had lost his parents in the war. The sailors named him Hon Yok and took care of his needs during the voyage to the South. "The little guy that we befriended, we got him to drinking coffee and he liked coffee real well," Chapman recalled, "but he didn't know what it was and he didn't like it at first, and then we put some sugar in it, and from then on, yeah, he wanted a cup of coffee but he wanted 'sugular' in it!" The kindness shown by the men of *Calvert* to the Vietnamese boy could not have escaped the notice of those Vietnamese aboard at the time.[27] Another *Calvert* sailor, Jim Daniels, summed up the American view of the sailors' commitment: "In America we do try to take care of people and help people out and we were just trying to help these people out and make them feel comfortable. They had a long trip. We were just trying to make them feel comfortable and fill them up."[28] The kindness of the American sailors to the Vietnamese who fled North Vietnam worked long toward reversing the Viet Minh propaganda. For many of the sailors, and most likely many of the Vietnamese, it had a lasting effect.

As of August 29, a total of 218,821 people had been evacuated from North Vietnam, including 34,905 Vietnamese civilians by the U.S. Navy. The French had also transported 21,213 tons of military and civilian equipment and 165 vehicles. Yet the situation remained perilous, and the success of the operation was still undecided. Although Ngo Ngoc Doi had been appointed by President Diem to coordinate the Vietnamese efforts with the United States and France, the South Vietnamese government was still reluctant to call upon the French or the Vietnamese army for assistance. General O'Daniel's efforts to have MAAG act as a fulcrum with the Vietnamese and the French eased some of the bureaucracy, but there was still much to be done in order to improve the evacuation and resettlement process. Life in the refugee camps in the North continued to be unsatisfactory, because the refugees' supplies of food, shelter, and medicine were still inadequate. The French continued to give the Vietnamese civilian population a low priority for transportation and provided little in the way of sanitation and other conveniences for those in the embarkation area. In Saigon the situation was not much better, although increased action by the United States and South Vietnam had resulted in some significant improvements.

Refugees arriving in Haiphong brought little with them and often suffered from prolonged disease. The Vietnamese and French facilities were not sufficient to care for the sick and injured, though with the addition of American assistance conditions had improved slightly. Officials within STEM and MAAG recognized the need for the Vietnamese to mobilize their public health and medical facilities to meet the challenges that would come in the following months. The Vietnamese abilities, and the success of the United States in assisting them to maximize their skills, would determine the ultimate success of the evacuation after the U.S. Navy departed. As August closed and the early confusion and disorganization of the great venture began to be resolved, the month of September promised to be a period of great movement and resettlement for the Vietnamese. U.S. officials recognized the need to focus on identifying and constructing resettlement sites and matching refugees with appropriate skills to the areas chosen. Health and sanitation remained high on the priority list, as did the coordination and funding of projects designed to ease the way of the Vietnamese on their passage to freedom. With the exchange of notes between the United States and Vietnam on voluntary agency relief in Vietnam, the two countries advanced to the next stage, and next month, of the evacuation—one that would prove critical to overall success.

CHAPTER 6

★★★★★★★★★★★★★★

Hanoi to Haiphong
The Circle Closes

*This operation in which we are now engaged is one of the most chal-
lenging I have ever faced in my whole Naval career, and I am thor-
oughly enjoying it. It has run the gamut of everything from delivering
babies to pulling 19 foot tape worms out of the refugees, to say nothing
of side issues such as political intrigues, sensitive situations and a lot
of headaches.* [1]

One of Admiral Sabin's first orders was to request from Admiral Stump
that Captain Rittenhouse continue as commander of Task Group 90 beyond his scheduled departure. Rittenhouse had volunteered to remain,
and as there were no other captains with comparable experience in the
debarkation area in Saigon, Admiral Stump granted permission for him
to remain.[2] By keeping Rittenhouse in place, Admiral Sabin was assured
better organization at the debarkation points in Saigon, a critical issue for
the United States as more refugees made the move south. One of Admiral Sabin's greatest concerns was organizing naval personnel in the mission and coordinating with the South Vietnamese. This was often more
difficult than he had anticipated.

It was difficult to organize such a complex operation when all of the
participants did not communicate with one another, even when the intentions were good. On September 1, Admiral Sabin learned that President
Diem had requested from the British minister at Saigon the use of Brit-

ish shipping without informing either the French or the Americans. The United States did not necessarily disapprove of British involvement in the operation, although logistics became more complicated with an increased number of nations and their ways of doing things. The British, with the approval of the UN commander for the Far East, released the British aircraft carrier HMS *Warrior*, which was scheduled to arrive at Haiphong on September 4. Although Admiral Sabin had never been informed of the British role in the operation and had not prepared for this addition, he agreed, after conferring with Ambassador Heath, to offer logistical support to the British. The British accepted the American offer but informed the admiral that *Warrior* would operate outside of the Task Force 90 command structure. Admiral Stump directed Admiral Sabin to cooperate and coordinate with the British contingent in transporting refugees and providing logistics and facilities as required.[3] The United States had control over some events, such as the inclusion of the British in the evacuation; others, however, were beyond the control of the Americans.

The situation in North Vietnam was critical at the end of August after a typhoon swept through Haiphong. Captain Winn reported that the camp sites at Haiphong had been cleared of broken glass and general debris. A few clear-skied days helped the clean-up process as mud holes dried and personnel removed debris. Winn soon learned, however, that other forces were causing damage to the camps. There was increased evidence that refugees were using tent stakes for firewood and the tents' manila lines for wrapping packages. Despite the problems, the construction of new camps and plans for sanitary improvements continued at an acceptable level. Captain Winn then inspected a seven-thousand-person refugee camp under construction and sites for water purification units.[4] The new camp would soon be put into use. With developments ashore progressing, Captain Winn then turned his attention to his ships; after reports of potential sabotage increased, he ordered patrols in the compartments that housed refugees and greater vigilance aboard the ships during their passage.

Evacuation operations continued in earnest at the beginning of September. USS *Montrose* loaded 2,340 Chinese Nung refugees on September 2, and USNS *Beauregard*, the first MSTS vessel to arrive in Indochina, began loading refugees, including a large number of fishermen with their equipment.[5] With the arrival of MSTS ships to aid the evacuation, Admiral Sabin initiated new procedures for quick turnaround between trips south, recommending that each T-AP and T-AK receive $5,000 to pay local clean-up crews. On a daily basis, these crews were required to maintain healthy and clean conditions in spaces used by the refugees. The funds were approved, allowing for a more efficient use of American personnel.

In a similar vein, to increase the efficiency in embarking the Vietnamese, the Americans discontinued DDT dusting aboard ships, as it was creating a bottleneck. The DDT spraying process was important. For the medical staff attached to the ships involved in the operation, one of the great concerns was the type of pestilence and disease carriers the Vietnamese might bring aboard the ship. DDT was in great supply, but the vehicle to transfer the chemical to the evacuees was not sufficient for the task. Early in the operation, *Montrose*'s doctor, Eugene Mauch, took care of that problem by taking a few of the big kettles from the ship's galley and using them to mix the DDT with flour. The substance was then inserted into some pump atomizers and given to his corpsmen to spray as the Vietnamese embarked. The process was an intrusive one, as he recalled: "We have to pull open shirts and blow this stuff inside and with the ladies we had open their skirts or pull their belts and, of course, that had to be embarrassing to say the least, but we had to blow this stuff around them as they walked on board."[6] Although the process was necessary, it did cause a bit of anxiety, especially because the Viet Minh had told many of the evacuees that the Americans would take them out to sea and dump them, and it also slowed down the embarkation process. As a result, sailors began dusting the refugees at the embarkation center before they boarded. The process was improved upon by the arrival in late August of *Skagit* with a supply of six tons of DDT talc for new gas-powered DDT dusting machines. It did not take long for DDT dusting operators to become proficient at their jobs in the embarkation area.

Even with more vessels operating in the mission and improved methods of embarkation, there were still bottlenecks. At least 92,200 Vietnamese had signed up in the Tonkin Delta for evacuation. Many who had registered remained in their villages because of the lack of accommodations in Hanoi and Haiphong as well as business, family, and other personal reasons such as the fear that families would become permanently

Fig. 6.1. PMU team dusts soldiers with DDT before they board
LST 901, September 1954. Photograph courtesy of the Douglas
Pike Photograph Collection, Vietnam Archive (VA000866).

divided unless they embarked on the same ship. To try to alleviate that
fear and lessen the bottleneck, Admiral Sabin ordered Captain Winn to
transport Vietnamese military personnel with their families in the same
LSTs, when possible. In addition to the growing number of refugees
waiting for the right time to leave North Vietnam, the French estimated
that approximately one hundred seventy-seven thousand tons of MDAP
equipment, as well as nineteen Vietnamese battalions, remained in the
Tonkin Delta.[7] The large number of Vietnamese wishing to leave and the
tonnage of materiel awaiting transportation provided the United States
with ample justification for remaining in Indochina.

While additional demands on U.S. shipping signaled more active participation, another growing concern in Haiphong was whether industrial
equipment would be transported out of the region before the Viet Minh
took control. Hubert Durand Chastel, the director of a large cement plant
in the North, approached STEM representatives about the prospect of

preventing his equipment from falling into Viet Minh possession.[8] In 1953, the Cimentaries d'Indochine (Indochina Cement Plant) produced three hundred thousand tons of cement—enough to satisfy the requirements of all Indochina. If the Viet Minh obtained the plant, it would provide a significant source of revenue for the DRV as well as strengthen the infrastructure of the war-torn Tonkin Delta. The cement plant, the coal mines at Hon Gay, the cotton mills at Nam Dinh, and the glazieries were the major industries of North Vietnam. All of Indochina consumed four hundred thousand tons of coal per year, and the cement plant accounted for one hundred fifty thousand tons of that total. Not only did the plant provide cement for all of Indochina, but it played a significant role in the stabilization of other major industries. Chastel also argued that the removal of the cement plant would cause a ripple effect among other industrialists who were undecided whether to leave North Vietnam. If equipment from the cement plant left, he argued, it was likely the coal mine equipment would follow rather than being surrendered into the hands of the Viet Minh. As a result, a majority of smaller industries would depart for the South in order to survive. It was clearly to the advantage of the United States to move these industries to the South. While the political-economic considerations played themselves out in Hanoi and Haiphong, the political-social dilemma of such a large-scale operation continued to resurface.

Captain Winn reported on September 6 that all available information in the North suggested that the total number of potential evacuees would be lower than anticipated, citing one village of 5,000 Catholics who had voted to remain in the North. The poor condition of the camps in Saigon influenced this group, and Viet Minh propaganda and obstacles also persuaded many to avoid the voyage. Aiding this decision was also the fact that the processing and completion of registration at Haiphong continued to proceed slowly and with little efficiency. Many Vietnamese in the embarkation area chose to stay in the camps rather than make the uncertain trip to the South until conditions improved. To counteract this trend, and encourage the departure of those refugees who might otherwise remain in Haiphong indefinitely, French officials threatened to eliminate fish and rice distribution.[9] The next day, Captain Winn reported a fourfold increase in registrations in Hanoi to 2,000, suggesting a reversal of the downward estimates of refugees. He also reported one of the smoothest loadings of refugees, of more than 4,250 civilians and military personnel. This was fortunate, as combat camera teams were filming the camps and medical aspects of the operation at Haiphong.

Not all operations were as smooth, though the movement of refugees continued to increase. USS *Comstock* and HMS *Warrior* took on 3,351 refugees in spite of a severe electrical storm with high winds and strong rains that uprooted trees and damaged a large number of tents in the embarkation area. Despite the storm, the Beachmaster Unit worked in the mud and rain to load an LCU with tanks and vehicles in time to clear the embarkation area during the daylight, which allowed the loading of the refugees. The loading of 1,200 civilians on *Warrior* proceeded quicker than expected, as a high degree of coordination existed between British consular officials and French and American personnel.[10]

Even when weather and coordination between the allies worked, American personnel still experienced challenges. On September 4, USS *Magoffin* reported that navy personnel had discovered two unexploded hand grenades hidden between boxes in a lower hold. *Magoffin*'s personnel found it impossible to conduct a thorough search of passengers during loading or after the refugees were aboard the ship and recommended that similar occurrences could be prevented only by a complete search of clothing and personal effects ashore. As a result, Admiral Sabin issued a warning to all of his subordinate commanders that the hand grenades suggested that planned sabotage was a real possibility. He cautioned them to watch for booby traps and instructed all personnel to exert extreme care and vigilance.[11] On September 14, General O'Daniel learned from the U.S. embassy that it had received an unconfirmed report from Mr. Compain, the French representative of the high commissioner in Hanoi, that the Hanoi Viet Minh administration and the Resistance Committee had coordinated with a similar committee in Haiphong in planning sabotage on U.S. ships involved in the evacuation operation. The operational orders for Passage to Freedom warned that Viet Minh sabotage was the greatest threat. That it did not occur with any frequency can be attributed to the diligence of the navy personnel involved in the operation.

While the American sailors were always conscious of the possibility of Viet Minh attempts at sabotage, they experienced very few cases that might be considered as acts against the United States' transport of Vietnamese to the south. Most transports inspected the baggage brought aboard before its owner was allowed entry. The Vietnamese had already gone through one screening at the embarkation point, which usually resulted in the confiscation of any weapons.[12] What might have been considered an act of sabotage by the Americans aboard *Montague* during its first trip was actually a misunderstanding by the Vietnamese. Some Vietnamese had brought wood with them and built a cooking fire aboard the ship. As soon as smoke was discovered, the crew quickly put out the fire and told the Vietnamese that such acts were prohibited. A similar episode happened aboard *Montrose*.[13] Despite the relative security during the operation, American sailors remained vigilant. At night the ships would illuminate the surrounding water to identify any foreign objects in the water and prevent a floating bomb from contacting the hull. An LCVP with 20mm machine guns also patrolled the water around the ships to discourage potential saboteurs.[14] This did not discourage local fishermen from bringing their sampans close to the ships to catch the fish that congregated in the shadows of the large hulls—until the Americans employed water hoses to keep the sampans at a safe distance.[15]

Even when sabotage was not a major concern, other problems occupied the attention of those who conducted the operation. USNS *Beauregard* reported that the Vietnamese priests did not assist in the organization of the civilians; they slept most of the time. Unlike the APAs and AKAs earlier in the operation, the MSTS ships did not need to construct above-deck sanitary facilities, preferring to rely on the existing facilities. But those sanitary facilities were not effective, and filth and refuse accumulated in the holds. Additionally, Vietnamese medical supplies brought aboard *Beauregard* were inadequate to meet the needs of the civilian population. Because the ship's officials were not authorized to pay overtime to the crew, there was no supervision of the passengers, which led to unsanitary conditions. On September 4, Admiral Sabin established a logistics support policy for MSTS ships. Unless there was an emergency, time-chartered ships would not replenish at Tourane through the logistics support group. All ships of that type would arrange for fuel, water, and supplies through their owners' agents and acquire unusual items from Admiral Gano's operation. Transports and cargo ships of the MSTS were to replenish in the same way as U.S. Navy ships but would stop only at Tourane when required. All MSTS ships had to arrange through the French for their own stevedores during replenishment at Tourane.[16] As a result of this new policy, on September 28, the logistics support group left Tourane and closed its operations in that city.

Captain Rittenhouse informed Admiral Sabin that he considered the officers and crews of the time-chartered ships as more severe and less sympathetic than navy personnel involved in the operation and suggested that the goodwill brought by the navy's participation in the operation would suffer as a result. With this information in hand, Admiral Sabin informed Admiral Stump that he would withdraw the time-chartered ships from the refugee evacuation as soon as possible. If difficulties continued, he argued that U.S. Navy personnel might be required aboard the MSTS ships, although he was reluctant to take that step unless it was absolutely necessary.[17] Just as transit to the South experienced problems, so did the embarkation camps. MAAG Haiphong informed O'Daniel that there was a serious shortage of control team personnel, especially doctors and interpreters, at Haiphong to oversee the arrival and organization of the evacuees in the embarkation camps. Despite assurances by Mr. Ham, the Vietnamese director of the evacuation, that teams aboard ships had been ordered to remain, the personnel disappeared upon arrival in Saigon.

On September 4, USS *Wantuck* became the first Task Force 90 ship to phase out of the Indochina operation. *Menard*, upon the completion of its unloading, would become the next. Admiral Sabin argued that any release of shipping other than the scheduled phase-out of amphibious ships would be premature. He preferred to wait until after October 10, when Hanoi would be turned over to the Viet Minh. The consensus of American officials involved in the operation was that the loss of Hanoi would not result in a large influx of refugees at Haiphong. One ship that did phase out of the operation was the hospital ship USS *Haven*. Captain Rittenhouse reported that *Haven*, at French insistence, would occupy Catinat Wharf in Saigon for three days while 725 wounded French POWs embarked. Other ships that would normally use the berthing area were moved to piers downstream to offload their passengers and equipment. *Haven* then traveled to France to return the soldiers.

In *Haven*'s place, USS *Consolation*, based in Tourane, served as the hospital ship for Task Force 90. The crew of *Consolation* did not know what to expect when the ship arrived in Indochina. Their initial understanding was that the ship would transport those difficult cases of French Union forces who had survived Dien Bien Phu to La Havre, France. *Consolation*

Fig. 6.2. Ceremony aboard USS *Menard.*
Photograph courtesy of Douglas Fraser, USS *Menard* (APA-201).

was eventually assigned to Tourane, where it spent approximately three weeks. Anne Peterson, who served as a nurse aboard *Consolation*, recalled that there were few sick people in the wards while the ship was on station. She and many of her colleagues did what they could during the time, providing more goodwill than anything else to those in need. "We were just heartbroken because we couldn't do anything to help them," Peterson remembered. "We took over food. We took over a little bit of clothing because we didn't have things for children, and we helped that way."[18] Like the sailors around her, Peterson did not speak Vietnamese or French, but she was able to communicate with the Vietnamese through smiles and care. *Consolation*'s role, though not directly involved in the transport of Vietnamese, did contribute to the overall mission of the U.S. Navy to care for the people of Vietnam.

On September 13, Admiral Stump agreed with Admiral Sabin's recommendations for phasing out a number of amphibious and MSTS ships as a result of the decreased number of refugees, but he advised Admiral

Sabin to remain prepared to handle any unforeseen refugee flow above the predicted rate. Admiral Sabin directed the T-APs to distribute gift items received from CTG 92.3 at Tourane to the refugee passengers. Five MSTS time-chartered ships were released in accordance with Admiral Stump's approval of Admiral Sabin's phase-out plan. On September 15, Admiral Sabin ordered *Montrose*, *Magoffin*, *Telfair*, and *Andromeda* to transfer five LCMs and two LCVPs to *Skagit* before their departure for Hong Kong upon phasing out of the operation. The Transportation Division, with the exception of *Calvert* and *Skagit*, were phased out of the operation. These vessels had been on their way back to the United States before the beginning of the operation and deserved a well-earned rest as a result of their participation.

Admiral Sabin did not want to decrease the size of his task force, but he was bothered by the number of idle American vessels involved in the operation. Earlier, on September 10, in a conference with MAAG Haiphong, Captain Winn, and Robert Adler of FOA, Sabin offered any assistance that might result in the immediate employment of the idle ships. Admiral Sabin's only alternative was to recommend to Admiral Stump that the idle ships be withdrawn. During the day of the conference, no American ships were engaged in the refugee evacuation, though HMS *Warrior* loaded 1,743 passengers. LST-822, having loaded the previous night, did depart for Tourane with 474 Vietnamese military personnel and family members, eighteen vehicles, and thirty tons of military cargo. Admiral Sabin outlined his position to the French and Vietnamese on September 11, after which he recommended to Admiral Stump that the United States reduce its passenger capacity to fifty thousand per month. Both MAAG Haiphong and General O'Daniel concurred with that assessment, estimating that twenty-five thousand refugees were ready for evacuation while another twenty-five thousand would be ready within thirty days. Neither French nor Vietnamese officials predicted a large increase in refugees as a result of the October 10 deadline to evacuate Hanoi, as outlined in the Geneva Agreements. The new U.S. shipping scheme envisioned by Admiral Sabin required thirty-six ships until September 28, when that number would be reduced to twenty-nine until October 19 and nineteen for the remainder of the operation. Admiral Sabin also recommended the five T-APs and three time-chartered ships scheduled for Indochina be canceled, that the two time-chartered ships en route be diverted to their normal duties, and that the five time-chartered ships in the area be released. Even as the rearranging of available shipping progressed, American personnel continued to revise the numbers of refugees and amount of material left to transport.

They estimated that of the three hundred forty-four thousand tons of military equipment ready for transport, two hundred thousand tons were of American origin, but it was almost impossible to distinguish the French from the American equipment. The French provided only two berths, and loading by lighterage became impractical because of the lack of stevedores, winchmen, and ferry service, all of which were supplied by the French. It was not until September 27 that Admiral Storrs, chief of staff to Admiral Stump, met with Captain Winn and MAAG Haiphong for a briefing on the situation. After the briefing and meetings with French and Vietnamese officials, he recommended that the United States place additional pressure at a government level to improve the situation and obtain a greater share of the port facilities at Haiphong.[19] Admiral Sabin maintained that he would need only four T-AKs and two time-chartered ships to handle the cargo. In the meantime, General O'Daniel would request from the French complete stevedoring for time-chartered ships for both loading and unloading. On September 14, LSMs successfully beached for loading instead of loading at the piers, which eased some of the congestion. Even as the logistical problems associated with the loading and transportation of equipment eased, as in every other aspect of the operation other obstacles surfaced to challenge Task Force 90.

Admiral Sabin informed Admiral Carney that they had not met the capacity of the piers at Haiphong of 4,000 tons per day because of disorganization and poor supervision by the French and a lack of stevedores. The Vietnamese stevedores had also held a work slowdown because many of them did not want all of the material and equipment moved to the South, leaving them with nothing. The two berths available to the United States resulted in the loading of only 250 to 300 tons per day. No passenger loading was expected for September 12, because the French planned to complete a lift of military personnel, making the debarkation area in Saigon unavailable. Instead, Captain Winn planned to load three LSTs with forty medium tanks, fifteen halftracks, three heavy vehicles, and 205 members of a Vietnamese tank regiment and related personnel for debarkation at Tourane. An additional two LSTs loaded with equipment, personnel, and vehicles of the 76th Vietnam Engineering Company, with the assistance of the beachmaster detachment, sailed for Tourane on September 15.

It was during this time that an incident aboard one of the LSTs reminded the American personnel that they were still in the middle of a war zone. The crew of LST-1148, en route to Tourane with Vietnamese troops and their families, reported an attempted plot by Vietnamese communists to incite a riot on the ship. A man armed with grenades had sought to take over the ship but was disarmed by the crew, and the LST received an escort to Tourane by USS *Begor* and LST-845.[20] The tension level increased as a result of the failed attempt, but it was magnified when LST-692 collided with the French merchant ship *Docteur Lavern* after the LST's stern anchor failed to hold in strong currents. The LST's collision with the port bow of the French ship caused no casualties and resulted in only minor damage.[21]

The French problem aside, the United States needed to focus on the flow of refugees from the North to the South, which had slackened. Admiral Sabin informed Admiral Stump that the sudden decrease in the number of refugees was the result of several factors. The most important reason was the failure to efficiently organize reception and resettlement centers. As a result, the Viet Minh propaganda had significance to the refugees who experienced the camps. The Viet Minh also were forcibly detaining refugees from leaving when their propaganda failed. The approach of the rice harvesting season also caused many farmers to delay their evacuation to the South, as their livelihood depended upon the success of the harvest. Finally, many in the Tonkin Delta conducted the majority of their business during the Tonkinese festival season. Like the farmers, a delay in departing would mean increased profits as well as more time to assess whether the South Vietnamese government was capable and willing to accommodate the large influx of refugees. As Admiral Sabin maintained, much improvement was required before many in the North would sacrifice everything for their passage to freedom.[22]

Only a very few of those refugees arriving in Hanoi and Haiphong were men of military age. On September 13, the South Vietnamese government reported that the reason for this absence was that most refugees had come from Catholic areas in North Vietnam. The Viet Minh had overrun those areas and had conscripted the young men. Those men who had not been conscripted by the Viet Minh had joined the Vietnamese military.[23] A Vietnamese army officer, Captain Man, suggested to Admiral Sabin that the decreased flow of refugees was a direct result of the disorganization for receiving and resettling the refugees. The evacuees had been promised a warm welcome, resettlement to villages in family or community units, and an opportunity to earn a living. Failure to fulfill these promises had allowed the Viet Minh to capitalize on South Vietnamese faults.[24] That the Viet Minh had halted the refugee flow into the embarkation areas is shown by the number of individuals who had registered on September 18 (517), September 20 (58), and September 23 (86).

American personnel suspected that the Viet Minh played a significant role in the lower number of individuals registering, but it was difficult to prove. Captain Winn informed Admiral Sabin that one of the U.S. Navy medical officers at Haiphong had a conversation with a Vietnamese man who wanted to discuss armistice violations to members of the International Control Commission.[25] The Vietnamese man, who claimed to be mayor of a village seventy miles southwest of Haiphong, told the American that five thousand refugees wished to evacuate to the South but were denied the opportunity by the Viet Minh, who had confiscated their sampans and the water buffalos used to draw carts. The mayor also reported that approximately thirty thousand Vietnamese wished to evacuate around Phu Ly, but there was no way to confirm the report. Other numbers came in from the countryside confirming that there were still Vietnamese with a desire to leave; getting them to Hanoi and Haiphong was the challenge.

At the beginning of September, Vietnamese sources listed between five and twenty thousand Vietnamese civilians in Hanoi who wished to go to the South.[26] On September 9, Colonel Sung, leader of the Nung minority group in North Vietnam, informed the Vietnamese, French, and Americans that he had thirteen thousand civilians and twenty-five thousand militia and their dependents awaiting evacuation from the Hon Gay area.[27] The French, as a result, had allocated one thousand seats each day on aircraft involved in the evacuation, and the United States began to concentrate on getting the refugees away from Hon Gay. If all the civilians had not been transported by September 20, the French planned to move the remaining refugees to Haiphong and continue the airlift from that city before the Viet Minh were allowed to take it over in accordance with the Geneva Conference Agreements. In addition to the civilians, the French were airlifting military refugees—Vietnamese troops and their families—at a rate of one thousand per day.

While the airlift proved the quickest way to leave North Vietnam, the sea route continued to be the most efficient and remained the primary means of departure for the majority of the evacuees in Hanoi and Haiphong. On September 13, 2,124 Chinese refugees embarked on USNS *General R. L. Howze* (T-AP-134), and the next day another 2,123 Chinese Nungs smoothly and quietly loaded aboard USNS *Marine Adder* (T-AP-193).[28] Captain Winn reported that he had canceled loading for September 15 because there were only 800 Nungs ready for embarkation, but on September 16, USNS *General A. W. Brewster* (T-AP-155) embarked 1,612 Catholic refugees, using LCTs and LSMs at Captha Port. The refugees had been transported to the point of embarkation in open coal cars. They arrived wet and dirty but still appreciative of the U.S. efforts to move them to safety. A total of 2,009 Nungs were loaded on USNS *General W. M. Black* (T-AP-135), while Vietnamese soldiers and equipment were loaded on an LST. There was confusion in the loading process when French drivers took vehicles to a different embarkation site and loaded the equipment onto a French LST. This caused the American LST to delay its start with less than a full cargo load. As the refugees embarked for their journey south, USS *Tortuga* (LSD-26) loaded seven barges containing 480 tons of equipment from the Vietnam Tank Regiment and sailed for Tourane. USNS *Fentress* (T-AK-180), the first MSTS cargo ship to engage actively in the operation, was loaded with MDAP equipment for departure to Saigon on September 17. USNS *Marine Lynx* (T-AP-194) loaded 2,982 refugees on September 18 and headed for Saigon. The process started anew with *General Howze*, whose return and loading of the next trip concluded on September 21. The onset of the monsoon season also played a role in the number of refugees available for transport. As Admiral Sabin reported his excess capacity, he also ordered Admiral Gano to move the Logistics Support Group from Tourane to Haiphong by September 28 with the onset of the northeast monsoon season.

The addition of these ships changed the ratio of supply and demand for the navy. Admiral Sabin reported to Admiral Stump on September 17 that Task Force 90 organization and ship capacity exceeded the number of refugees and amount of equipment predicted for the operation.[29] By September 22, General O'Daniel was able to report to the Department of State that the recovery of MDAP equipment in the Haiphong and Hanoi areas was proceeding as scheduled. Hanoi had very little equipment left, and the French had assured General O'Daniel that all would be moved by October 10, when the Viet Minh were to take over the city. According to the French master plan, the movement of equipment was six days ahead of schedule, and the remaining equipment, one hundred eighty thousand tons of general cargo and fifty thousand tons of vehicles, would be transported to the South by the end of March. By providing military personnel as stevedores, the French were able to maintain their schedule and confidence of completing their objective. While General O'Daniel had no cause for alarm that the material would not get moved, he reassured the Department of State that MAAG would remain vigilant.

Coordinating the movement of the large task force with the tens of thousands of refugees required a great deal of skill and patience. As was often the case with such an operation, the attention of American personnel was often divided. On September 18, Admiral Sabin reported that the matting issued to the refugees was too loosely woven, and they rejected it. Many of the ships' captains believed the mats were a fire hazard and had refused to carry them aboard during the transit. The captains also reported that the Vietnamese in sampans in Haiphong and Hai Long Bay also refused the mats when they were offered as gifts. After his examination of the mats, Admiral Sabin agreed that the mats were unsatisfactory and should be discontinued. When Admiral Gano requested the destruction of the mats, Admiral Sabin responded by challenging his staff to find another use for them.[30] The mats were finally used at the debarkation centers by the Vietnamese refugee commissions. An issue such as matting might seem trivial, but at the time one of the principal goals of American personnel in this humanitarian operation was to promote a better understanding between the two peoples. This objective was often tested.

Mr. Ngo Van Cuong, a correspondent for the *Agence Vietnam Presse* and the Saigon French daily *Journal D'Extreme-Orient* who complained of conditions aboard USS *Montrose* during his time aboard the ship from September 9 to September 12, stated that Captain Andrews, whom he misnamed as Summerville, failed to provide him with a desk or table to write stories and made him eat with the enlisted men while the captain entertained two white Russians. Cuong presented a letter of introduction from R. W. Hamelin, MAAG Haiphong, but the captain, he claimed, refused to acknowledge it and treated him badly. He also complained that he and a Vietnamese army officer were required to stand in line for their food and wash their trays. He also mentioned the poor quality of the food—noting the rice was not cooked properly—and the unpalatable canned fish he was fed five times a day. He informed U.S. officials that many people became sick below deck because they were forced to stay below where the air circulation was inadequate. Cuong told Edward Stansburg of USIS that he was surprised by the conditions and had been urged by the refugees aboard to write stories about the poor conditions.

Although Cuong's statement was passed through the lines of command, the reporting officer doubted the extent of his claims and believed that Cuong's experience could be explained in more simple terms tempered by his not being treated as a first-class passenger.[31] The story later relayed to Admiral Sabin by Captain Andrews was that the two white Russians were an elderly couple who had eaten in the wardroom as the personal guests of one of the officers and had paid their own mess bill. Food aboard the U.S. Navy ships was not free of charge, and all officers were responsible for the food provided at meals. Captain Andrews also informed Admiral Sabin that Cuong was quartered with the control team and assigned to the troop officer staterooms, in which there was a desk. The incident passed without further comment.[32] Even as Cuong's remarks became public, the navy decided to decrease its public relations efforts in Indochina. On September 18, Admiral Stump learned that the Pacific Fleet public information officers assigned to Indochina would be withdrawn because there was not enough navy activity to warrant coverage. As MSTS ships and personnel replaced U.S. Navy ships and personnel, Admiral Stump ordered the public information office teams to return to their normal duties.

Although there was negative publicity on the American side of the operation, there was enough positive feedback to counter it. On September 14, Francis Cardinal Spellman sent a message to Admiral Sabin: "Wish express heartfelt demonstration of Christian charity in evacuating clergy and laity from Haiphong to freedom in South Vietnam. Highest tradition

Fig. 6.3. American sailor helps feed a small refugee aboard USS *Magoffin* (APA-199), September 1954. Photograph courtesy of the Douglas Pike Photograph Collection, Vietnam Archive (VA000867).

of U.S. Navy has been matched in the thrilling achievement of liberating a sorely pressed people."[33] American support for the operation was positive even if it was limited to those few who were directly involved in the Vietnam situation. For U.S. personnel the support from home was valued, but the reward from the Vietnamese and the satisfaction of a job well done was greater. For many of those sailors directly involved in the transpor-

Fig. 6.4. Ambassador Donald R. Heath and Admiral Lorenzo S. Sabin look on as the mayor of Saigon gives a welcoming speech at the arrival of the one hundred thousandth refugee from Haiphong, September 24, 1954. Photograph courtesy of the Douglas Pike Photograph Collection, Vietnam Archive (VA000884).

tation of the Vietnamese, the experience was life-defining. "It was something different," USS *Calvert* coxswain Roy Constant recalled. "My own personal feelings, you couldn't help feeling sorry for those people. That's the way I felt; I'm not sure how everybody else felt about it. I felt sorry for them. From what I'd heard then and what they'd been through."[34] Stan Coito, aboard *Montague*, summed up the general feeling of those sailors who participated: "I used to talk to them. They spoke their language and I spoke mine, but there's a way of communicating. . . . I really warmed up to all of them people. I really liked them, you know. I saw personalities in them. We would talk and they would laugh. I don't know whether they knew what we were saying or not."[35] The young sailors involved in the operation were not dealing in abstractions of Cold War mentality but in the concreteness of a humanitarian effort that directly affected their lives and the lives of the tens of thousands of Vietnamese under their care.

Sources of concern about the operation did not originate only in connection with American participation. The operation was continually hampered by the inability of the French and Vietnamese to communicate with one another. This problem enhanced the lack of organization and coordination in an operation that required both for success. The American officials involved in the operation found themselves in the middle of these two competing forces as they filled their role in the region. Admiral Sabin shared with Admiral Stump the problems he experienced—situations that helped increase the already strong tension.[36] Even when events were ripe for positive propaganda, a problem always lurked in the background. On September 21, *Estes* left Haiphong with the one hundred thousandth refugee, a tobacco and cloth salesman with his family.[37] *Estes* arrived at Catinat Wharf in Saigon on September 24 to a ceremony to commemorate the lift. The ceremony was attended by Vietnamese, French, and American officials and diplomatic representatives, and it included a presentation of a Vietnamese scroll of appreciation from President Diem to Admiral Sabin and gifts for the refugee family, including 6,642 piasters collected from the staff and crew of *Estes*. Afterward, Admiral Sabin gave a luncheon aboard for the high-level French and Vietnamese officials in Saigon. In return for this courtesy, the senior Vietnamese present at the luncheon invited Admiral Sabin to dinner, but at the dinner no French officials were present, and efforts to discuss the French role in the operation by Admiral Sabin were pushed aside. The next day, the commander in chief of French naval forces in the Far East, Vice Admiral Philippe Auboyneau, invited Admiral Sabin to dinner, but in this case no Vietnamese were present. The same failure to communicate or cooperate occurred during Admiral Sabin's visit to Nha Trang on his return trip to the North. While in Tourane, Admiral Gano experienced the same animosities between the French and Vietnamese as he tried to coordinate the logistical side of the operation. Regardless, Americans continued to perform their duty despite Vietnamese or French lack of cooperation.

If communication between the Vietnamese and the French had been the only problem, then the operation would have been easy. The scope of such an operation resulted in a number of issues that threatened morale and the efficiency of the transport. On September 18, Admiral Sabin discovered that personnel from USNS *Marine Adder* had charged the control team members for their meals. Captain Rittenhouse informed the admiral that this was the first time, to his knowledge, that this had occurred and that all other ships had provided free food.[38] After the incident, Admiral Sabin officially ordered all MSTS ships carrying passengers not to charge for food because it hurt American goodwill and impaired the role of the teams, who had few available resources. Admiral Sabin informed Captain Rittenhouse that these expenses would be paid with existing naval funds. Not all the news was bad, as Captain Rittenhouse reported that the MSTS T-APs were maintaining a high standard of conduct in their interaction with the civilians during the operation, although debarkation procedures continued to be difficult at Cap St. Jacques. Aboard USNS *General A. W. Brewster*, priests used the loudspeakers to warn the refugees not to leave the ship because of conditions at the camps. Despite this attempt at subterfuge, the refugees finally debarked and loaded onto trucks after some cajoling by other priests who were better informed of the conditions in the camps.

The clash of American and Vietnamese cultures also presented interesting side stories throughout the operation. On September 21, the crew of USNS *Marine Lynx* discovered opium and smoking paraphernalia aboard ship.[39] Narcotic use was not illegal in Vietnam, and opium was often a more plentiful cash crop than rice. But the presence of opium spurred the commander of *Marine Lynx* to warn his crew against using opium and ordered them not to collect it, fearing that some of the substance might remain on the ship after it was released from the operation. Because these narcotics violated U.S. Navy regulations and American law, General O'Daniel worried that a disagreement might arise between the two countries that could potentially hamper the evacuation operation. As a result, he ordered the immediate confiscation of all narcotics. Hoping to quell this problem before the refugees reached the navy transports, Admiral Sabin informed both French and Vietnamese officials of the navy's regulations, American law, and the necessity of refugee searches. Navy policy was to confiscate any narcotics aboard its ships but then return the property to the Vietnamese upon debarkation. Opium was a problem on some of the ships, while the chewing of betel nuts, also used as a sedative, caused some consternation among the sailors. Carl Benning remembered: "This root turned their teeth black. When they smiled they looked strange to someone used to seeing white teeth. Most of the refugees also dressed in black clothes so that their teeth matched their clothes."[40] This example of the clash of cultures did not diminish the energy or commitment of the American sailors.

The embarkation and debarkation areas had a set of unique problems for the navy. One example of the difficulties involved in using Vietnamese stevedores was the unpredictability of their abilities. USNS *Pembina* (T-AK-200) took thirteen days to load its cargo in Haiphong, and on September 25, when it arrived in Tourane, only 80 of the 2,000 tons were offloaded in six and one-half hours, and only 80 additional tons were offloaded on September 26. It was estimated that, given this schedule, it would take five or six weeks to transport 2,000 tons—a clearly unacceptable timetable. By September 30, USNS *Muskingum* had loaded 1,217 tons of cargo. The problem of finding berthing space and stevedores in the North was repeated in the South. The lack of pier space, lighterage, and stevedores limited the amount of cargo that could be offloaded at Tourane. *Pembina* and *Muskingum*, as a result, were not able to discharge their cargo in a timely manner and became the last two heavy cargo ships to offload at that city.

Another example of the difficulties in transporting cargo occurred on September 29, during the offloading of LST-901. The LST was first delayed because the French did not make a beach site available for it; then there was some confusion about the cargo, because the cargo report did not indicate that the equipment aboard belonged to STEM, and the STEM vehicles on the LST were not reported to the MSTS representative in charge of the area. To make matters worse, the keys to the vehicles had been misplaced, so the vehicles had to be winched off the LST. The stevedores involved in the offloading took a three-hour siesta and left at 6 p.m. without permission and without completing their job. Finally, French Legionnaire equipment was placed among the STEM equipment, adding to the confusion. The LST was not able to offload all of the equipment before the French demanded the beach site used by the LST, and, thus, the LST sailed for Haiphong still carrying fifteen tons of STEM equipment. The loading of cargo continued, despite the ever-changing obstacles, while the problems of the operation were balanced with some good news in mid-September.

By September 20, there was some indication that the Viet Minh had eased their campaign to deny refugees access to the embarkation areas. One explanation for that change was the presence of International

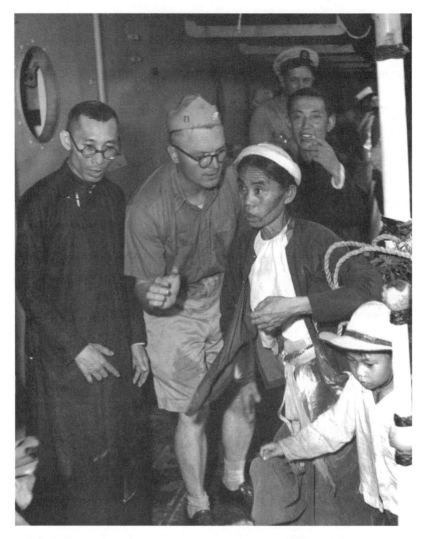

Fig. 6.5. Vietnamese Catholic priests served as leaders and interpreters
as well as being refugees. Photograph courtesy of the Douglas Pike
Photograph Collection, Vietnam Archive (VA000865).

Commission members in Phat Diem and Bui Chu, two predominately
Catholic provinces where there were many potential evacuees. While the
influx of refugees from these provinces would cause an increase in the
embarkation areas, Admiral Sabin saw no need for increased shipping—
especially as the French had improved the loading procedures with the

introduction of French military personnel as stevedores. Admiral Sabin also maintained that the potential increase in the cargo load would not necessitate additional shipping, as the *Pembina* had been loading since September 9. Admiral Sabin recommended the temporary release of the personnel carriers USNS *General S. D. Sturgis* (T-AP-137) and USNS *Marine Serpent* (T-AP-202) until October 10, as well as two cargo carriers should they be required after the withdrawal from Hanoi.[41]

Even as Admiral Sabin juggled the navy and MSTS ships involved in the operation, the LST remained the workhorse of Operation Passage to Freedom. LSTs were involved in moving all types of equipment and personnel, from mobile surgical teams with their equipment to military personnel with their equipment and families. Anything that could fit into an LST was carried during the course of the operation, and life was always busy for the crews. These ships not only served as cargo carriers but also transported military and civilian personnel throughout the operation. Because the LST had the ability to land on the beach, it was subject to greater security risk, although its mission was more flexible. It was not uncommon for navy personnel on the LSTs to carry sidearms because of the risks involved with their duties.[42]

Morris Smith, who served on LST-887, recalled the situation on the beach as Vietnamese refugees were organized to embark on the LST. Spraying with DDT was an important part of the process, as was inspection of goods brought aboard to ensure there was no contraband. Aboard LST-901, Ted Zeigler witnessed the condition of the Vietnamese as they embarked: "They would come on by the dozens. . . . Half of the men's heads had all these scabs and sores and stuff, and most of the people, the women and men, had just terrible teeth, just terrible teeth."[43] Despite the questionable healthiness of the Vietnamese, Zeigler and his shipmates were continually amazed by the strength of the evacuees. "They were loading rice bags on their [LST] and I think those things weighed about 200 pounds and these little Vietnam guys would throw that thing up on their back and carry that thing up the tank deck there, and so we were going to try and help them. It took two sailors carrying this thing to get that thing up there and these little guys were carrying it up there like it wasn't nothing."[44] Just as the Vietnamese continued to amaze the sailors of the LSTs, so did the goodwill exhibited by the Americans earn the trust of the Vietnamese.

No passengers were loaded on September 22, nor were there enough for September 23, although LST-901 did depart Haiphong with 80 tons of equipment and 25 vehicles. Inside the ship were 650 drums of DDT, four hundred cases of medical equipment, and three hundred first aid kits. Eighteen of the vehicles belonged to the Health Services Division of STEM. Only 1,200 refugees remained at Camp de la Pagoda, situated near Haiphong, and none had arrived from Hanoi. Two hundred seven military and 254 medical personnel and their equipment were loaded onto an LST, but no refugees were loaded on September 25. On September 27, USNS *Marine Adder* and one LST loaded 153 refugees and 2,764 military personnel, 801 tons of cargo, and 120 vehicles. *Marine Adder* sailed for Tourane, while the LST sailed for Nha Trang.

At the same time, personnel and equipment moved to the South, the French and Polish were involved in transporting those who wished to go to the north. The French had allocated approximately ten ships for Viet Minh transportation and had estimated that sixteen thousand of the possible one hundred fifty thousand personnel had already completed the trip north.[45] Captain Winn reported that the actual ship requirements would be less and the operation would be complete by November 1, because many Viet Minh were reluctant to leave their homes in the South. Many of them did not want to leave their families and livelihood, while others were ordered to remain in the South to continue to fight should the Geneva Conference Agreements fail. The French had the capacity to move all of their cargo and, with additional French military personnel acting as stevedores, could increase the cargo capacity of Haiphong from seventy-five thousand tons per month to ninety thousand per month. Admiral Sabin did not agree with General O'Daniel's recommendation to provide the French with five or six LSTs until the end of May 1955, even though the French would blame the United States if they failed to transport all of their equipment from the North. Admiral Sabin argued that holding LSTs beyond their scheduled rotation out of the operation was against navy policy. He also maintained that available U.S. and French shipping was more than enough to handle the military and other equipment in Hanoi and Haiphong, and he suggested that the navy focus on getting the French to be more efficient in their shore organization, use of lighterage, and finding additional stevedores.

As of September 27, the United States and the French had evacuated

Table 6.1. Number of Days Each Ship Type Served in the Operation

Ship Type	Total Days	Principal Mission
APA	264	Civilian Transport
AKA	167	Civilian Transport
AGC	51	Flagships
APD	129	Flagships for Task Group Commanders
LST	651	Equipment, Military, and Civilian Transport
LSD	193	Equipment and Military Transport
LCU	579	Military and Civilian Transfer to APA, AKA, LSD
AF	53	Logistic Support
AH	37	Medical Support
AKL	56	Logistic Support
AKS	12	Logistic Support

more than three hundred seventy-three thousand people from North Vietnam by all methods of transportation. The two countries had also transported 62,239 vehicles and 55,248 tons of cargo. The total number of days American ships served in the operation was impressive, as shown in Table 6.1.[46]

On September 30, Captain Winn visited Hanoi to assess the equipment and refugee situation before October 10, the deadline for Viet Minh occupation of the city.[47] Because no refugees had arrived for two days, the American personnel in the debarkation centers struck the remaining tents and relocated to Haiphong. While this was being done, French personnel removed all salvageable equipment from their airfield and relieved the Vietnamese police in Hanoi. The city clearly showed the effects of the transfer of power, as the white cars of the International Control Commission and armed French troops positioned themselves at every intersection.

Earlier, a priest who had escaped by sampan from Thai Benh told American officials that twenty thousand civilians from that district and fifty thousand from neighboring districts wanted to leave for the South but were denied transit to Haiphong by the Viet Minh.[48] The Vietnamese propaganda officer in Hanoi informed CTG 90.8 that he did not have enough money or personnel to conduct an effective anticommunist campaign or to counter the propaganda being distributed by the Viet Minh. On October 1, two thousand refugees arrived at Camp Pagoda in Haiphong after a seventy-mile journey through Viet Minh–held territory aboard twenty-seven sampans. The new arrivals informed camp officials that another fifty sampans were behind them trying to make their way to the embarkation point.

While operations were gearing up for the withdrawal from Hanoi, U.S. personnel in the South also transitioned to the next phase of the operation. On October 3 Commander A. E. Teall relieved Captain B. N. Rittenhouse as commander of Task Group 90.9 in Saigon. Commander Teall faced his first challenge after being on the job for only a few days. On October 5, USNS *General W. M. Black* arrived in Saigon to disembark its Vietnamese passengers. During the trip, the Vietnamese refugees were given American gift packages, only to have these tokens of goodwill confiscated by Vietnamese customs officials as they inspected the refugees. The customs officials then started taking the personal effects from *General Black*'s crew as the sailors departed the ship. The U.S. consul issued a note of protest and successfully returned most of the items before *General Black* departed Saigon.

Confiscation was not repeated in such a flagrant violation of the sailors' or refugees' rights, but on October 6, Chinese refugees who had arrived on *General Howze* were required to pass through customs inspections. Even though American officials were present during these inspections, they could not stop confiscation and were not able to determine the extent of it. Later in the operation, American personnel learned that the customs officials were searching for opium and gold leaf. After the *General Black* incident, American officials rebuked the Vietnamese customs officials, and the crew of *General Howze* was spared similar treatment. Despite this improvement, refugees were still targeted for more detailed inspection, the effects of which were not lost on the new arrivals to South Vietnam, who lamented any loss of personal items, whether contraband or not.[49]

As the deadline for evacuating Hanoi approached, General O'Daniel informed the Department of State that American personnel had moved all available equipment from Hanoi less than a week before the October 10 deadline, as specified in the Geneva Agreements. This included all salvageable materials, including nonworking but repairable items that the Viet Minh could use. All remaining items were to be destroyed.[50] By the October 10 deadline, the United States had completed its evacuation of Hanoi. Typhoon Nancy served as the greatest threat to the Americans, and the navy ordered its ships to the heavy-weather anchorage in

Henriette Passe or out to sea. On October 11, the typhoon passed the Haiphong area. Hanoi was in Viet Minh hands, but evacuees wishing to escape the North still had Haiphong. The next stage of the operation would prove just as challenging, as the area of operation had shrunk and less than half of the total number of those who would eventually evacuate had completed the journey.

Ending this phase of the operation, President Ngo Dinh Diem awarded Admiral Sabin the Presidential Citation with Ribbon of Friendship in a surprise ceremony at the presidential palace in Saigon. Admiral Sabin accepted the citation subject to the approval of his commanders.[51] As the first phase ended, Ambassador Heath sent a letter to Admiral Sabin in which he repeated his appreciation for the professional manner in which Task Force 90 had conducted itself in the evacuation. He offered his highest praise for the navy's officers and men in dealing with the refugees, suggesting that their work had left a lasting impression on all involved in the operation. "This mission," Heath maintained, "has been carried out in the best tradition of the Naval service."[52]

CHAPTER 7

Resettling a Nation

One of the greatest concerns for the United States was working with the South Vietnamese to ensure that their contribution to the operation was coordinated and visible to those involved. On September 2, members of the STEM staff met with a Dr. Vien, who served as deputy to Commissar of Refugees Ngo Ngoc Doi.[1] During a one-and-one-half-hour meeting, Vien discussed the South Vietnamese government's plan for resettling the refugees. He informed the group that all refugees would be registered in Haiphong or aboard their transport in order to facilitate their logical resettlement once they arrived in the South. The South Vietnamese government had adopted criteria for selecting land for resettlement. It had to be owned by the government, have access to a main road or the ability to connect to a main road after construction, be well-drained, and be suitable for farming, small industry, or other refugee occupation.[2] Vien stressed, as had STEM officials before him, that it was imperative that the refugees have an opportunity to make a living for themselves, their families, and preferably an entire village group. A significant worry for the Saigon government was the influx of refugees in Saigon and its ability to move these refugees out of temporary housing, especially the schools, before September 30, when the school year began.

During this meeting as well as the many that would follow, American personnel worked at the foundations of nation building. This was a difficult task in ordinary times, but especially difficult with the influx of thousands of refugees, many of whom had fled the North without the capital to start anew. The government planned to use the area around Bien Hoa for resettlement; it had already transferred five thousand refugees there to a small compound across the road from the mental health hospital. Future refugees who were resettled in the Bien Hoa area would be escorted by their priests, provided with tents for temporary shelter, and given the materials to construct their own permanent houses at an estimated cost of 3,000 piasters apiece. Vien informed the group that the French had assumed responsibility for clearing and grading the land as well as providing access to the main roads and installing water and sanitation facilities.

The South Vietnamese government had decided to resettle refugees on higher ground rather than rice land because growing rice would take them longer to become self-sufficient. A rice harvest would take six months to mature, whereas the refugees could plant other crops with a shorter time to harvest. Additionally, higher ground would afford a greater opportunity for the refugees to cut their own wood, especially bamboo, which was needed for permanent housing. Vien indicated that the government had set aside twenty-six hectares of land for twenty thousand families, or land for approximately one hundred thousand people. The refugees were expected to construct their own housing and provide the tools for this process, while the provincial chief and bishop of Bien Hoa would aid in the construction of other village structures, feed the refugees until they were self-sufficient, and provide security. The South Vietnamese government would transport some food—rice, fish, and salt—to Bien Hoa. Vien informed the group that there was still a great need for bulldozers; drillers; small tools such as axes, adzes, and machetes; and hurricane lamps; and that malaria control items such as spray and netting were in short supply.

Just as Admiral Sabin came to understand the difficulties involved in coordinating with the South Vietnamese, so did members of the STEM team discover the same problems in synchronizing American and South Vietnamese operations. In Cap St. Jacques, the situation continued to be tenuous. The medical chief of the province had no additional personnel to spare, and the medical lieutenant in charge of the 150-bed hospital and refugee camp was not able to do the job alone.[3] Other problems also emerged, such as the hospital's arrival in Cap St. Jacques without instructions on how to assemble it and the arrival of five drums of DDT without sprayers. STEM officials had already assisted the province chief in constructing the camp; locating the tents, wells, and latrines; and clearing and grading the area. MAAG officials had helped with the assignment of Vietnamese troops in the resettlement area and oversaw the reception of refugees, materials, and equipment. In addition, MAAG took charge of the whole operation at Cap St. Jacques, which resulted in its becoming a significant area of debarkation for the operation.

STEM's role had been under internal review in early September, and its future usefulness was questioned because much of its advice had been ignored while its money was spent by the Vietnamese.[4] Richard Brown characterized the mission in the North as nothing more than a "listening post" and assumed the position of a handyman—that is, fixing what did not work in the refugee settlements—and he complained that their efforts to organize and coordinate the registration and improve camp conditions and sanitary facilities had failed.

Another note of concern was the nature of Operation Passage to Freedom. In the hands of Task Force 90, its objective was to get the refugees from point A (the North) to point B (the South) as quickly as possible without care for their welfare at the point of embarkation or their future after debarkation. Attempts to rectify the situation, according to Brown, had been either ignored or refused, resulting in miscommunication; idle ships, trucks, and wharf crews; and poor conditions for those the United States was trying to help. Brown cited an example in Haiphong when STEM representatives responded to a request for wells and privies only to be told by MAAG officials that STEM assistance was not needed, only later to have MAAG officials request that STEM increase its assistance in providing these very facilities. While this occurred, MAAG officials openly criticized the STEM officials for not being cooperative. Brown argued that STEM had already made a significant investment in money, materials, and technical support to the South Vietnamese government and the refugees. It now faced the problem of losing all it had invested because MAAG had assumed too much control over the operation and had different objectives than STEM.

While MAAG officials believed it was important to move as many people as possible, according to Brown it was STEM's opinion that speed over organization resulted in too many forced, unplanned, and ill-conceived resettlements in areas chosen for availability. This resulted in resettlement areas without adequate health, water, and sanitation provisions. Brown was pleased to hear Dr. Vien's assessment of the situation, even though the plan he presented was independent of the South Vietnamese agencies with which STEM had been working. The result was that STEM's advice and expertise were minimized. Brown questioned to what extent STEM should invest in activities for which it had no control but would ultimately be held accountable should the result fail. This assessment signaled one of the growing areas of frustration for Americans in Vietnam. The size and scope of the operation were much larger than the United States had anticipated. Unlike the French, who in August had requested American assistance, there was no one else to turn to for help, which resulted in greater attention to detail and a renewed sense of energy and urgency to see the task complete.

In addition to the internal problem the United States experienced with the scope of the refugee problem, the Americans were also hampered by various obstacles imposed by the French. On September 3, O'Daniel informed Admiral Stump that the French did not intend to pay the pilotage fees accumulated by U.S. Navy ships for French pilots used to navigate the Saigon River. Ambassador Heath planned to present the bill to the Vietnamese government, and if it refused payment, O'Daniel would begin plans to have STEM pay the bill.[5] Another problem that emerged with the French was in connection with the use of berths in Haiphong. Captain Winn informed Admiral Sabin on September 9 that twenty-one French ships were involved in the cargo lift.[6] For every U.S. ship in a Haiphong berth, it meant a French ship was idle, with a corresponding loss of revenue. As a result, the French were not willing to relinquish space for American ships, and Captain Winn recommended that no additional ships load cargo at Haiphong other than the ones already present. Even as the United States tried to obtain more berths for embarkation and debarkation, the port rates for Task Force 90 ships increased.

When STEM officials were not worrying about fees and berths, they concentrated on the day-to-day problems of the operation, such as the shortage of tents for those refugees who needed housing. The main disembarkation camp had 445 tents available, 25 of which were used by administrative and Vietnamese military personnel. This left 420 tents for the maximum of twelve thousand refugees expected in the camp at any one time. The construction of tents had been a continual problem in both the reception and resettlement centers since early August. STEM's Community Development Division sought to rectify the problem by training young Vietnamese men in the skills of pitching twenty-man tents for refugee shelters.[7] The plan was to use U.S. and Vietnamese military personnel to demonstrate the erection of a tent to sixty Vietnamese civilians at the Hippodrome. Once these men learned how to set up a tent, they would be dispersed throughout the camps in South Vietnam with the responsibility of establishing temporary shelter for refugees until permanent shelter was constructed. Not only would this program assist in increasing the number of tent shelters, but it would also use camp labor, open up space in the camps, and help the Vietnamese understand that they needed to help themselves.

In Hue, on September 4, John Thelen consulted with local leaders on the refugee problem at the end of August. The Vietnamese officials believed they had the refugee situation under control, with the exception of some minor sanitation problems. Thelen learned that the question of permanent resettlement had not been resolved, although the plan was to resettle refugees in areas most suitable to their former occupation in the North. The French had already informed the Community Development Division that it had finalized plans to provide for three hundred families in and around Ban Me Thout.[8] These families would be divided into three groups of one hundred families each and permanently resettled where there was sufficient building material and available work, but there was no indication that their occupation was a factor in the relocation. Ban Me Thuot was a reasonable area for resettlement of refugee families, but it certainly satisfied only a small number of those from the North. The United States and South Vietnamese desired a thousand Ban Me Thuots; it found many fewer.

Because Quin Hon was a regrouping area for the Viet Minh, the three thousand refugees from that region who were temporarily in Nha Trang would return once the Viet Minh had been transported to the North. Thelen stressed the need for registration of refugees, though the effect of his words was not determined. During his trip Thelen learned that central Vietnam was ready for resettlement work as soon as the Vietnamese government released funds for the project. The Vietnamese officials had received only six million of the sixty million piasters promised and had used this money to sustain the refugees in their temporary shelters. The remainder of the money would provide for permanent resettlement. Officials in Hue were worried about the loss of time caused by the delays in receiving funding and feared that the monsoon season with its heavy rains and flooding would hamper the operation and significantly decrease the morale of the refugees in the region.

In an effort to improve the overcrowded situation in Saigon and Cap St. Jacques, O'Daniel recommended to Admiral Sabin on September 6 that only one ship with fewer than twenty-five hundred civilians arrive daily in one of those ports from September 11 to 25. General O'Daniel suggested that, for that period, Task Force 90 focus on transporting cargo in appropriate ships. Admiral Sabin agreed, if such actions were necessary, though he warned O'Daniel that one ship daily would result in idle shipping and an unnecessary overcrowding of the embarkation area in Haiphong. This, in turn, would discourage those seeking evacuation and could result in negative publicity and increased Viet Minh propaganda. Additionally, the United States had only two berths available at Haiphong, and if Task Force 90 concentrated on only cargo, those berths would fall well short of the ships' capabilities. On September 7, Admiral Sabin informed General O'Daniel that he was concerned about the proposed reduction in refugee transportation, especially in light of the increase in registration in Hanoi and the arrival of MSTS transports with capacity for 3,500 passengers. These new elements, he argued, increased the necessity of maintaining Saigon as a point of debarkation and the need to establish alternate areas in Nha Trang or Tourane to relieve the pressures of overcrowding.

Admiral Sabin received significant support from Admiral Stump and informed O'Daniel that interrupting the normal schedule would not be prudent.[9] On September 8, MAAG Haiphong informed O'Daniel that recent visits to refugee camps in and around Haiphong had reinforced their estimates of the number of refugees available for evacuation.[10] There was little to suggest that the number would increase and more evidence of a decrease in the flow of refugees to the embarkation area. Two Catholic militias had been suspected of joining the Viet Minh with their weapons intact, which added to the pessimistic assessment, for Catholics were the primary population fleeing the Viet Minh. Captain Winn agreed with the MAAG Haiphong assessment. Of the twenty-two thousand refugees from Haiduong, only two thousand remained. Captain Winn, therefore, intended to load only one ship per day if there were sufficient numbers of refugees available in the evacuation camp. As a result of these conflicting reports on the number of refugees available for evacuation in the Tonkin Delta, Admiral Sabin organized conferences with MAAG Haiphong, Captain Winn, and French and Vietnamese officials to determine shipping requirements. Admiral Sabin, however, was of the opinion that it was not necessary to keep a large number of ships in Indochina on "suppositions, uncertainties, and irregular schedules." General O'Daniel informed Admiral Stump that the failure to move refugees away from the southern reception centers had resulted in overcrowding and the inability to handle an increased influx of evacuees.

Matters were not improved by isolated Vietnamese Catholic priests who balked at their resettlement options. In Cap St. Jacques, priests had refused their charges from using tents constructed by the French army. Twenty-five hundred refugees had planned to resettle in Tay Ninh, but priests in charge of the group refused transportation because of potential religious conflicts with others occupying the area. O'Daniel believed there was only a small chance that any significant number of refugees would leave the camps until American officials could get the Vietnamese refugee leaders organized. In response to Admiral Sabin's concern for diminished capacity of Task Force 90 ships, O'Daniel maintained that the French airlift could make up for any decrease to keep the flow of refugees coming to the South. STEM officials believed the continuation of the airlift was an unnecessary expense, as there were idle U.S. Navy ships in the North and adequate shelter at the embarkation facilities in Haiphong. MAAG Haiphong agreed with the STEM assessment, prompting both sides to reassess the situation as it stood in mid-September.[11]

On September 11, the chiefs of provinces of South Vietnam met in Saigon at the Ministry of the Interior at the request of Ngo Ngoc Doi, commissioner general for refugees.[12] At the time of the conference, more than two hundred seventy thousand refugees had been evacuated from the North, and another one hundred forty thousand were expected. This would prove to be almost four hundred thousand short of the actual number. Through the meeting, attended by Lavergne and Thelen, MAAG and STEM officials learned much about the Vietnamese perspective of the operation. There was general agreement that the success of the resettlement effort depended upon the cadence of arrival from the North. The province chief of Bien Hoa reported that thirty thousand refugees were currently resettled in the province, which had capacity for another seventy thousand individuals. The first twenty thousand could be absorbed immediately, though it would take an additional three months before the province accommodated the remaining fifty thousand. Thu Dau Mot province had capacity for twenty thousand refugees, even though it had no rice land. Although previous refugees assigned to that area had rebelled against permanent settlement in the province, the province chief believed resettlement would be successful.

The Cap St. Jacques representative informed the group that his area was useful only as a reception area, whereas Baria, to the northwest, had three thousand hectares for six thousand refugees and rice land for another ten thousand. Tay Ninh province had room for thirty thousand individuals, though the Caodaists believed that one hundred thousand could be resettled in the area. Long Xuyen had been reserved for military personnel, although fifteen hundred civilian refugees had settled in the area; it had reached its capacity. The area around Vinh Long was also filled to capacity with twenty-five hundred refugees. In Gia Dinh two thousand refugees were housed in schools, but the province chief maintained that all would be moved before the beginning of school, and the province could handle another nineteen thousand after October 1. In the Mekong Delta, My Tho presented a security risk but could handle six thousand refugees, and Can Tho offered twenty-five thousand hectares for refugee resettlement. Other smaller provinces in the Delta, including Soc Trang, which was reserved for military refugee families, Tra Vinh, Ta Nan, Rach Gia, Bac Klieu, and Sa Dec, made land available to the evacuation operation. When the totals were added, the province chiefs accounted for four hundred thousand refugees in South Vietnam. STEM officials estimated that it would cost 1,205,000,000 piasters to take care of the refugees in the southern part of Vietnam before they could become self-sufficient. Rehabilitation costs for central Vietnam were an additional 1 billion piasters. On October 10, the day the Viet Minh took over Hanoi, the number of refugees in central Vietnam stood at 71,925, as shown in Table 7.1.

Table 7.1. Refugee Status in Central Vietnam

Quang Tri	7,564
Thua Thien (Hue)	27,080
Da Nanh (Tourance)	11,539
Quang Nam (Faifoo)	4,114
Phu Yen (Song Can)	285
Khanh Hoa (Nha Trang)	11,397
Ninh Than (Phon Rong)	2,891
Binh Thuan (Phon Thiet)	6,235

W. A. Dymsza, STEM program officer and acting representative to central Vietnam, reported to Lavergne on September 28 on the progress in central Vietnam, complaining of the central Vietnamese officials' inability to coordinate and affect positive leadership.[13] The problem with refugee resettlement in early September had been the lack of funds. This was not the problem at the end of September; rather, as Dymsza reported, it was the failure of government services to work together in a coordinated effort. Dymsza learned that province chiefs maintained that they could not build resettlement shelters for 4,000 piasters—the cost established per home—and had failed to work with other local officials in constructing community facilities that adhered to STEM's standard. Province chiefs also planned to resettle farmers on privately held, abandoned land even though it was suspected that the absentee landlords would return and demand a high rent for the land cultivated by the refugees.

In the southern provinces of central Vietnam, the Vietnamese government planned to resettle 3,300 families in Nha Trang, 650 families in Phan Rang, and 6,000 families in Phan Thiet.[14] Half of Phan Thiet was reserved for forty thousand Montagnards from the North. The Montagnards were supposed to be taken care of by the French, but, after receiving complaints, the Vietnamese government initiated its own relief. On September 13, the director of Social Action Service assured STEM officials that these estimates were very conservative and that the provinces could absorb a larger number of refugees even though temporary shelter would be a problem. In a meeting between Dymsza and Mr. Duyen, government delegate in central Vietnam, the two agreed that the Vietnamese government needed to increase construction of permanent housing for refugees in central Vietnam before more refugees started to arrive and school started at the end of September, at which time school buildings would no longer be available.

In its first phase, Ben Tre had two thousand hectares for five thousand to seventy-five hundred families. Ben Tre's population exceeded two hundred thousand, with the primary wealth coming from cultivation, coconuts, fruits, salt, and fishing.[15] Its high ground produced mulberry trees and silkworms, cotton, peanuts, and tobacco. It was a perfect area for resettlement, because the job opportunities for refugees were plentiful. STEM had already allocated 10 million piasters for the completion of phase one on September 22 and was considering an additional 3 million piasters to increase the refugee total to ten thousand individuals and possibly twenty thousand individuals in a third phase. Before the second and third phases, it was necessary to construct roads throughout the area to ensure security, economic prosperity, and military transportation. Because the Viet Minh had used Ben Tre as a military base of operations during the First Indochina War, it was important to keep a continual Vietnamese military presence in the area. Ben Tre had many advantages for the refugees; the primary one was the ease with which they could be absorbed into the local economy. It was estimated that an individual could earn 50 piasters daily while spending only 20 on essential supplies such as wood, fish, and vegetables, which were plentiful. The saving of 30 piasters multiplied by four thousand refugee families resulted in 36 million piasters by November 1955. This did not take into account what other members of the family might earn and promised a successful resettlement project. Militarily, Ben Tre was an attractive area to Catholics from the North because of the previous influence of the Viet Minh during the First Indochina War. As the chief of the province, Huynh Van Suu, would argue, resettled refugees would be the first to suppress an attempt by the Viet Minh to reassert their military presence.

Just as Ben Tre was an attractive place to resettle, so were the original debarkation points of Saigon and Cap St. Jacques, despite the Vietnamese government's unwillingness to let the refugees stay. Many refugees in the reception camps in Saigon and Cap St. Jacques refused to be resettled, instead demanding that they be allowed to remain in the camp, where food and shelter were guaranteed. Furthermore, camp officials in Cap St. Jacques found it difficult to organize forty refugees to act as a ship cleaning detail. The refugees, most of them fishermen, earned more fishing and refused the lower pay, and lower-status position, of clean-up personnel.[16] On September 13, the total refugee population at the Cap St. Jacques debarkation camp was 17,194, and no refugees were scheduled to relocate into resettlement camps or permanent villages.

In Cap St. Jacques, STEM, French, and Vietnamese officials worked toward improving the medical and sanitary conditions in the camps.[17] Poindexter reported on September 13 that the French doctors had designed a logical medical plan for the refugees, including three tents to house the 150-bed hospital: one tent each for maternity, contagious diseases, and diagnostic laboratory services. Major surgeries would be performed at the military hospital in Cap St. Jacques, when needed, while postoperative convalescence would be in the camps. The preventive medicine plan called for a public health nurse and tent visiting nurses who emphasized social services and health education and coordinated an immunization plan. Milk distribution was organized for infants, children, pregnant and nursing women, and sick and hospitalized patients. The permanent dispensary in the camps remained and would house an outpatient clinic and ambulatory treatment center. The doctors organized a chemical bucket brigade for collecting feces and other body waste and constructed a special incinerator for disposing of the waste. Dr. Poindexter recommended the immediate additions of a professional health educator and a malaria control unit and eventual organization of schools, a fire control brigade, and recreational facilities. Cap St. Jacques, he recommended, would provide an excellent opportunity to create a model public health program the Ministry of Health could reproduce throughout the rest of South Vietnam.

On September 17, Captain Rittenhouse reported that the camp at Cap St. Jacques was almost permanent and full, although it possibly could absorb an additional two thousand refugees a day for one week if absolutely necessary. Rittenhouse requested no further arrivals until after the completion of two additional camps in the debarkation area.

As more and more refugees flooded the South, certain areas emerged as logistical concentration points. Bien Hoa province became one of the major centers for refugee resettlement in South Vietnam. It suffered, on a larger scale, the results of this influx of people into the existing community.[18] There were two common problems in all refugee resettlement areas, though in Bien Hoa both were enhanced. First, the cost of living increased with the arrival of large numbers of North Vietnamese refugees as well as families of French and Vietnamese military personnel. In order to combat inflationary factors, the province chief, Ho Bao Thanh, ordered police to exercise strict control of market prices and punish speculators and entrepreneurs who charged more than the fixed price set by the Vietnamese government. The province chief did not want to decrease the number of new inhabitants; rather, he called for an increase in production. He called for the cancellation of war taxes and the free transportation of rice and other foodstuffs from Saigon to Bien Hoa. The second problem to emerge in Bien Hoa was the different standards set for northern and southern Vietnamese refugees. The Minister of the Interior had ordered that each refugee family from North Vietnam receive one hectare. Southern refugee families, who had also lost their homes and livelihood, were not entitled to one hectare. This caused much discontent among the southern refugees resettled in Bien Hoa. The province chief proposed a plan to split each hectare between northern and southern refugee families as well as put the southern refugee families on the same basis as that of the northern families.

For the STEM chief of the Agriculture and Natural Resources Division, Bien Hoa represented not a permanent resettlement area but one of temporary expedience in this stage of the evacuation effort. Bien Hoa had been an area of historically limited settlement for a reason. It was a nonagricultural province with little to offer the refugees. He maintained, however, that the Vietnamese government had to employ this marginal area for emergency resettlement of northern refugees. The upland area of Bien Hoa allowed immediate exploitation of some crops and timber until December, after which the dry season made it nearly impossible for the refugees to be self-sustaining. Although this temporary area was a necessity, he argued that the USOM needed to develop plans for more permanent settlements if the new population in South Vietnam were to thrive. Holiday, who also visited Bien Hoa in September, recognized that there were problems concerning access to water and sanitary facilities but did not understand why other members of STEM criticized the Vietnamese efforts in the area. Bien Hoa had seen an influx of refugees, some thirty thousand in the first few weeks of the evacuation, and did not have adequate time to prepare. The Vietnamese officials in Bien Hoa had made the best of a difficult situation.[19]

The problem of Bien Hoa was not unique to the overall situation in South Vietnam. At the September 24 STEM division chiefs' meeting, Lavergne, acting deputy director for refugee affairs, presented a committee report from his unit that examined past plans for refugee resettlement with an understanding of the conditions as they appeared at the end of September.[20] The report stressed the basic concepts that evacuees and displaced persons in Vietnam shared common values, required the opportunity to earn a minimum livelihood as soon as possible, and needed to be comfortable in their new environment. It was also important that the Vietnamese government take a positive, active role in ensuring the maximum use of personnel and resources to the benefit of the refugee and displaced person population. The tenor of the report, as conditions in Bien Hoa demonstrated, was that the first phase of the resettlement operation was over and the second phase needed to begin. The first phase dealt with the emergency resettlement of refugees from the North and was seen as nothing more than a stop-gap measure. The second phase dealt with the rehabilitation of the lands and other resources in South Vietnam to accommodate the new population. This required careful planning and coordination for success, as its effects would be long term. The role STEM would play in this phase was critical as the Vietnamese government struggled with internal division and political intrigue, which took focus away from the refugees.

By the beginning of October 1954, the resettlement program in Vietnam was gaining momentum and had reached a point at which the United States needed to reorganize and concentrate its efforts. The United States had no project agreement with the Republic of Vietnam that covered the resettlement of Vietnamese in the South. The provisions of the most recent project funded the evacuation of the refugees and their reception in the South. The Vietnamese government, however, continued to spend money on the resettlement problem with the understanding that the United States would reimburse it for these past, present, and future expenditures. It was also generally thought that the Vietnamese government had not been spending its money—and thus the United States' money—efficiently and economically and had little hope of achieving economic independence and integration of the refugees into their permanent resettlement areas.[21]

To overcome these obstacles, the U.S. economic mission in Vietnam recommended a reevaluation of requirements for temporary assistance to refugees and a division of aid between temporary relocation and permanent resettlement. It also recognized a need to renew coordination and consultation between various Vietnamese government agencies and the USOM technical division in order to use available U.S. assistance more effectively. Another concern at this time was the distinction between refugees from the North and displaced persons in the South. The majority of focus was on the refugees, but it was understood that a solution for the displaced persons was required before the Republic of Vietnam could hope for a stable political, economic, and social environment.

The plan of action for the project was distributed on October 12, the day after Hanoi was returned to the Viet Minh. The plan called for the evacuation and resettlement of an estimated five to six hundred thousand Vietnamese through the end of May 1955—an estimate that fell short by 30 percent.[22] The plan's program of activity outlined the budgetary requirements for the evacuation to the South, reception of the refugees, subsidies while the refugees were in the reception camps, and permanent resettlement. The amount was estimated at one billion piasters. Additional equipment costs of nearly $16 million included tents, welcoming kits, and materials for construction of the temporary resettlement areas in the South. The resolution of the project plan was greeted with other positive news.

There were some indications that the reception camps were achieving a certain degree of success. In the camp at Phu Tho there were approximately thirteen thousand civilians and twenty-eight hundred military personnel, most of whom were Catholic and had been in the camp for approximately one month. The camp was well organized and reasonably clean. It had had an effective program of inoculation and a program of action for sanitation that included assistance from the public health section of the Vietnamese government. The sanitation plan also provided incentives and rewards for those in the camp who maintained their areas and sanctions for those who did not.[23] The camp had the appearance of returning to normalcy. Inside the camp, tents were transformed into businesses, with barbers, tailors, notions shops, soft goods dealers, wooden shoe fitters, fish hook and net makers, and soft drink vendors. There was also a self-starting drugstore and other convenience stores. In his tour of the camp, H. M. Pascal received only two complaints: the refugees wanted a chapel, and one person had been denied permission by the camp commander to build a house on the camp site.

The theme of evacuees dealing with many of their own problems, albeit with American financial and technical assistance, was repeated throughout the early part of October 1954. In a memorandum planning for a meeting with Commissioner General for Refugees Ngo Ngoc Doi, the division chiefs within USOM were called upon to provide recommendations for basic minimum housing, sanitation, education, and relief, with the understanding that even the minimum might not be attainable. As one STEM official would argue, "Much can and will be done by the evacuees themselves if they are left to their own devices. It should be our aim to assist the Vietnamese to channel latent forces into lines of communal development and solidarity."[24]

A clearer understanding of some of the difficulties encountered by STEM officials in the refugee camps is best described in a report from sanitation engineer Morton S. Hilbert to the chief of the Health and Sanitation Division on October 12. Between October 5 and 8, Hilbert visited fifteen established and proposed camp sites in the northern part of central Vietnam. [25] The supplying of fresh water for the camps had been a primary concern from the beginning and had run into innumerable obstacles. Hand pumps used to extract fresh water often broke, resulting in no water for the community, and the discussion of building and maintaining wells was measured in not hours or days but weeks. In several camps the open wells were inadequate in both quality and quantity. The wells attracted mosquitoes and other pests that exposed the refugees to disease or dirtied the water supply. The creation and maintenance of privy facilities also was a constant battle. In addition to the construction of the units—expensive when materials, transportation, and labor were taken into account but necessary for the health of the refugees—there was the added challenge of health education and reinforcement of proper hygienic practices. Hilbert's recommendations echoed those of the model camp at Phu Tho and STEM division chiefs' meetings. A combination of incentives and active participation by the Vietnamese who would be using the camps on a day-to-day basis was much more effective than any other strategy currently in use.

Voluntary agencies played a prominent role in the relief of refugees throughout the operation. The major problem, however, was the ability of these agencies to coordinate their activities to achieve maximum effect. On September 15 and 16, STEM organized a meeting of all volunteer agencies to better coordinate their roles.[26] STEM agreed to provide offices for volunteer agencies, free of charge, on the fifth floor of the Perchoir building in Saigon. It also agreed to provide office supplies and support for those involved in the agencies. In return, ten agencies supplemented U.S. assistance. The Cooperative for American Remittances Everywhere (CARE) had purchased and distributed 815 cases of condensed sweetened milk for the Saigon debarkation center and had ordered ten thousand food packages for distribution against STEM remittance. CARE officials also had plans for twenty-five hundred clothing packages for distribution against STEM remittance. The National Catholic Welfare Conference (NCWC) had plans for a milk distribution center at a dozen reception camps. Six of the centers were in operation with 400,000 pounds of dried milk. The NCWC had twelve hundred bales of used clothing and 436 additional pounds of dried milk en route to Indochina and had plans for another 1 million pounds of powered milk and 900,000 pounds of butter oil, vegetable oil, and cheese. The NCWC had thirteen nurses, under the Brothers of St. John of God, assigned to the reception and resettlement camps. The Vietnamese Red Cross had purchased medical supplies and services for the reception centers. Other organizations, such as the Mennonite Central Committee, the Church World Service, the Philippine Jaycees, UNICEF, and the American Women's Association had provided supplies or planned to supplement the relief effort in Indochina.

With the end of Passage to Freedom's first phase, as well as the withdrawal of American, French, and Vietnamese from Hanoi, attempts to relocate and resettle refugees south of the seventeenth parallel had mixed results. Debarkation points had achieved a certain degree of orderliness, though it was apparent that much work needed to be done to maintain livable conditions. Such conditions could be achieved only by the coordinated efforts of all involved. Considering the condition of South Vietnam, a country only a few months old, the conditions were acceptable, but more would be necessary as the flow of refugees continued to find their way to the South.

CHAPTER 8

★★★★★★★★★★★★★★

Hanoi to Haiphong
A Country in Transition

With the evacuation of Hanoi complete on October 10, the first significant phase of the operation was complete. Originally, Admiral Sabin
had requested that all U.S. ships begin their final phase-out after Hanoi
was turned over to the Viet Minh, as it was believed that the majority of
evacuees would have been transferred at that point. With the concurrence of the commander in chief of the Pacific Fleet (CINCPACFLT),
the admiral recommended against a final phase-out date, however, until
mid-November, when a better assessment of transportation needs would
be available. The transition to the next stage in the operation brought
with it new challenges to gathering and settling the refugee population
and countering Viet Minh propaganda. Even with the loss of Hanoi, the
mission remained the same—deliver to the South as many Vietnamese
as wanted to make the journey.

The flow of refugees into the embarkation areas around Haiphong had
been decreasing during the month of October, especially after the Viet
Minh takeover of Hanoi. CTG 90.8 learned on October 16 that there were
four primary reasons why the Vietnamese who had expressed an interest in moving to the South delayed their departure.[1] First, some were
curious to see what would develop in Hanoi after the Viet Minh took
over the city. Some held the belief that if the Viet Minh behaved well,
there would be no reason to journey away from their ancestral lands to an
area of the country foreign to them. Second, others were concerned for

the state of the South Vietnamese government, which seemed to be at a crossroads as political intrigue threatened to disrupt the young republic. Third, of more immediate concern, was the rice harvest, which was to be completed in mid-November. The harvest, a source of livelihood and survival, had been the focal point of much of the Red River Delta community. Associated with the rice harvest were festivals and a general sense of contentment, and it was difficult for many to abandon their harvest when it was so near, especially when it meant a journey with an uncertain end. Finally, many wanted to wait until the Tet holiday to liquidate their business interests.[2] On October 18, CTG 90.8 revealed another factor influencing the reduced refugee flow: 150 refugees arrived at the embarkation area in Haiphong in two sampans and two rafts, guided to the site by an eighty-five-year-old patriarch. During their journey the refugees had dodged Viet Minh patrols intent on denying them access to Haiphong. Viet Minh obstruction was one of the primary reasons why there was a reduction in refugees in the embarkation point.

As a result of the slowdown, Admiral Sabin called for a conference of U.S., French, and Vietnamese officials to determine requirements for American shipping in Indochina in order to recommend the phasing out of U.S. ships. At the October 19 meeting, Admiral Sabin found the French officials cooperative, stressing the need for "unity of purpose and maximum effort."[3] The next day, the French agreed to pay for the pilot and port fees incurred by the United States in Saigon, finally resolving that particular problem between the U.S. Navy and French officials in Vietnam, an issue that had been outstanding since the beginning of the operation. The official word was that the French government wished to waive the fees because of the generous assistance provided by the United States at its own expense. It was also agreed that MSTS vessels in service would begin rotating out of the theater of operations beginning with *General Brewster* and *General Black*, which departed the Indochina theater on November 2 and 3, respectively. The remaining MSTS transport ships were to phase out at Admiral Sabin's discretion.[4] Before its departure on October 29, *General Black* loaded 5,224 Vietnamese, the largest number of evacuees embarked on any one ship during the operation.

The problem of evacuees reaching the embarkation point remained a critical issue. The obstacles placed by the Viet Minh were not the first faced by the Vietnamese who wished to leave North Vietnam. In late September 1954, three separate incidents demonstrated Viet Minh strategy.[5] On September 26, more than two thousand Vietnamese from Hai Hau district in Bui Chu were denied access to the Nam Dinh ferry, effectively ending their attempt to reach Haiphong. The refugees were forced to camp on the opposite side of the river while they waited for the Viet Minh to relent. After a week, they returned to their homes when it became clear the Viet Minh would not leave the ferry. On the same day, approximately three thousand Vietnamese on their way to Hanoi from Phat Diem and Bui Chu were stopped by Viet Minh agents at Phu Ly.[6] The Viet Minh agents organized a mob and, with poles and sugarcane sticks, forced the refugees back to their villages. When the International Control Commission (ICC) finally was able to investigate the incident on November 12, it was not surprising that it found no evidence of Viet Minh violations. Such was the totality of Viet Minh control of the population that the ICC brought back three thousand complaints lodged by the local inhabitants against the French instead of any Viet Minh violations.

On September 29, approximately two to three thousand Vietnamese from Thai Binh province arrived at the Nam Giang ferry only to be denied access by Viet Minh forces. After a week, out of supplies, the group was forced to return to their village. Phu Ly was the scene of another confrontation on October 4 between three thousand Vietnamese and ten thousand Viet Minh and their supporters, which resulted in the death of a pregnant woman and a four-year-old child.[7] On October 6, three to four hundred Vietnamese from Son Tay met a Viet Minh force that took their baggage and forced them to return to their village. Three thousand Vietnamese arrived at the Ninh Giang ferry only to discover that the Viet Minh would not let them cross. After waiting for fifteen days while the Viet Minh keep the ferry operating but denied them access, they were forced to return to their village. This type of obstruction continued throughout the three-hundred-day period and provided additional incentive for many to leave North Vietnam behind.

There were many reasons for delays in Haiphong, some caused by poor organization, less-than-cooperative French and Vietnamese officials, the weather, and reluctance on the part of the Vietnamese refugees. One reason that came to the surface in October was the question of currency. Many refugees fleeing North Vietnam had been in occupied areas and carried only Viet Minh piasters, and others who had to travel to Haiphong were required to purchase Viet Minh piasters in order to make their way across Viet Minh territory. As a result, many carried a currency that would have no value once they were transported to the South. The idea of losing what little money they had was too much for many of the refugees, especially for a people who had little in the way of personal possessions. Michael Adler advised STEM and MAAG officials that an attempt to force the refugees to evacuate before their currency was converted was politically inadvisable and would jeopardize future evacuation plans. He reported that estimates suggested that the Vietnamese refugees had 1.25 million Viet Minh piasters.[8] It was not likely that the South Vietnamese government had the financial resources or ability to organize a currency exchange in Haiphong, and Adler recommended that an official exchange in Saigon take care of the problem. On October 27, Adler reported that Haiphong officials were collecting Viet Minh piasters from refugees and giving them receipts for reimbursement in Vietnam piasters when they arrived in Saigon. Many refugees refused to leave the North, however, until they received assurances of the exchange. The United States agreed to help organize the Saigon exchange, which satisfied many of the refugees and allowed the evacuation to proceed.[9]

Viet Minh hindrance to the free movement of those wishing to leave the North did not stop the determined few whose need to leave outweighed the threats of the Viet Minh. On October 23, a French landing ship retrieved Vietnamese from beaches near Van Ly, approximately fifty miles south of Haiphong. Although this area was in Viet Minh territory, the French picked up the refugees, most of whom originated from Bui Chi. The Vietnamese had wanted to leave Bui Chi but had been stopped. When they were allowed to proceed, the Viet Minh required them, most of them Catholic, to pay a transit fee of 15,000 Viet Minh piasters (equivalent to approximately 500 RVN piasters) for their passage in sampans and rafts. The majority of the refugees did not have that amount of money, and some who did were not allowed passage to Haiphong because of their position within the Vietnamese community. The French landing ship transferred the Vietnamese to another French ship off the coast of Van Ly. Admiral Sabin, in response to the number of refugees seeking passage via this new route, offered to station a transport ship three miles off the coast to relieve the French ship. The T-AP had a greater passenger capacity than the French transport. The Vietnamese continued to arrive on the beaches the next day as a French LST, an LSM, and the French ship *Pimodon* transferred them to the T-AP for their passage to freedom. Other French ships, including *Bois Belleau, Captricieuse* (F-745), *Giraud* (F-755), *Glaive* (P-632), *Cassequet* (P-633), *Vulcai* (A-656), LSSLS *Pertiuisame*, LSSLS *Hallebare*, and LCM 9052, participated in the rescue operations.

On October 27, the French LST arrived in Haiphong with a load of eighteen hundred Vietnamese from Van Ly, all of them rescued from sampans and bamboo rafts. The refugees reported that many in the group had been detained and beaten by the Viet Minh before their escape. Two of these refugees who were wounded by the Viet Minh as they escaped by raft from Bui Chu were treated by Lieutenant (junior grade) Thomas A. Dooley, M.D., and Vietnamese Roman Catholic priest Father Khue at the Haiphong hospital. A Viet Minh patrol found the two Vietnamese trying to reach Haiphong. After the patrol failed to convince the couple to return to their village, they closed in on the pair and wounded the man in the head and his wife in the arm. Dooley and Khue took pictures of the wounds, and the couple gave evidence of their mistreatment to present to the ICC as examples of Viet Minh violations of the Geneva Agreements. For Dooley, this experience, repeated so many times through his tenure in Vietnam, altered his future. He committed himself to the welfare of the people of Southeast Asia until his death in 1961.[10]

The ICC released its results on November 3, though the findings were not made available to the U.S. officials in Haiphong until November 8. As in many of the dealings with the ICC during the three hundred days, American requests for action were met with limited response or frustrating regulations that punished the evacuees and pardoned the Viet Minh. On October 30, on its return trip to the North, *General Brewster* picked up 1,209 Vietnamese from French vessels at Van Ly before returning to Haiphong. From October 16 to November 6, between 16,000 and 19,500 refugees arrived in Haiphong aboard French ships that had picked them up along the coast. One thousand of them had spotted French ships a few miles off the coast and had decided to swim for an island from which the French could pick them up rather than face the Viet Minh patrols that had increased as a result of the new evacuation routes. Even though the

Viet Minh chased the fleeing Vietnamese, all but three children who had drowned made it to the island and passage to Haiphong.

It was frustrating for MAAG and navy officials to know that all the refugees who wanted to leave North Vietnam were not given the opportunity and that U.S. Navy ships were not being used to their fullest as a result. The Americans and South Vietnamese gathered as much data as possible on Viet Minh violations of article 15 of the Geneva Agreements to present to the ICC. U.S. officials turned over their data to the South Vietnamese government so it could report the violations to the ICC, which it did in a report made public by the Vietnamese embassy in Washington, D.C.[11] The stories of the Vietnamese provide insight into not only the obstacles they had to face from the Viet Minh but also the strength of conviction that helped them go on this passage to freedom. Mr. Tran Van Tru, a fifty-six-year-old Catholic farmer from Hai Hau district, Bui Chu province, told what the eight people in his family went through to arrive in Haiphong:

> We abandoned our house, our garden, our rice field to flee South. We arrived November 2, 1954, without having been able to bring anything with us. We had intended to leave for a long time, but our eldest son, employed aboard a transport at Nan Dinh, was arrested by the Viet Minh and we were obliged to wait for his liberation. He was liberated October 1, 1954, and we immediately constructed bamboo rafts and left the region at the same time as 500 others with their children. We went through the hamlet of Linh Co to get to the village of Co Le, but there we were detained by Viet Minh agents. Our son, Tran Van Xuyen, was again imprisoned on the charge of having organized the evacuation. Our convoy dispersed. So our first try at evacuation failed.[12]

The family made a second attempt two days later when the son was released by the Viet Minh and made it to Haiphong after paying for boat transportation at 10,000 Viet Minh piasters per person. Everyone from Tran Van Tru's village of two hundred made it to Haiphong and rode on U.S. Navy ships to South Vietnam.

Mr. Vu Viet Ty, a sixty-two-year-old salt maker from Ha Trai in Hai Hau district, Bui Chu province, recalled how his family of nineteen abandoned all that they had to flee the Viet Minh: "If in spite of my great age I decided to leave the village where I was born, it is because the Viet Minh regime is too severe and their taxes excessive; our hard labor yields us annually 600 baskets of salt, of which we must pay 250 for the production tax. The Viet Minh forbids me to sell the other 350 baskets. If they should authorize the sale, I would have other taxes to pay on the transaction, so that in the end nothing would be left to support my family."[13] Vu Viet Ty's situation was not unique, as many who left North Vietnam did so because they, too, believed that they would not be able to continue their livelihood.

Others left because they feared the Viet Minh regime. Mr. Pham Van Khue was only eighteen years old when he fled North Vietnam, though the decision had been made for him in 1952: "My father was assassinated by the Viet Minh toward the end of 1952 for having organized an anti–Viet Minh Catholic youth group. After his death, I had to escape to a relative's house in the village of Con Tron and for five days I had to hide in a hole in the ground. The Viet Minh arrested my mother, mistreated her, and attempted to force her to summon me back."[14] Pham Van Khue was arrested by the Viet Minh in 1952 and spent two years in a prison camp. After the signing of the Geneva Agreements, the Viet Minh released him, and he made it back to his village to find that all of his possessions had been confiscated by the Viet Minh. On August 8, Khue helped to organize the village to go to the embarkation area, but the refugees were forced back by the Viet Minh. It was not until October 10 that he and the three remaining members of his family were able to escape for the price of 20,000 Viet Minh piasters per person, leaving for South Vietnam on October 16. The United States recognized the propaganda value of the Vietnamese stories for the American public. The objective became one of exposing the Viet Minh in a negative way and increasing international pressure on the Viet Minh to stop the truce violations.

In response to the French effort to evacuate the refugees from coastal waters, the Viet Minh accused them of entering North Vietnamese territorial waters and violating the Geneva Agreements.[15] The French countered that they were in international waters and were in the area only to help the Vietnamese refugees who were fleeing the Viet Minh in small boats. The French based their action upon international law that governed sea rescue in case of distress. Although the ICC promised to investigate the Viet Minh obstructions as well as the claim that the French had violated international waters, the U.S. State Department did not believe any positive results would materialize. The Indian delegate demanded unanimity in ICC decisions, and the Polish delegate had previously been obstinate on decisions against the Viet Minh.

Viet Minh obstruction of the refugee movement to the South was not the only complaint lodged by the United States, the Republic of Vietnam, and France. U.S. officials believed the Viet Minh put on the appearance of adhering to the Geneva Agreements while employing delaying tactics, subterfuge, and outright contempt in their violations of the agreements.[16] The United States cited several major violations, including the process of leaving Viet Minh cadre in South Vietnam instead of regrouping them in the North. The cease-fire agreement called for the disarmament of the Viet Minh in Cambodia, Laos, and South Vietnam, but the French had evidence that the Khmer–Viet Minh forces in Cambodia had not been disarmed, and the United States had reports that the Viet Minh had moved heavy artillery and Soviet-made rocket launchers into Laos. American officials suspected that the Viet Minh regular forces in South Vietnam kept enough weapons to equip one artillery division and four infantry divisions. Those Viet Minh who had reported to the gathering points in South Vietnam carried few weapons—most of which were obsolete. The United States also had documentation to suspect that the Viet Minh were forcibly recruiting Lao youth into the Pathet Lao forces but failed to convince the ICC. The United States also worried about the two northern provinces in Laos that were not turned over to the Laotian government as prescribed in the Geneva Agreements and was concerned about the Polish members of the ICC, who appeared to be obstructing investigation into Viet Minh violations.

In Cambodia the first group of Viet Minh boarded French navy landing craft at the Neakluong ferry point on the Mekong River on October 12. The group of 525 Viet Minh came from the Battambang and Kampong provinces. Four additional lifts occurred on October 18, when another 900 Viet Minh, including 10 women, were removed. The final lift transported the remaining Viet Minh. It was estimated that between 2,500 and 2,800 of the 4,050 Viet Minh identified in Cambodia had traveled north of the seventeenth parallel. The ICC expressed satisfaction with the Viet Minh evacuation of Cambodia despite the fact that the total number of evacuees was between 1,200 and 1,500 less than the figure announced earlier by the Viet Minh—only half of the French estimate and only one-fourth of the unofficial Indian estimate.[17]

There was a general anxiety within U.S. circles that the ICC did not recognize the serious threat the unfulfilled evacuation would cause to the balance of power in Cambodia. Although U.S. officials were not satisfied with the situation in Cambodia, they were even less sanguine about the Viet Minh evacuation of Vietnam. The Viet Minh had announced that twenty thousand personnel would assemble in the Plaine des Joncs provisional assembly area by the October 10 deadline established during the agreements at the Geneva Conference. But the French had estimated that only fourteen thousand Viet Minh had entered the area for transportation to the North. The remaining cadres were thought to have either deserted the Viet Minh or stayed in South Vietnam to continue the insurgency if necessary. While the Viet Minh organized their withdrawal from the South, the French evacuation of the Red River Delta proceeded as planned. By October 14, thirty-two thousand French Union soldiers and forty-two thousand Vietnamese army troops and militia had withdrawn from the North with an estimated sixty-five thousand tons of equipment and materiel and seven thousand military vehicles. In the southernmost part of the Mekong Delta at Ca Mau, the French had estimated thirty thousand Viet Minh would regroup for transit north.[18] The French agreed to move the Viet Minh to a deepwater port to the north to board the one Polish and two Russian ships assigned to move the Viet Minh forces to North Vietnam.

The ICC was incapable of dealing with violations of the Geneva Agreements and the inconsistency of Viet Minh relocation. The Polish delegation never failed to block American and South Vietnamese concerns about the Viet Minh, while the North Vietnamese perceived the Canadian representative to be nothing more than a puppet of the United States. The Canadian members of the ICC were not reluctant to mention the difficulties in working with the Polish representatives of the ICC. In a conversation with Ainalie Kerr, Ottawa correspondent for the Catholic weekly *Ensign*, several Canadian delegates confided in the reporter that they were faced with insurmountable obstacles with the ICC.[19] The Canadians knew the Viet Minh were sending weapons and personnel to their once-held territory for those who did not travel north and understood that the Viet Minh persecuted Vietnamese refugees who wished to leave North Vietnam. In addition to the problem of the Polish representatives' blocking unanimous decisions was the inadequate way the French and

Vietnamese reported Viet Minh violations. This continually frustrated the American officials in Vietnam as they worked to expose the Viet Minh. The South Vietnamese government representative in North Vietnam demanded that the ICC investigate Viet Minh violations in Nam Diem even though the French had received intelligence from the Catholic clergy stationed in that area that there were no violations—especially when compared to those in Phat Diem and Bui Chu. French officials informed MAAG representatives that the request was either one of stupidity or of a sinister nature to distract the ICC. Officials with the U.S. Department of State had an additional perspective on the poor handling of the Viet Minh violations—the belief that the French were reluctant to expose the Viet Minh because they feared their own violations would also be exposed and publicized by the Viet Minh.

Although the failure of the ICC caused many problems for the United States, that was not the only concern. Operation Passage to Freedom presented itself as a unique opportunity to export American ideals and resources through the day-to-day actions of American personnel involved in the operation; reporting those successes was much more difficult. In a letter to Vice Admiral T. G. W. Settle, commander of the Amphibious Force, Pacific Fleet, Admiral Sabin lamented over the poor coverage the evacuation had received from the navy's Public Information Office (PIO) and the civilian press in the United States.[20]

Admiral Sabin found himself in a quandary. He recognized that the press coverage for the operation was insufficient, but he risked the charge that he was furthering his own career ambitions if he protested the lack of coverage. While adhering to command orders to let the PIO orchestrate the publicity for the operation, Admiral Sabin was constantly reminded of the public relations failure. At the American consulate in Hanoi, Admiral Sabin was told over the telephone by a correspondent that his operation was "an historical event—a story which has all sorts of possibilities in human interest." The admiral replied that he would provide information as it became available. When he requested guidance on how to handle questions from correspondents, the official word returned to him was that his remarks should be confined to a general statement that the United States was involved in the operation at the request of the French and Vietnamese governments. Ambassador Heath, after learning of Admiral Sabin's instructions, informed him that that was not enough and arranged for a press conference, arguing that the navy "would be short-sighted indeed if it didn't capitalize on this."

After the press conference, interest in the operation increased, though not as much as expected. Don Huth, chief of the Manila bureau of the Associated Press (AP), traveled on *Estes* with Admiral Sabin to Haiphong, filing daily dispatches and covering an early embarkation of refugees. The New York office of the AP informed Huth that the story was not generating interest in the United States and ordered him back to covering the SEATO conference. A Time-Life correspondent expressed similar interest and filed a story without success.

Admiral Sabin believed that the navy had failed a tremendous opportunity to reap the benefits of the humanitarian effort. When Sabin's flagship brought the hundred thousandth refugee to Saigon to present to President Diem, Ambassador Heath, the accredited diplomatic corps of those nations involved in Vietnam, and several high-ranking officers, the navy's public information officer filed a story but never followed through to ensure its publication. Sabin's feelings mirrored those of many who were involved in the operation: "I feel that somewhere along the line the navy has muffed an opportunity of a lifetime." When compared to the United Kingdom's coverage of the carrier *Warrior*'s participation in the evacuation, the lack of coverage in the United States became even more appalling, as the British involvement made every paper in the United Kingdom and many other media outlets in Southeast Asia.[21]

Just as the plight of the refugees and the war of words and actions consumed the naval personnel involved in the operation, so did the constant challenges of resettling tens of thousands of new arrivals in the South occupy the time of the USOM, which worked with the young Saigon government to enable the transition of its newest citizens. On a field trip to Bien Hoa on October 18, Walter Ross, community development division officer with STEM, reported on the condition of the housing in the area.[22] Ross found that, despite ample time for preparation, Vietnamese officials in Bien Hoa had failed to realize the complexity involved in planning the resettlement of thirty to forty thousand refugees into a small city. He was not able to determine, from the information provided by the Vietnamese, what areas had been set aside for resettlement and the basic characteristics of the area identified. No records of landownership were available to review. Without this basic information, he concluded that it was impossible to provide adequate technical advice and assistance in the planning and creation of housing in the resettlement area. He recommended that STEM suspend aid until basic conditions were met. The Vietnamese had to provide planning and design counterparts for the city and assemble basic information about the proposed sites. They also had to clarify the terms of landownership and who would provide future administrative support for the city. Finally, Ross recommended a plan to use Aided Self Help Housing rather than contract construction to further enable the refugees and provide a sense of ownership of the land.[23]

Herman Holiday, who also traveled to Bien Hoa, shared Ross' views. Holiday argued that the Vietnamese authorities responsible for refugee resettlement needed to understand the importance of quick and effective planning, taking into account security, environmental concerns, and possibilities for employment and rehabilitation. Holiday, who had been involved in resettlement issues for four years, strongly urged USOM to insist that Vietnamese officials use all of their existing technical experts to solve the problem of resettlement. Without complete and total mobilization, the Vietnamese government was destined to fail.

A trip by STEM and civilian aid workers to central North Vietnam revealed similar problems with the resettlement camps in that region.[24] F. C. Bruhns, refugee adviser to STEM, reported on the group's four-day trip with a summary of basic needs for the camps. Foremost, he stated that the Vietnamese needed funds and advice for community development. Sanitation, clean water wells, dispensaries, schools, churches, communal houses, and roads were all necessary in order to make the camps function, and the Vietnamese in charge needed American advice on how to develop the infrastructure. Once a plan was created, the United States would need to provide equipment and technical training and maintenance to ensure the growth and expansion of the resettlement areas.

There were some exceptions to the rule. At Luong Dien, approximately thirty kilometers south of Hue, the group found a well-developed camp under the management of a Vietnamese priest. All that was required was basic farming equipment and material to ensure adequate crop development. The settlement at Tourane, which held 133 families, did not fare was well, however. The land surrounding the camp was not suitable for farming, and the group found very poor sanitary conditions. In addition, the village was prone to flooding during heavy rains. The village needed

at least three new wells, an infirmary, a school, and a church. The Vietnamese leadership complained that they had requested funding for these
projects but had not received positive results. Despite repeated American
insistence, the Vietnamese were often slow or obstinate about effecting
change in the refugee camps. Something as simple as the purchase of an-
tiseptic products for the refugee camps, requested early in October, had
received no attention from Vietnamese officials despite their knowledge
that the product would help improve sanitary conditions and reduce disease in the crowded areas.[25]

An October 27 census of the refugee situation found that more than
one hundred thirty-five thousand refugees had left the reception centers
in Saigon and Cap St. Jacques for the thirty-seven resettlement centers
and eleven provinces throughout South Vietnam, while an additional sev-
enty-one thousand refugees had been resettled in central Vietnam. Of
those refugees, approximately 30 percent required some kind of medical attention. As a member of the Health and Sanitation Division within
STEM, Hildrus Poindexter headed the team in charge of refugees at Cap
St. Jacques. He conducted a survey of refugee reception camps in the
area on November 2 and 3 with a less than satisfactory opinion of the
existing conditions.[26] While the camps had better overall administration
and were not as crowded as they had been the previous month, no camps
had adequate sanitary facilities, and in only one camp, Long Tan, was a
good environmental sanitation facility being planned and constructed.
The camps had the necessary medical personnel to handle the situation
but had been short of medicine since the beginning of the operation. He
also learned that some of the medical personnel had not been paid in
two months. Poindexter recommended that first aid kits and a moderate
supply of antibiotics be sent to the chief of medicine in Baria and that
STEM establish a health unit at Long Tan and provide additional health
education in the region.

The work toward the health and welfare of the Vietnamese refugees
was not a burden shared only by the Americans, French, and Vietnamese. Under Operation Brotherhood, Jaycees from the Philippines worked
to relieve the suffering of the Vietnamese people by providing medical
assistance and supplies in the refugee areas.[27] The Jaycees set up two
medical centers in South Vietnam to relieve the medical suffering of the
Vietnamese. The Saigon unit worked out of the dispensary at Phu Tho

Table 8.1. Central Vietnam Refugee Census

Bien Hoa		Thu Dau Mot	
Ho Nai	26,912	Bec Suc	2,140
Lac An	9,252	Rach Kien	3,914
Gia Kiem	10,107	Rach Bat	7,903
Phuoc Ly	9,237	Ben Cat	538
Phuoc Khanh	1,332		
Trung Tam Cu Tru	252	**Vinh Long**	
Ben Co	238	Tinh Ly	413
Cay Co	32	Tam Binh	1,190
Tan Mai	4,691	Vung Liem	900
My Tho		**Cholon**	
Long Dinh	2,478	Hoa Khanh	7,305
Thanh Phu	417	Luong Hoa	925
An Duc	1,021	Duc Hoa	90
An Hoa	446		
		Gia Dinh	
Tay Ninh		Tan Phu Throng	2,706
Chef Lieu	8,565	Tan An Hoi	301
Cam Giang	6,732	Xuan Truong	2,194
Rach Re	226	Go Cong	2,369
		Cho Go	50
Ben Tre		Xom Moi	8,606
Than Thuy	1,280	Go Vap	288
Ba Tri	1,000	Ba Vhieu	361
		Thi Nghe	119
P.M.S.		Tan Binh	1,689
Blao	1,420	Cu Chi	4,196
		Ba Gia	1,650
Ba Ria			
Phuoc Le	460	**Sa Dec**	250
Long Tan	940		

with two doctors and one nurse, seeing an average of 150 patients a day. This medical team visited the four major reception centers daily to dispense medical treatment. The second unit traveled from Saigon to Bien Hoa, approximately twenty miles from Saigon, daily and examined from 350 to 450 patients each day. The Jaycees experienced three major problems: they were not staffed to meet the medical needs of the Vietnamese, they did not have enough time to care for the refugees because of long days of traveling, and they lacked enough medical drugs and supplies. The last problem was further aggravated by the rigid customs regulations of South Vietnam. Only the Red Cross and CARE were allowed to import medical supplies without duty. As a result, all of the supplies sent by the Jaycees had not reached the doctors because of customs. When the Jaycees tried to use the Red Cross to import their drugs and other

supplies, the Red Cross agreed to help but only if a portion of those supplies remained with the Red Cross. The Jaycees then successfully turned
to CARE for assistance, though the importation of medical supplies remained an issue. Despite the problems the work of the Jaycees in Operation Brotherhood achieved a certain amount of success. By November
4, the Jaycees' personnel had seen and treated more than thirty-five hundred patients and had received good coverage with the press. The Philippine representatives of Operation Brotherhood provided much needed
relief and demonstrated to the South Vietnamese and their northern
refugees that they were not alone.

During November the personnel involved in Operation Passage to
Freedom again experienced a series of events that would test their resolve, as epidemics and a typhoon once again visited the U.S. Navy in
Indochina. On November 4, the entire crew of USNS *Hennepin* (T-AK-
187) reported being infected with scabies. The crew received treatment
in Hai Long Bay, and the disease did not stop *Hennepin* from loading 100
tons of fibro-cement, 109 tons of fertilizer, 10 tons of vocational school
equipment, 15 tons of typographical equipment, two jeeps, and one station wagon, all of which was delivered to Saigon on November 9. As Hennepin loaded, Typhoon Pamela caused all of the Task Force 90 ships in
the Haiphong area to sortie out to sea for evasive maneuvers. Almost all
of the loading in Haiphong was suspended the next day and resumed on
November 7, when Task Force 90 ships were allowed to return to the embarkation area. Despite such challenges, the rewards were always worth
the effort. Although not every Task Force 90 ship had direct contact with
the Vietnamese refugees during the evacuation, all were directly connected with the plight of these people and contributed to the best of their
abilities. The crew of USS *Askari* (ARL-30), a repair support ship, donated
clothing for distribution to the Vietnamese refugees in Haiphong. The
crew received thank-you notes for their generous gift. The notes were
gratifying, but the work of rescuing those in need served as even more
incentive to continue.

Starting on November 6 and in an operation lasting forty-eight hours,
the French rescued nearly forty-two hundred refugees who had attempted to escape to a sand island at the mouth of the Tra Ly River near Phat
Diem.[28] The French planned to send ships and planes to provide relief
for the Vietnamese and assist in their evacuation even though the Viet

Fig. 8.1. Fireman, Engineman Striker James I. Hart was declared the winner of the beard contest conducted among the sailors in the operation, August 1954. Photograph courtesy of the Douglas Pike Photograph Collection, Vietnam Archive (VA000842).

Minh had increased its troop strength in the area to discourage this escape route. As a result of this increased influx, the ICC decided to send a "Committee on Freedom" to the area to help those refugees who wished to leave. Representatives of the DRV insisted that each Vietnamese wishing to leave provide a set of motives for his or her decision, but the ICC replied that a Vietnamese citizen had only to express a desire to leave to receive assistance. The ICC requested a DRV team to accompany the committee in order to facilitate and approve the necessary paperwork for departure. Although the DRV was forced to comply, it did refuse a French offer of assistance and transportation facilities to ease the burden. When the ICC was finally able to get its committee to Phat Diem and the sand islands, there was no evidence of inhabitants on the south side of the island, while soldiers, apparently Viet Minh, guarded the population on the northern side and refused any contact with the ICC. When

Fig. 8.2. A small boy lends a helping hand to an experienced sailor on board
USS *Bayfield* (APA-33), September 7, 1954. Photograph courtesy of the
Douglas Pike Photograph Collection, Vietnam Archive (VA000891).

the committee returned to Phat Diem on November 13, the situation was critical. The DRV reluctantly agreed to set up a permit office to process applications to leave North Vietnam, but the Polish delegate argued that the people who had assembled at Phat Diem were under the influence of French propaganda and had not applied for permission from local authorities to go to the South. For many refugees in Phat Diem, the presence of the ICC helped, but others were scared of the Viet Minh and unsure of what would happen once the ICC left the area.

While conditions in the north continued to be perilous for those who wanted to leave, STEM officials had their share of problems with the refugee community. On October 19, a Vietnamese nationalist attempted to board USNS *Marine Lynx* while it was moored at Saigon. South Vietnamese soldiers caught the individual stealing and beat him before turning him over to the French. The man later died of internal injuries. The U.S. government did not become involved in the incident after the French investigated it. The incident was unfortunate, but it did not lessen a few of the notable achievements that occurred about the same time. On October 21, the MSTS time-chartered ship SS *Culucundis* completed a test loading in less than twenty-two hours. A combination of U.S. sailors, merchant seamen, and French Foreign Legion stevedores loaded 359 vehicles, the equivalent of six LST loads. French officials in Haiphong informed Admiral Sabin that they would release an additional battalion of Legionnaires for stevedoring. By that time the Americans had completed a survey of equipment that remained in Haiphong.[29]

Almost all of the American Economic Aid (AEA) equipment and supplies had been transferred to the South except a small quantity of super-phosphate fertilizer, fiber asbestos cement reefing, and a few vehicles used for operations. Also, approximately three thousand tons of AEA asphalt and twenty-five thousand tons of asphalt owned by the French military were left in Haiphong. According to the Geneva Agreements, a minimum amount of operating utilities was to be left in Haiphong. This did not cover the equipment of privately owned corporations, and Michael Adler, USOM representative for Haiphong, was careful to ensure that all of that type of equipment received clearance to move to the South. Adler had a difficult task because Vietnamese bureaucrats at all levels wanted to handle the equipment and materials belonging to their own interests rather than allowing the United States to oversee the transfer. This resulted in poor handling of the materials, security breaches, and Viet Minh accusations that the United States and France were aiding in the removal of equipment promised them by the Geneva Agreements. The situation became even more delicate for Adler because the list of privately held equipment was still extensive and included the Haiphong cement plant, the Carbondage du Tonkin, and the equipment of several smaller secondary industries.

On October 28, a MAAG representative traveled to the Haiduong sector between Hanoi and Haiphong in preparation for the final abandonment of the camp there. The French had a few pieces of equipment left for evacuation after they had cleared the abandoned forts, emptied the barracks, and burned or destroyed anything that the Viet Minh might find useful. On October 31, the French turned over the city to the Viet Minh without incident. The official areas available for embarkation had now shrunk to an area around Haiphong with its border twenty-four kilometers to the west. With the circle closing around Haiphong, the MSTS cargo ships began moving nonmilitary equipment in order to keep it out of the hands of the Viet Minh. SS *José Martí* had loaded a number of pieces of public works equipment on October 25, including sweepers, bulldozers, graders, cement mixers, generators, spare parts, and other materials that were too valuable to be destroyed or left for the Viet Minh.[30]

On October 31, French General Ely responded to an October 8 MAAG request for information concerning the requirements of U.S. shipping through January 1955.[31] Ely argued that the American troop ships were no longer required, as the number of refugees had been considerably reduced and the transport of Vietnamese Popular Army units suppressed. He argued that this would remain true as long as the number of Vietnamese refugees requesting transportation remained low, because French shipping was sufficient to provide transport to the French Expeditionary Corps as well as several thousand Vietnamese refugees per month. The French plan also called for the removal of one hundred fifty thousand tons of equipment (plus another fifteen thousand tons of organic cargo) and thirteen hundred vehicles by the end of January 1955 and requested the retention of the four U.S. cargo ships in Indochina. Ely also called for the retention of ten LSTs in order to evacuate all the MDAP equipment still in the North. He informed MAAG officials that his staff was studying the procedures by which the remaining three thousand vehicles in North Vietnam would be removed between February and May 1955 as French Expeditionary Corps units left the area. The suggestion in the report was that the United States would play some role in the removal of the vehicles. Finally, Ely recommended that one American LSD remain at Haiphong to assist in the transportation of lighterage facilities and floating equipment from February through May 1955. General O'Daniel concurred with Ely's request even though he had previously approved of Admiral Sabin's phase-out plan that called for the removal of the LSTs because the French had sufficient cargo capacity. Admirals Carney and Stump agreed with Admiral Sabin and overrode General O'Daniel, allowing the phase-out to proceed as planned.[32]

In early November 1954, a typhoid epidemic broke out in Phan Ri. Hildrus Poindexter investigated the incident on November 5 and 6 and found thirty-five cases, with five persons already dead. The French military had been furnishing medical care to the refugees at the time. Poindexter made arrangements to immunize the population—something that should already have been done—and provided one thousand capsules of typhoid vaccine. In the northern Pays Montagnard du Sud (Montagnard Country of the South; PMS) it was estimated that 30 percent of the population had been sick with malaria. Although that was down from 60 percent of the population in 1949–1950, it still represented a significant portion of the population. One of the reasons for the high number was the inability of the French and American doctors to convince the Montagnards that antimalaria drugs would virtually eliminate the negative effects of the disease. The villages within the PMS were remote, with difficult access points, and it was almost impossible to provide routine checks for education, vaccination, or follow-through on medicine dispensed. Harry Stage, a vector control specialist with STEM, reported two DDT spray teams active in the area for mosquito eradication, but insurmountable obstacles prevented access to the villages.[33] The DDT teams had adequate supplies but lacked proper training. Stage reported that one team was observed mixing the DDT with their bare hands. Despite these medical situations, STEM members had made remarkable progress in the improvement of conditions for the refugee population. They were also rewarded on November 6 when STEM learned that the budget for the refugee project would continue into fiscal year 1955 with $25 million for the resettlement effort and $5 million for the sealift.[34] FOA director Harold Stassen indicated that another $5 million could be allocated to the sealift when needed. At the request of STEM Saigon, Stassen placed an additional five million piasters in reserve for unforeseen requirements in the refugee project.

Mid-November saw a major transition in Indochina with the departure of Ambassador Donald R. Heath and the turnover of command by Admiral Sabin. On November 10, Admiral Sabin and the commander of Task Group 90.8, Commander J. H. Davis, held a briefing for Ambassador Heath and the newly arrived Ambassador J. Lawton Collins. Both Sabin and Heath had been involved in the American side of the evacuation from its inception. Now both would depart at the same time, having overseen a remarkable humanitarian achievement. Admiral Sabin transferred command of the embarkation unit in Haiphong to Commander Davis on November 14 and released the logistical support group at Tourane Bay from the Indochina operation before departing for Hong Kong on USS *Estes* the next day. Captain Frank, who had broken his pennant in USS

Balduck (APD-132) on November 5, assumed local command of the sea phase of the operation, while Admiral Sabin retained overall command. Admiral Stump offered the following to Admiral Sabin: "On the occasion of your departure from the Indo China area I want to extend to you my congratulations for the magnificent job that you and your command, including both fleet and MSTS ships, have done and continue to do in carrying out the Indo China refugee evacuation and the relocation of MDAP equipment from the Tonkin Delta. Well Done."[35]

There is no question that the operation had a profound effect on Admiral Sabin as well as the many men and women who served in one capacity or another in Task Force 90 during Operation Passage to Freedom. "When we encounter people to whom those cherished principles have been denied and see their determination not to submit to such denial," he wrote to Francis Cardinal Spellman, archbishop of New York, "it brings home to us with forcible eloquence the realization that we Americans are enjoying those precious benefits because our forefathers were imbued with the same spirit and determination we witnessed in those refugees."[36] Despite the change in leadership at the top, the work continued with diligence and awareness that the success or failure of such an operation would have a lasting and significant impact on the future of Indochina.

CHAPTER 9

★ ★ ★ ★ ★ ★ ★ ★ ★ ★ ★ ★ ★ ★ ★

Transitions and Change

The departure of Admiral Sabin from the Indochina area did not signal an end to the operation, nor did it lessen the importance for the United States of moving the evacuees. For the remainder of the year, there was a constant flow of Vietnamese—approximately three hundred per day—to the embarkation area around Haiphong, and the first weeks of 1955 saw that number increase to about five hundred a day. Many of the refugees who arrived in Haiphong had difficulty reaching their objective, although reports indicated that the refugees were becoming savvier in dealing with the Viet Minh. Although Hanoi and Haiduong were no longer under French control, the refugees used those cities to their advantage by legitimately traveling to one, taking a train to the outskirts of Haiphong, and then entering the reception centers on foot. Refugees from Phat Diem, an area under Viet Minh control but also with a heavy concentration of Catholics, continued to arrive through a more difficult route by sea. During this period there also emerged a new motivation, as the French announced that after February 1, 1955, they would not guarantee security in Haiphong or orderly transport to the South. This caused an upswing in refugees wanting to evacuate the region in advance of the new deadline as well as additional American support to meet the challenge. At that time the U.S. Navy transported 38,861 civilians and 822 military personnel as well as 31,054 short tons of equipment and 952 vehicles from North Vietnam. While the sealift progressed, American personnel in Saigon changed their focus from dealing with the evacuation from the North to resettlement of those refugees who had already arrived in the South. The influx of so many refugees taxed the Saigon government and challenged the United States in its effort to generate goodwill among the Vietnamese. Moving the evacuee population was a tremendous under-taking, but settling them proved even more difficult and more politically significant for long-term U.S.–Vietnamese relations.

The resettlement of the Vietnamese refugees was based upon several considerations, the first of which was economics. A good plan needed to divide the refugees among the rice fields and forests for maximum cultivation and exploitation of those resources. The refugees had certain expertise in all fields, and matching them accordingly would increase integration of the new population into the existing society. The military view argued that the refugees should be relocated in places that the Viet Minh had evacuated in order to maintain security and stability for the government. The people leaving North Vietnam would be less likely to support the Viet Minh and more willing to defend themselves against any encroachment. Resettlement of the refugees also had a political com-ponent. It was important to disperse the refugees among the southern Vietnamese to ensure absorption into that population. The worry was that large concentrations of refugees would create new political groups that would resemble feudal societies. Finally, there was a religious com-ponent to the resettlement issue; priests who had brought their villages or districts to the South would require maintenance of their groups in the South for religious coherence. These were just some of the problems facing resettlement as the evacuation reached its halfway point.

The departure of Admiral Sabin also signaled a greater shift from navy to MSTS ships involved in the operation. Task Force 90.8, the embar-kation force in Haiphong, consisted of USS *Balduck* and four LSTs as well as three MSTS T-APs and three MSTS T-AKs. LST-855 embarked the remaining beachmaster and boat unit personnel in Haiphong as it was released from service, leaving only three LSTs available, while *Ma-rine Adder*'s release dropped the number of T-APs to only two. USNS *Herkimer* (T-AK-188) arrived the next day and reported to Task Force 90.8. As *Herkimer* arrived, LST-772 was release from the operation and departed the Indochina area. At this point in the operation, the U.S. Navy had transported 153,807 civilians and 13,657 military personnel, with an additional count of ninety-two births aboard U.S. ships to offset the forty-eight deaths. The navy had also transported 27,977 short tons of equipment and 5,791 vehicles. Despite these accomplishments, the total number of refugees in Haiphong camps stood at 11,127 on November 15, with more arriving daily. There was still work to be done.

The number of refugees in the Haiphong camps would increase on November 16, 1954, with the first arrivals from Phat Diem, all of whom were brought by boat and truck. Although the first group of sixty-one individuals was small, an additional ten to twelve thousand from the Phat Diem region would make their way into Haiphong over the next ten days. The United States did not realize the Phat Diem contingent would be as prolonged or extensive, but that did not deter the continued release of U.S. ships from the operation. After discussions with the French and MAAG in Haiphong, the commander of TF 90.8, Captain Frank, released USNS *Marine Lynx* and USNS *Fentress*. The French had three landing craft and the United States had one T-AP, but as there was only one loading berth for each of the French landing craft, and the flow of refugees had been minimized as a result of Viet Minh interference, the shipping contingent seemed satisfactory. On November 18, 1954, the day two hundred additional Phat Diem refugees arrived, LST-840 was released and was soon followed by LST-1159.

The populations in the two major camps in Haiphong—Shell and Pagode—numbered 5,000, but only 1,700 of the refugees there were willing to leave Haiphong. Many of those who wanted to remain were waiting to exchange Viet Minh piasters or for family members to arrive in order to depart together. The Phat Diem refugees continued to enter Haiphong, although U.S. and French officials believed that only a token number would reach the embarkation area because of the Viet Minh.[1] A November 16, 1954, communiqué from U.S. Army officials in Haiphong estimated that 20,000 to 30,000 Vietnamese from Phat Diem desired evacuation to the South, although, because of Viet Minh obstacles, only five thousand of them probably would be delivered.[2] On November 20, 1954, 128 refugees arrived from Phat Diem to the embarkation area, 60 by junk through Bui Chu and the remainder on Viet Minh transportation through Hanoi. The ICC investigated the complaints brought by these evacuees and publicized by the South Vietnamese and discovered that the Viet Minh were allowing passage and providing transportation, but through a roundabout route.[3] The Viet Minh charged for the transportation, organized demonstrations, and spread propaganda to influence the refugees to remain in the North. When the final numbers were tallied, approximately 12,000 Vietnamese from Phat Diem escaped.

The French navy had also begun discussions with Vietnamese Catholic leaders to conduct an operation off the coast of Vinh similar to the Bui Chu operation. Catholics around Vinh had been receiving a constant stream of propaganda and intimidation from the Viet Minh on the routes south of the seventeenth parallel. Many had been refused passports to travel in Viet Minh territory or were required to pay up to 7,000 piasters for transportation even though transportation was supposed to be free in accord with the Geneva Agreements. News reached Haiphong that the Viet Minh were issuing passports to only twenty families per day and were continually harassing those who made the trip to Haiphong. When eight hundred additional Phat Diem refugees arrived on November 24, 1954, the United States established a temporary refugee camp at the Kien An church, seven miles southwest of Haiphong. It was at this time that reports of the Viet Minh obstruction reached American officials. The Viet Minh had told the Vietnamese that if they went to Haiphong, the French would forcibly recruit them into the French Foreign Legion and they would be sent to Algeria to fight in that emerging war. Another refugee from Phat Diem, a Catholic priest, relayed to the Americans how he was tortured by Chinese army officers, who had jammed chopsticks into his ears and had beaten him with bamboo poles after he had tried to organize the people of Phat Diem in the evacuation. Other refugees informed MAAG and USOM officials that they wanted to leave North Vietnam for religious reasons. The Catholics from Phat Diem departed because the Viet Minh were forcing them to work without pay or charging high taxes on profits made in commerce. The people of Phat Diem also wanted to leave the region because the Viet Minh were not enforcing the law and were pushing communism.

The United States continued to advance the call for international recognition of the Viet Minh violations to the Geneva Conference. This held a twofold advantage to the American effort in Indochina. It publicized the nature of Viet Minh rule in North Vietnam and further justified the tremendous amount of resources expended in the evacuation effort. On November 15, 1954, the Department of State issued a directive to the embassies and consulates in Hanoi, Saigon, Vientiane, and Phnom Penh. These posts were ordered to continue gathering and reporting Viet Minh violations of the Geneva Conference as well as other actions that might be construed as a breach of international law.[4] The items seen as potential violations were the introduction of foreign weapons and personnel, forced recruitment in Laos, and the failure to disperse military cadre in the South. Concerning the evacuation, embassy and consulate officials were ordered to document restrictions on refugee and ICC movement, religious persecutions, and the continued Viet Minh control of northern Laos. The United States had made a significant push in exploiting these violations in previous months with little success outside traditionally pro-American countries. Even as American personnel documented Viet Minh violations, they also moved to counter South Vietnamese actions that destroyed the goodwill generated by Operation Passage to Freedom.

The resettlement of refugees in the PMS suffered a minor setback in November when RVN soldiers vandalized portions of the camps at Ban Me Thuot. Daniel J. Weiner, chief engineer in the Health and Sanitation Division, conducted an inspection tour in mid-November 1954 of Ban Me Thuot, Dalat, and Djiring.[5] Weiner recommended greater policing of the camps to prevent further destruction. There is no question that American officials were frustrated with South Vietnamese handling of the refugee crisis. It was difficult to prove to the new residents that the Republic of Vietnam offered a better alternative to the North when camps were poorly constructed and maintained, suffered vandalism by the hands of those tasked with protecting them, and gave indications of corruption within the new government. It was not helpful that Viet Minh cadre who remained in the South had penetrated the refugee settlements to help spread discontent in the overcrowded camps. The Catholic organizations were the only counterforce available to thwart the Viet Minh.

The South Vietnamese Army and the Viet Minh were not the only problems in November. STEM program observer Bette Moyle learned that the refugees at Phat Diem camp in the Gia Kiem resettlement area had not received the medicine provided by American Aid.[6] Vietnamese medical officials diverted the supplies from the refugees for political gains or profit. The refugees did not know why they had not received the medicine, only that it had been promised by the United States and had not been delivered. The situation became so critical that the USOM representative offered to "personally deliver the supplies by pony cart and dog team" if the Vietnamese continued to create obstacles to the dissemination of the medicine.[7]

Public relations remained a priority for the operation, although the United States experienced a mild setback in mid-November when *Washington Post* correspondent Ferdinand Kuhn's assessment of the resettlement effort made the front page. Kuhn wrote of the horrors he witnessed in Bien Hoa, where, he observed, fifteen thousand Vietnamese had been resettled on land unfit to cultivate and had been left without shelter and water. Kuhn's article set the FOA in motion to demonstrate that the situation was not as bad as Kuhn had described. Harold Stassen worried that the *Washington Post* article and others printed in November, though not balanced and focused only on the refugee camps and resettlement, were undermining the positive value of the evacuation. Stassen called upon his STEM team to make an effort to show news correspondents the better side of the camps and the U.S. presence in working with the refugees.[8] Though the *Washington Post* and others might have had a legitimate concern in the resettlement camps of November 1954, it is difficult to justify any criticism of the American effort to organize the best possible conditions. The story reached Indochina at the same time another STEM field trip searched for a prime resettlement area.

Walter E. Ross, urban low-cost housing adviser in the Community Development Division, traveled to Nha Trang in search of adequate space for a new camp.[9] The area around Nha Trang had the capacity to accommodate up to forty thousand refugees, but although it had great potential, there still was political and military unrest in the area. In time, Nha Trang would become an area heavily saturated with refugees. STEM officials did not end their search with Nha Trang. Just as Ross surveyed the Nha Trang area, John Thelen conducted similar studies over the southern and central portion of the Plaine des Joncs. They would not be satisfied until all those who wished to come to the South had the proper quality of life. By mid-November the U.S. Overseas Mission shifted its focus from evacuation to resettlement as that became the priority.

The refugee and resettlement program was smaller in scope in central Vietnam than in South Vietnam, though it still experienced many of the same problems. William Dymsza reported to D. C. Lavergne that there were many significant problems with the project. The South Vietnamese government had spent too much money building homes, indicating a lack of planning and control over the resettlement operation. The focus on home building deflected resources from other important community-based projects such as schools, medical facilities, and infrastructure, all of which assisted in the development and reintegration of the refugee population. The second obstacle in central Vietnam was the lack of leadership. The Vietnamese government could not retain its commissioner for evacuation in central Vietnam for a long duration, nor did that office receive adequate funds or support from Saigon. If the resettlement effort was to succeed, the United States needed to work within the South Vietnamese framework but also help guide it with the technical and organizational expertise the Vietnamese lacked.

Dymsza also complained of the growing conflict between the government and the army in central Vietnam.[10] The dissension had resulted in poor morale and an increased ineffectiveness in government officials in carrying out their duties, as they were too concerned with the rivalry with military personnel. Many of the army forces in central Vietnam opposed Diem's policy and rule in South Vietnam. The situation was bad enough that a planned trip by Diem to the area was canceled because of the threat of army-inspired demonstrations. The enormity of the refugee resettlement problem, though smaller in central Vietnam, could not afford the diversion of attention and resources caused by internal Vietnamese rivalry. This was especially true because the United States had been given warning that refugee movement would increase.

On November 20, 1954, two French fishing contractors arrived in Haiphong requesting U.S. assistance to evacuate approximately one hundred Chinese fishing families from Hai Long Bay to the South. The one condition the fishermen had was that they wanted to take their boats. Up to that time none of the fishermen around Haiphong had given any indication that they wished to leave. The French navy proposed sailing the fishing boat fleet in April under escort. The United States rejected this plan because Viet Minh infiltrators had already penetrated the community, and it was feared that the Viet Minh would be entrenched in the community by April and that none of the fishermen would want, or be able, to leave. The navy began studying the feasibility of transporting the fishermen, their families, and boats by French landing craft.[11] At a conference to discuss the matter, the French also informed the Americans that they required four additional LSTs for use between Haiphong and Tourane to remove an additional fifteen hundred vehicles more than had been planned by General Ely. The French also reported to the Americans that some of their available shipping would depart to redeploy their troops to France. General O'Daniel agreed with the French plan and requested that all U.S. shipping remain in the area with the addition of four MSTS LSTs for a period of six weeks between December 15, 1954, and January 31, 1955. Captain Frank agreed with O'Daniel so long as the French agreed to assign berths for the ships in Haiphong.

When Captain Winn visited the fishermen in Hai Long Bay to assess the size of their boats, he concluded that it was impossible to move them by French landing craft. The shape and size of the boats precluded hoisting them or storing them on deck or in a hold for the trip to the South. Only LSDs were capable of transporting the fishing boats, but Captain Winn did not believe the cargo warranted the expense of using an LSD. He maintained, however, that the fishermen needed to be evacuated as soon as possible, as they were increasingly fearful of Viet Minh retribution. Captain Frank recommended that the problem of the fishermen was solvable if the French fishing contractor who had initiated the movement arranged for transport or the French transported the fleet between the monsoon seasons. Either way, Captain Frank did not believe the United States should become involved in the mission. The problem arose again on December 9, 1954, when the owners of 180 registered fishing boats informed the French and American officials that they would not be ready to leave until the end of April 1955.

Other conditions around Haiphong also created obstacles for the evacuation. Vietnamese workers in the acetylene plant went on strike on November 22, 1954, after the French began removing equipment from the facility. The workers claimed, with some logic, that the removal of equipment would mean the end of their employment. The French, however, were convinced that the strike was a communist-inspired event to hamper removal of equipment to the South. Both sides held accurate views of the situation, though the correctness of each perspective only heightened the tension in Haiphong. Vietnamese officials abandoned an attempt to remove dental and x-ray equipment from a dental clinic at the city hospital after hundreds of nurses, technicians, employees, and their families demonstrated against the loss of their jobs. Again, the French

Table 9.1. North Vietnamese Refugees Evacuated to South Vietnam as of November 26, 1954, and Repartition of Refugees in Resettlement Areas

North Vietnamese Refugees Evacuated to South Vietnam as of November 26, 1954[1]		
Saigon reception camps	16,000	6%
Other reception camps	50,000	18%
Resettlement areas	208,000	76%
Repartition of Refugees in Resettlement Areas		
Reinstalled in cultivation areas	125,000	60%
Remained in cities as nonspecialized workers, laborers, craftsmen, traders, or civil servants	26,000	12%
Artisan centers	36,000	18%
Fishing zones	21,000	10%

1. Report of the Commissariat General aux Refugees, S.P. 99.619, November 26, 1954, Folder 1, "Refugee Program," Box 3, Series 1452, Classified Subject Files, 1953–1958, Field Service, Resettlement and Rehabilitation Division, RG 469, NA.

and Vietnamese suspected Viet Minh organizers of rallying the people against the removal of the equipment. Strikes were not limited to the North, however. USNS *Hennepin* was delayed three days in Saigon because of a stevedore strike directed against one of the shipping companies using the Saigon docks.

Strikes were not the only new problem in the operation. On November 26, 1954, American officials learned that the Dominicans, who had remained in Haiphong to assist in the evacuation of the Vietnamese, had been ordered to depart the city permanently. The Dominican priests had served as translators and had often eased the worried minds of newly arrived refugees who had learned about the Americans through Viet Minh propaganda.

Always a great concern for the United States was the first contact between American personnel and Vietnamese evacuees. In the North, this took place in the reception centers of Haiphong, and great care was taken to ensure that these camps were presentable. On November 29, the sanitary conditions in the Haiphong camps were rated as good after U.S. Navy medical units sprayed Lindane and DDT. Under the command of Dr. Thomas Dooley, the camps improved over time. Dooley closed the refugee camp that had been set up in the kindergarten in Haiphong and established a new camp near the cement plant at the outskirts of the city. With new facilities, Dooley and the sanitary unit were able to organize camps as they wished. The same day the camps received the rating, a family of forty-two arrived in Haiphong led by the 102-year-old patriarch of the family. The five generations in the family had traveled ten weeks to Haiphong from the village of Thanh Hoa in Phat Diem. The refugees in the Haiphong camps numbered 10,123—most of them from Phat Diem—with only 3,550 willing to leave. The remainder wished to wait until the rest of their family arrived in the embarkation area. The refugee camp would have been larger had it not been that the majority of the young men in the camps joined the South Vietnamese army or assimilated into the Haiphong population.

With the arrival of December 1954, the atmosphere in Haiphong took on a new urgency. General Cogny assumed all civil government functions for the French and announced through the press that the French would not be responsible for military security or the structured evacuation of French nationals after February 1, 1955. As a result of this announcement, a number of stores in Haiphong closed as French nationals who had remained in Haiphong to take advantage of the situation started the process of leaving the former French colony. Cogny had assumed control from Mr. Compaigne, who had, the USOM learned on December 2, 1954, been negotiating a financial settlement with the Viet Minh to salvage French business property. O'Daniel issued instructions to MAAG Haiphong that under no circumstances should the United States transport civilian equipment before all of the MDAP materiel had been evacuated.[12] He ordered both MAAG Haiphong and MAAG Saigon to coordinate MSTS shipments of civilian equipment with the French to lessen the potential losses to the French while at the same time ensuring that all usable equipment was denied to the Viet Minh when the three-hundred-day period was completed. By December 6, 1954, the French had prepared only three LST loads for the four MSTS LSTs scheduled to arrive later in the month. STEM officials were able to load all of their equipment onto the MSTS ships for passage south, anticipating the February deadline when security would no longer be guaranteed. The tension heightened in Haiphong as a result of the French announcement, which the emergency sealift off of Vinh did not ease.

The evacuation off of Vinh was complicated by a number of factors. The pickup scheduled for December 12, 1954, failed to produce results because of the rough weather that prohibited sampans and other small craft from traveling out to the waiting American ships. The surf also prevented landing craft from going to the beach to load the refugees. The scheduled pickup the next week was again postponed because of rough seas. Despite the delays in the Vinh operation, an average of five hundred refugees arrived in Haiphong during the period. Most of the refugees entering the embarkation area had arrived on false or reused transit passes. A total of 10,223 refugees remained in the camps on December 19, though only 2,900 were ready to depart. The French stationed two ships off of Vinh on December 20, but no refugees were retrieved during the night. The French had retrieved 525 individuals the previous night. For these refugees, the passage to freedom took the long route up to Haiphong and back down past Vinh and to Tourane, Cap St. Jacques, and Saigon. The arrival of 2,300 Vietnamese from the Vinh region on December 23 did not upset the balance in the Haiphong camp, as the French continued to airlift approximately three hundred refugees per day to keep the camp population down. The decrease of three hundred per day by airlift was supplemented by another one hundred per day who joined the South Vietnamese Army and still another two hundred who left the embarkation area to search for missing family members in the Viet Minh zone. The French dispatched a navy frigate to Vinh for another refugee pickup without success. While French, Vietnamese, and American officials agreed that there were still refugees who wanted to leave the area, the increased Viet Minh patrolling prohibited further extraction. They concluded that this evacuation route had been exhausted. The last French ship left the Vinh area and returned to Haiphong on January 2, 1955.

The decreased flow of evacuees was noted by all involved in the operation, and the French developed a plan to use the existing American transport ships to evacuate the remainder of the refugee population. A conference the next day between French army and navy officers and Captain Frank resulted in the recommendation that the United States provide one LSD from January 10 to March 1 and one LSD, and possibility one AKA, around May 1 if needed. Admiral Sabin and Admiral Carney approved Captain Frank's recommendation, and three MSTS LSTs arrived in Haiphong for duty. On December 15, 1954, LST-520 joined LST-47, LST-176, and LST-546 in Haiphong. LST-176 completed the first evacuation load, followed by LST-546 and LST-520. All three ships headed to Tourane on December 17, while LST-147 loaded and sailed for Tourane the next day. The French army had been able to load an average of 1,527 long tons of equipment per day for the first fifteen days in December. Although this was below the goal of 2,000 long tons set for December, it was above the November average of 1,500 long tons. The French guaranteed that there would be loads for the LSTs throughout their deployment to Indochina.

USOM officials devised three potential plans to increase the flow of refugees, whom they believed were less obstructed by poor weather than by the Viet Minh. The Viet Minh isolated villagers who had indicated a desire to leave by selling their water buffalo or household goods.[13] The Viet Minh also prohibited large groups of people in an effort to prevent mass exodus from villages. The first plan was to resume the LST landings near Tra Ly, where Catholic priests had assured the United States they would have evacuees ready to embark for Haiphong. Weather and Viet Minh patrols were the greatest concern for this plan. A second plan called for evacuees to congregate around the Hanoi cathedral on Christmas morning, under the auspices of a Canadian ICC observer, and to board a train for Haiphong. The third scheme sought the use of Tiger Island, three miles off the coast at the nineteenth parallel. Evacuees would have to make their way to the island, where French ships would pick them up and take them to Haiphong. However, a French LSM had picked up four refugees on the Ba Lang coast on January 19 and had taken them to Haiphong. The area had been the scene of clashes between the Viet Minh and large groups of Vietnamese protesting against the DRV. The French reported that the Viet Minh had placed a number of mortar batteries along the coast, making it impossible to retrieve refugees from the beaches.

The crew working in the Haiphong theater received a welcome treat on December 24 when Captain Frank returned to USS *Balduck* with twelve hundred pounds of Christmas mail, but the general goodwill was offset by increased security in Haiphong as rumors of Viet Minh demonstrations increased. Although no demonstrations occurred during the Christmas holiday, the streets of Haiphong took on the appearance of an armed camp as special military policemen patrolled the city, and American personnel were restricted to their billets. French army intelligence reported to American officials in Haiphong that the Viet Minh had formulated a policy toward the evacuation of equipment and infrastructure from Haiphong. The Viet Minh would oppose all removal of capital with propaganda, strikes, and peaceful demonstrations. There was no indication that any violent method was contemplated to retain material.

USNS *Sword Knot* and SS *Codington* arrived in Haiphong in relief of *Hennepin* and USNS *Fentress*, and both cargo ships were put to work on December 28 as *Sword Knot* began to load asphalt purchased through USOM funds and *Codington* loaded cement. *Codington*'s load was the last of three left in Haiphong, and *Herkimer* and USNS *Captain Arlo L. Olson* (T-AK-245) took on the last two loads on January 3, 1955. *General Howze* returned to Haiphong and loaded approximately five hundred Chinese from Hon Gay and eight hundred Haiphong residents. The Haiphong residents were the first sizeable group to leave the city after the French urged early departure. Many of them brought with them large packages and boxes, which delayed loading of the ship. MAAG Haiphong officials informed Captain Frank that with the shipment of goods in early January, only sixteen thousand tons remained for transport for the remainder of January, and an expected influx of thirty thousand refugees might require an additional transport. American materiel was not the only equipment ready for departure and vying for American attention. On January 16, MAAG Haiphong officials learned of the request of the French private enterprise Charbonnage du Tonkin to ship a hundred pieces of heavy equipment out of Haiphong during March, April, and May. The French owners of Charbonnage du Tonkin had tried to convince the United States to purchase its equipment in late November 1954 without success. The French officials had negotiated the release of the equipment, all of which had been paid for by the United States, from the Viet Minh, though the list to be shipped did not include all of the American-purchased equipment. Captain Frank met with MAAG Saigon representatives and USOM officials to confirm the number of refugees making the trip to the South by the end of February. It was estimated that twenty thousand Vietnamese would take their passage to freedom if members of the ICC were able to patrol the Viet Minh territory effectively and deter violations of the Geneva Agreements.

In South Vietnam new problems emerged as refugees refused to redistribute according to the plans of the South Vietnamese government. Catholic clergy insisted on moving their congregations to Bien Hoa province, refusing to relocate to established resettlement camps with houses and ready agricultural land outside the province.[14] The South Vietnamese also continued to have difficulty establishing lands for cultivation. The commission general did not want to take over abandoned rice lands for refugee use and lacked the organization to distribute farming tools for refugees to clear their new land and plant their first crops. By the end of December, with a possible two hundred thousand additional refugees from Haiphong, U.S. officials recognized the potential disaster looming over South Vietnam. When the High Board for Refugees Commission met on December 6, it focused on these problems. It also discussed how to create a permanent subsistence for the new population.[15] The commission recommended that refugees be resettled in areas similar to the ones they had left in North Vietnam, but it did not offer a plan by which this could be accomplished. The Vietnamese knew what needed to be done but did not have the expertise to reach those goals. As a result, refugees were often ill-placed, which caused frustration for them as well as for U.S. officials who were forced to provide temporary solutions to short-term problems rather than providing long-term answers to the problems of evacuation. The lack of a national plan that coordinated all of the offices available in South Vietnam continued to plague the evacuation process. The results were staggering. Through December, 60 percent of the refugees resettled in South Vietnam listed their occupation as farmer, while another 10 percent were fishermen; artisans and civil servants completed the list. Seventy percent of the refugees were placed in forest areas, 10 percent in cleared highlands, and only 20 percent in rice and other farming areas. The strength and value of the refugee population was not being fully employed.[16]

The critical nature of the Bien Hoa situation was seen in the refugee population at Ho Nai. The original camp could accommodate ten thousand refugees, but by December 17, there were more than forty-one thousand refugees in the camp. Overcrowded camps caused a number of problems. In addition to the health considerations for so many people in a small area, there was also the real likelihood that not all of the South Vietnamese government's promises could be kept. This caused some dissatisfaction among the Ho Nai population, even though they were not supposed to be in that province. Overcrowding the refugees from the North while trying to meet their demands was one of the many problems the United States inherited from the South Vietnamese as the problem switched from being one of moving the Vietnamese to one of resettling them. USOM officials continued to pressure the South Vietnamese to issue a decree that would allow the government the ability to take over uncultivated rice land and farmland for distribution among the refugee population. This would have the dual purpose of easing the overcrowding in Bien Hoa while fulfilling the promises of a new start for those who had made the journey to the South. Despite the apparent advantages, USOM officials did not believe the South Vietnamese would issue the decree.[17] The lack of faith by American personnel in their South Vietnamese counterparts was not strengthened by the rotation of Vietnamese officials in charge of the refugee situation.

Pham Van Huyen took over as commissioner general for refugees on December 7, requiring STEM officials to reintroduce their proposals for refugee resettlement, although he was more than willing to listen to them. One plan that had merit was the use of the leprosarium sawmill in Ban Me Thuot to provide lumber for the flood of housing requirements in the region. By using existing resources with an ample labor and lumber supply, the sawmill supplemented the resources of the U.S. government and provided for better resettlement housing. The resettlement effort also received a boost from Australia, which provided much-needed farming equipment, under the Colombo Plan, as well as instructors to train the South Vietnamese in the equipment's use and maintenance.[18]

At the end of 1954, the U.S. Navy had transported 175,227 civilian passengers and another 14,089 military personnel. The navy had moved 6,388 vehicles from North Vietnam as well as 50,238 short tons of equipment and materiel. Navy personnel had recorded 54 deaths during the operation though that was offset with 111 births aboard U.S. ships. The navy's evacuation totals equaled approximately one-third of the total number of individuals evacuated. Although almost all military cargo had been transported to the South, the one U.S. Navy and ten navy-controlled ships would continue to evacuate military personnel and nonmilitary cargo until May 1955. The new year began as the old had ended, though many of the American personnel involved in the operation now came from the MSTS.

General Howze returned to Haiphong on January 4, 1955, after dropping off its passengers in six days—a record turnaround for the operation. The next load included five hundred members of the Vietnamese Confederation of Christian Workers, the largest labor union in Vietnam. It was estimated that these five hundred Vietnamese were the first of twenty-five thousand possible evacuees from the union. The union members presented some problems for the crew of *General Howze*, because many of them did not feel that they should have to take care of their own belongings and refused to clean up their rooms when finished with them, despite clear orders to the contrary. The rest of the passenger load on *General Howze*, a combination of Chinese merchants and Nungs, behaved well. The ship was delayed from leaving for Saigon by weather on January 10, and then another day as the Chinese merchants continued to bring large cargo boxes aboard the ship, in the amount of two hundred long tons.

USS *Gunston Hall* (LSD-5) arrived in Haiphong on January 10 to begin service in the operation. The LSD would remain on station until the end of February, making several trips from Haiphong to Saigon. One of the continuing problems for the ships in Task Force 90 was maintenance, and the LSTs—the workhorses of the navy—suffered the worst. In a period of two days, January 9 and 10, 1955, LST-546 suffered a crack in its main deck and damage to its radio equipment and gyrocompass as a result of rough seas, while LST-47 suffered hull damage. The rough weather forced LST-176 to return to Cap St. Jacques, USNS *Captain Arlo L. Olson* to anchor eighty miles north of the city, and *General Howze* to delay its scheduled departure. The weather continued to be a problem the next day, stranding ships in Saigon because of high seas. LST-176 became the third MSTS LST to suffer a crack in its hull while trying to return to Haiphong. While the weather played havoc with American shipping, the French and Vietnamese continued to argue about the size of the refugee population left in North Vietnam, and Vietnamese police took a more authoritarian role in Haiphong. There was some justification for the vigilance; the French confiscated seven large junks, loaded with cement, gasoline, and lubricants, on the Song Ria River headed toward Viet Minh territory.

On January 20, Captain A. R. St. Angelo, aboard USS *Cook* (APD-130), arrived in Haiphong to relieve Captain Frank as the commander of Task Group 90.8. After the transfer of personnel, *Balduck* departed for Kobe, Japan. Captain Frank remained for a few days to welcome Admiral Sabin back to Indochina, then departed by air. During the change of command, *General Howze* took on board the two hundred thousandth passenger loaded aboard U.S. ships during Operation Passage to Freedom. Tension

Table 9.2. Task Group 90.8, January 1955

USS *Cook* (APD 130)	USNS *General R. L. Howze* (T-AP 134)
USS *Gunston Hall* (LSD 5)	USNS *Marine Serpent* (T-AP 202)
MSTS LST-47	USNS *Captain Arlo L. Olson* (T-AK 245)
MSTS LST-176	USNS *Sword Knot*
MSTS LST-520	SS *Codington*
MSTS LST-546	

was also mounting at this time as Buddhists joined with Catholics in protesting the Viet Minh government. The numbers in the camps remained the same, as a result of an increased French airlift to an average of five hundred individuals per day, but the French did request the continuation of the MSTS LSTs beyond their departure date to finish loading and transporting the originally planned loads south of the seventeenth parallel.

On January 23, as Captain St. Angelo officially relieved Captain Frank as commander of Task Group 90.8, the United States suspended operations for a period of four days for the Tet holiday. The only exception was USNS *Marine Serpent*, which was offloading in Saigon. At the end of Tet, Task Group 90.8 consisted of the ships listed in Table 9.2.

February 7, 1955, was the two hundredth day of the evacuation. With one hundred days left, it was clear that there were still many Vietnamese in North Vietnam who wanted to resettle in the South. The Second Interim Report of the International Commission for Supervision and Control in Vietnam (ICSC), released just three days after this milestone, reported that the situation was progressing, but not as smoothly as desired. The ICSC reported that each party to the Geneva Conference was concerned more with denouncing the other side than with working together to ensure an effective process. The situation was further hampered by the fact that local officials in both North and South Vietnam distrusted both the French and DRV officials, causing additional delays or indifference to the evacuees.[19] Both the French and North Vietnamese continued to complain to the ICSC about violations, in most instances taking their cases to the public and press before approaching the commission. It was clear that, despite any legitimacy in the cases, both sides were prone to exploit propaganda value anywhere it appeared.

CONCLUSION

★★★★★★★★★★★★★★★

The Bamboo Curtain Falls

The final push during Operation Passage to Freedom can best be characterized by alternating brief periods of frenzied anxiety and relative calm. Tense moments occurred as the American and French forces prepared for the handover of Haiphong to the Viet Minh with the knowledge that some potential evacuees might be left behind. These final months were difficult for those who ran the camps in both the North and the South, as Viet Minh agitators made frequent appearances, and political opponents of Ngo Dinh Diem stepped up the intensity of their challenge to his rule. These events also brought long periods of calm in the movement of the refugee population from Haiphong. During the latter part of April, the number of evacuees reached an all-time low. Despite the ebb and flow of the operation during these final days, American personnel in charge of the evacuation continued to provide the necessary talent to ensure a peaceful resolution of the three-hundred-day period of free movement. Their accomplishment was one of the most remarkable events of modern military humanitarianism.

In his report to the new director of mission, Leland Barrows, the chief of the Community Development Division, Herman J. Holiday, urged several reforms for the final evacuation push. Of immediate concern was the lack of a comprehensive organizational plan for USOM. USOM officials had been working independently of one another in their dealings with the Vietnamese government, which had caused some inefficiency. Holiday called for the registration of all refugees with complete histories, the employment of all able-bodied individuals toward public works, and more coordination with the Vietnamese and local government to ensure that the refugee population, as well as the southern population who had endured eight years of war, were well taken care of with the money the United States was spending in South Vietnam. Holiday was particularly concerned, as were many of the Americans in South Vietnam, that the Vietnamese government cooperate with the United States and USOM in maximizing their efforts to improve South Vietnam and limit the wasteful and corrupt practices that had developed in 1954.[1]

In the North, the Tet holiday slowed down evacuation processes even though the usually festive environment was subdued. USOM officials found it difficult to accomplish goals and were not able to obtain from the Vietnamese normal intelligence on the status of the evacuation. At the end of Tet, there were approximately 14,000 refugees in the three embarkation camps—Shell, Pagoda, and Cement—around Haiphong, with the daily influx averaging 550 people. In addition to the refugees, MAAG Detachment Haiphong reported eighteen thousand tons of cargo and five thousand vehicles left for evacuation.[2] Before its departure from Indochina, *General Howze* was scheduled to make two trips to Saigon to empty the camps in preparation for the post-Tet push, but because of the Tet lull it completed only one trip. Among the 4,253 refugees evacuated by *General Howze* was its fifty thousandth person, making that ship the most used during the operation. To that date it had carried nearly one of every four evacuees. Despite larger than desired numbers in the camps, the general morale was good, in part because of the work of Dr. Dooley, who organized the cleaning of the camps and ensured a constant source of fresh water for the refugees. During the final push, Dooley, whose work would eventually earn him the honor "Officer de l'Orde Nationale de Viet Nam," awarded by Ngo Dinh Diem on May 12, 1955, assisted in the temporary closing of camps to clean them out and redistribute the evacuees awaiting transportation. This resulted in much more sanitary conditions and in addition disrupted the plans of agitators within the camps. Dooley also began a campaign to organize additional non-military American assistance for the refugee population. On February

24, the Pfizer pharmaceutical company donated one hundred thousand magnamycin tablets to Dooley for his use in the refugee camps to treat infections of the skin, respiratory tract, and bone.

The Tet holiday did not mean the situation was peaceful in Haiphong. On January 26, a riot occurred at the waterworks when French army personnel attempted to remove one of their standby generators. Nearly one thousand Vietnamese rallied in front of the ICC offices to protest the removal of the generator before the Indian representative, V. K. Krishna Menon, defused the situation with the assistance of additional French troops. Violence was thwarted during the confrontation when French soldiers subdued a Vietnamese in the process of throwing a grenade at Menon. There was no question in U.S. and French circles that the Viet Minh organized the demonstration.[3]

The Viet Minh did not cause all the problems in Haiphong, however. The French required authorization from Paris for the removal of all American equipment under their direct control and created obstacles to American operations. On February 1, USOM officials attempted to remove five refrigerators and two washing machines from the Haiphong hospital, only to be stopped by the fixed bayonets of the French Foreign Legion.[4] French officials had cleared the equipment for evacuation but did not inform the Legionnaires of the decision.[5] This was but one in a long series of miscommunications between American and French personnel in Vietnam. Fortunately, there were no casualties.

Another situation hampering evacuation operations was the hesitancy of Vietnamese evacuees to leave the transit camps in Haiphong. Early in the operation, refugees waited for family members or assurances that life in the South would be better than life in the North. By February 1955, many of the Vietnamese remaining in the camps stayed to collect the cash per diem provided by the United States. For the naval side of the operation, this meant that *Marine Serpent* was the only ship to carry passengers during the month; it made two trips on February 8 and 16, carrying 5,266 and 5,170 passengers, respectively. Two days after the last trip, the refugee committee in charge of the embarkation point officially closed registration for sealift until March 1 in order to process the remaining refugees as well as provide a psychological effect for those hedging their decision to depart North Vietnam.[6] Haiphong officials had not pressed the Vietnamese to embark earlier in the operation, and as a result several

Vietnamese businesses had been established around the camps. The refugees in those businesses earned a solid living and had little incentive to leave Haiphong until the last moment.[7] This was particularly a problem at Cement Camp, where Father Khue served as an agitator. President Ngo Dinh Diem had sent Khue to Haiphong as an unofficial adviser. With that backing Khue began to assert his authority, taking command of the Vietnamese part of the evacuation as well as creating a militia from the young men populating the camps. He used the militia to organize demonstrations and curry favors for Catholics in the camps. Khue threatened the official Vietnamese representative and disrupted USOM meetings with the Vietnamese. USOM officials in Haiphong worked hard to get Khue out of Haiphong, but they had little success.[8] On February 4, with the number of refugees in the Haiphong evacuation area at seven thousand, the United States decided to evacuate Cement Camp to diffuse Father Khue's influence. Governor Le Quang Luat ordered Khue to return to the South in mid-March, which eliminated one obstruction to USOM.

USOM officials also worked hard during the final push to ensure that no usable American equipment remained in Haiphong after the end of the three-hundred-day period. The United States justified these actions because it had not signed the Geneva Agreements, which legally allowed it to push forward with evacuation of materiel. By February all significant American equipment had been evacuated to the South, and French materiel was schedule for removal before May. The situation was such that Admiral Sabin could report with confidence that the phasing out was proceeding as planned. The evacuation of North Vietnam would not be a repeat of the situation that had occurred in China when that country had turned to communism in 1949.[9] There were still Vietnamese manufacturers with equipment in Haiphong without enough money to pay for its removal. The French continued to remove this equipment, including the material from the coal mine, cement plant, and battery factory. During February the French military also completed the removal of the radio station. There was little organized opposition by the Viet Minh to these moves. These actions of, and cooperation by, the French received praise from the USOM officials in Haiphong. During the final three months, the U.S. personnel organized financial aid and strategic cargo lift using USS *Gunston Hall* and LSTs to remove all that was valuable.[10] On February 8, General Cogny issued an official proclamation warning French civilians in North Vietnam that failure to evacuate through Haiphong by April 15 signified the individual's desire to stay in the North after the French withdrew. The French had issued a similar proclamation in December 1954 for a final deadline of February 1, but it did not have the effect anticipated. The April 15 deadline signaled to those remaining in Haiphong that the end of the French empire was near.[11]

At the beginning of March 1955, approximately forty thousand Vietnamese in Haiphong had signed up to travel to the South, though they appeared to be in no great hurry to leave. These individuals were in addition to the refugees already in the embarkation area. USOM officials decided to close all three embarkation camps around Haiphong by the middle of the month, transferring the remaining inhabitants into Haiphong. On March 7, the ICC authorized final approval for the removal of the remaining AEA equipment in Haiphong, with the exception of two ambulances at the Haiphong hospital that were released less than a week later.[12] *Sword Knot*, *Marine Serpent*, and *Marine Adder*, all MSTS transports, carried the bulk of the American equipment during the final stages. These vessels, along with more cooperative French officials, were given special recognition by the USOM officials. *Marine Adder* embarked the five hundred thousandth Vietnamese seeking a new life in South Vietnam on its March 6 trip with the appropriate fanfare: a band, gifts for the refugees, and a formal ceremony. The event, despite its significance, did not attract the attention of the news media, who were more interested in covering the evacuation of the Tachen Islands. Admiral Sabin could never reconcile the failure of the news media with the efforts of the U.S. Navy: "I was proud of our performance at Tachen. . . . But I feel a greater pride in our people for their accomplishments in Indo-China where they labored month after month in a stinking climate, under health hazards and continuous problems ranging from everyday occurrences of an unclassified nature to Top Secret tasks requiring the utmost in security preservation."[13] Operation Passage to Freedom succeeded in all of its objectives save using the situation to publicize to the world the plight of the Vietnamese people fleeing the Viet Minh.

It was during this time that another problem arose. During the chaotic situation in the North, as entire villages concentrated at the embarkation points, families were often separated. This growing population, when added to the children made orphan by the war, created a unique problem for the Vietnamese and Americans. A large orphanage had been established in Haiphong to care for the young population. Madam Vu Thi Ngai had taken a personal interest in the children and had "charmed" U.S. officials into helping her and her charges. As the orphanage planned to move to the South, the question arose whether the government or the city owned the orphanage's property. The ICC had been reluctant to move what it considered welfare items from the city and would not authorize the removal of the orphanage property until the matter had been settled. Roger Ackley, the USOM Haiphong representative, came up with the solution of "nationalizing" the orphanage. Madam Ngai declared that she was the owner of everything, which allowed the United States to transport her personal property as necessary. Essentially, Madam Ngai's declaration cast her beyond the reach of the ICC. The first load of orphanage equipment was loaded on USNS *Sword Knot*, and, although Madam Ngai feared ICC intervention, loading proceeded without incident. Madam Ngai's work had a significant impact on all American personnel in Haiphong, and all worked to ensure that she had the means to continue her mission in the South. A little American ingenuity allowed that to happen.[14]

Ingenuity was not limited to American personnel. As the evacuation slowed, the Viet Minh increased their use of U.S. and French ships to transport personnel, materiel, and intelligence from North to South Vietnam. Operation Trojan Horse, as it was known within American circles, had been prevalent throughout Operation Passage to Freedom. This operation saw Polish and Russian ships carry Viet Minh cadre from South to North Vietnam. After receiving instructions in the North, these same cadres would blend in with the refugee populations and enter the embarkation points. Because there was no way to distinguish whether a Vietnamese was Viet Minh unless he or she was identified, the cadres were able to use free transport back to the South to deliver orders from the North. American and French officials attempted to identify Viet Minh who had made more than one trip to the South, but with very little success. Not only did these cadres use the free transportation, but they also gathered intelligence along the way. They were able to assess Vietnamese-American interaction and thwart it when possible, as well as target disembarkation and temporary resettlement areas for further agitation. There is no question that the Viet Minh took advantage of Operation Passage to Freedom to move their own personnel and intelligence between the two countries.

Ackley ended his assignment in mid-March and was replaced by Norman Poulin. The transition between Ackley and Poulin was smooth, even though many in Haiphong sought to take advantage of the new representative. These included British Hong Kong subjects seeking free air passage out of Haiphong—they claimed Ackley had promised it—and Father Khue, who attempted to reassert his authority in the embarkation area with his Legion of Social Workers, described by Ackley as a rogue militia. Other Vietnamese tried to convince Poulin that materiel already evacuated was still in Haiphong and that he needed to act on it. These left-behind items were in fact personal property for which the Vietnamese needed to pay for transportation.[15] Poulin was able to sort the true from the false while preparing for the final days of the USOM in Haiphong.

On March 30, *Marine Adder* loaded 1,991 refugees; the lowest total for the year, much to the disappointment of the American personnel in Haiphong. *Marine Adder* had had some setbacks in early voyages, including a food shortage on one trip and questionable actions by its personnel on another. French personnel aboard the LSMs that transferred refugees from the shore to the ship confirmed the less-than-gentle treatment. These events, relayed by those who had made the trip to relatives in the North, damaged the ship's reputation.[16] The Viet Minh exploited this isolated situation and continued to spread rumors that the Americans cut off the left hand of all newborn babies, threw women and children overboard, and forced the men to work as slave labor in the rubber plantations of South Vietnam. The LSTs also looked like monsters to the Vietnamese when their payload doors were ajar. The Viet Minh played on this fear and told the refugees that, once at sea, the U.S. Navy would open the doors to drown them. The Viet Minh propaganda had some effect, but not enough to slow down the final push.

Another sign of the operation's end was the change, on April 1, of the numerical designator of forces involved in Operation Passage to Freedom from Task Force 90 to Task Group 50.1, with a similar restructuring down the line of command, although personnel and number and type of ships remained the same. The change signified the beginning of the end for the Indochina evacuation. On April 11, Captain Walter C. Winn relieved Admiral Sabin as commander of TG 50.1, although Admiral Sabin would play a role until the very end. He in part had committed himself to seeing to the operation's end and was determined to ensure its successful completion. During the month, *Marine Serpent* and *Marine Adder* operated as passenger transports on an eight-day cycle to maintain the regular flow of refugees. Also on April 11, representatives of the French Union forces and the PAVN signed Protocol 29 "concerning the transfer of the Civil Administration in the perimeter of Hai Phong."[17] The protocol outlined the acts of the French departure and end of Passage to Freedom, which was scheduled to take place the following month. Much of the protocol mirrored the issues that had concerned the USOM during the operation, including the final transfer of municipal property and assurance that the final transition would be peaceful. The publication of the protocol, coupled with the impending French deadline of April 15, saw a marked increased in Vietnamese leaving for the South. *Marine Serpent* carried an operational record 6,289 refugees from Haiphong on April 12, while SS *Marine Adder* carried 4,006 and 4,968 on April 7 and 15, respectively. The T-LSTs 535, 548, 578, and 629 arrived on station toward the end of April to begin transporting the remaining equipment in Haiphong, which at that point consisted of military and civilian vehicles and military personnel.

During the first few days of May, few civilians were transported to the South. On May 2, Camp Marine closed in preparation for the final evacuation of Haiphong, leaving only the 9 Rue Bonal refugee camp in operation. Vietnamese still occupied the abandoned camps, waiting until the last minute to depart. One of the major concerns for those remaining was the disruption in Saigon caused by the Binh Xuyen, which had engaged in open conflict with the South Vietnamese army and supporters of Ngo Dinh Diem. The Binh Xuyen stepped up its aggression in Saigon with the objective of overthrowing Diem, who had been diffusing the organization's power in and around Saigon and Cholon as he consolidated and stabilized South Vietnamese politics. Although the Binh Xuyen crisis was important to the survival of Ngo Dinh Diem and his government, it had little influence on the close of the evacuation.

An advanced administrative party of Viet Minh officials arrived in Haiphong on May 5 to begin the transfer of Haiphong to the Viet Minh. The 350 Viet Minh, led by Nguyen Thai, began the takeover process in order to be ready for the official administrative transfer on May 9, followed by the occupation of the city by the Viet Minh. The advance party acted in a very professional way, treating the citizens with respect and courtesy—something noted by the remaining American personnel. Despite some apprehension on the part of the remaining Americans, the Haiphong residents did not appear concerned or anxious with the imminent arrival of the Viet Minh.[18]

The final inspection by U.S. personnel in Haiphong on May 8 indicated that no MDAP or other American-funded equipment remained in Haiphong. With the Viet Minh marching on the city, the last of the Americans retreated to the Do Son Peninsula. Dr. Dooley recalled that it was relatively quiet during the transition: "The Navy Base closes today, the piers are gone, the buildings are emptied. There is nothing left in my warehouse there, all has been transferred to the ship."[19] The handover was accomplished on May 9 without any serious incident despite the fact that USOM officials were forced to abandoned their offices and unable to centralize the evacuation process. The French, under Admiral Querville and his Deuxieme Bureau, rounded up the last-minute refugee stragglers and housed them at the French marine barracks. Those evacuees made up the last list of passengers on USNS *General Brewster*.

After the evacuation of Haiphong, the allied perimeter would continue to shrink with the transfer of the area surrounding Haiphong on May 13 and Do Son Peninsula on May 15; the tip of Do Son Peninsula was evacuated on May 16. The last American ship, *General Brewster*, departed Haiphong on schedule on May 13, making its way to Do Son to participate in the final embarkation of French security forces and equipment as well as the last group of ten refugees who had fled the Viet Minh. Among this last group were a Vietnamese father and daughter who had been delayed in Hanoi because the mother of the family refused to leave North Vietnam. The father and daughter, the last official refugees to leave under the Geneva Agreements, left the mother in Hanoi rather than live under Viet Minh rule. This division of the family symbolized the period 1954 to 1955 as Indochina divided into North and South. Most who traveled to the South left some family member or family cemetery behind. For those Vietnamese the country was truly divided and would be whole again only when the Viet Minh were defeated and they could return to their place of origin. For those Vietnamese, this dream would never come true, and for many who survived the war until April 30, 1975, the experience of Passage to Freedom—on a much more violent and disorganized scale—would repeat itself. Those Vietnamese who left the North in 1954 had lost their home. In 1975 they had lost their country.

Table 10.1. Evacuation Totals, May 1955

	French Airlift	French Vessels	USN Vessels	Self Evacuated	Totals
Vietnamese Civilians	172,783	101,239	293,002	41,328	608,352
French Civilians	11,206	26,818	0	0	38,024
Vietnamese Military	6,187	37,838	14,868	0	58,893
French Military	23,459	69,080	2,978	0	95,517
Totals	213,635	234,975	310,848	41,328	800,786

After the evacuation of Do Son, all American and French ships moved to the Baie de Lanha. This was a period of anxiety for many aboard who were unsure of the possible Viet Minh threat, but it was also a time of relief and good weather. American crews took advantage of the lull for a last run at beach and swimming parties and "a last look of the scenic splendors of the world now passing behind the bamboo curtain."[20] All the Americans left for the Viet Minh were empty beer cans and cartons. U.S. and French ships moved farther away to Cac Ba, Surprise, Union, and the Paix Islands on May 18. The French ships on station, led by Admiral Querville aboard *Jules Verne* and reinforced by two carriers—*Lafayette* and *Bois Belleau*—and the cruiser *Montcalm*, joined by USS *Cook*, USS *Diachenko* (APD-123), USNS *General Brewster*, and USNS *Marine Adder*, handled the remaining evacuation. These ships, along with transports, remained off the coast of Do Son until the last minute. *Marine Adder* stayed on station until May 18, the final day of the operation, and departed for Saigon with no civilian passengers aboard. When the last French military forces evacuated from the mainland on May 15, the total number of those who had been transported stood at 800,786.[21]

During the course of the evacuation there were 184 recorded births and 66 deaths among the refugee population. The U.S. forces suffered no fatalities and only a few casualties, all of which were noncombat-related. The passage of the three-hundred-day period for free movement across the DMZ at the seventeenth parallel did not signal an end to the movement of the Vietnamese people.[22] In June it was estimated that approximately six to seven thousand refugees had worked their way to the South through the Viet Minh checkpoints or through Laos. Typically, these refugees were found in the DMZ and brought to Quang Tri for transportation down to Tourane. The estimated three Viet Minh companies patrolling the DMZ allowed this movement, in part to continue the process of reinfiltrating its cadres into South Vietnam to keep its lines of communication open. The RVN officials in central Vietnam did not have the organizational structure in place to thwart this violation of the Geneva Agreements.

The plight of the refugees who had resettled in the South did not end with the close of the operation. The evacuees represented a strong bloc of individuals who, despite the fact that they had voted against the Viet Minh by leaving the North, were vulnerable to the political intrigues that developed the Hoa Hao, Cao Dai, and Binh Xuyen factions, each of which challenged the Diem regime. In Tay Ninh, home to thirty-eight thousand refugees, government officials expressed grave concern to the remaining American officials about Cao Dai interference in the resettlement camps. The Cao Daists controlled half of the territory around Tay Ninh and used their influence to foster discontent among the refugees against the government officials who were trying to administer relief.[23] The Viet Minh also continued to threaten the new southern residents with attacks against individuals and by burning villages in a continued effort to intimidate refugees. The Viet Minh, disguised as elements of the remaining French Union forces, targeted village priests and government officials in an effort to disrupt the transition period of resettlement. In Bien Hoa province, USOM representatives documented several cases of Viet Minh interference. In Gia Dinh province, USOM representatives noted numerous attempts by the Viet Minh to infiltrate the refugee camps, to intimidate through threats of bodily harm or material destruction, and to spread anti-Diem pamphlets and propaganda. The Binh Xuyen stepped up their antigovernment postures during the summer months with attacks against resettlement areas in Baria province.

North Vietnamese evacuees experienced hardships after making the decision to leave their homelands. The difficulties of the movement from homestead through Viet Minh territory to board a ship to a new region, often without benefit of finances to establish themselves, continued as the refugee population became the targets of internal disputes emerging as South Vietnam sought to claim its national identity.

In the months that followed, as Diem consolidated his power and began to shape his vision for South Vietnam, the refugees suffered further. Diem used the refugees as a foundation for his power, but that did not provide them immunity from future troubles. A group of refugees settled in Nha Trang were successful in becoming immediately self-supporting. As Nha Trang grew around the refugee settlement, it became necessary to move them. Because the group was comfortable in the area, it resisted, and the provincial police forcibly removed them, destroying their homes, furniture, and equipment; injuring those who physically resisted; and imprisoning those who stood in the way. Many of the refugees pleaded for USOM interference, though the Americans thought it best not to interfere with what appeared to be an internal matter. In areas such as Dalat, often considered the resort region of South Vietnam, resettlement camps were often forced to relocate in order to preserve the original use of the land. Diem became furious upon learning that the refugees were ruining the forests around Dalat and ordered their transfer to the central highlands. Diem planned to return the city to being a tourist center for South Vietnam and to preserve the area as a governmental summer retreat. It was enough for refugees to have to worry about the Viet Minh and the three sects, but the added anxiety of overzealous government officials strained the refugee population even further.[24]

Roger K. Ackley, one of the last members of USOM to be directly involved in Passage to Freedom, outlined what was a deciding factor in continued U.S. involvement in Vietnam and one of the chief legacies of Operation Passage to Freedom. In many respects, his sense of moral obligation helped to justify the United States' attempt at nation building in the Republic of Vietnam in the 1950s and to explain an underlying factor that influenced American escalation policy in the 1960s:

> What would happen if southern Vietnam fell? Of course it is our policy to do everything in our power to be sure it does not fall, and, true enough, the situation is improving, but what if it does fall. I am convinced that morally as well as politically, we are bound to take steps to assist as many as possible in whatever time is permitted to avoid fearful retribution at the hands of the Communists. Be it right or wrong, we have declared ourselves to these people and to the world as encouraging their flight to freedom, and, participating in it. We have therefore, morally married a long term responsibility. Even politically, we must not lose face in the Far East by selling these people short.[25]

On September 9, 1955, Admiral Sabin received the Distinguished Service Medal from the secretary of the navy.[26] During his opening remarks the secretary highlighted the difficulties of such an operation, which was conducted in adverse weather, in a restrictive political climate, and with an unknown country and population. The secretary enumerated the other problems associated with the operation, including the language barrier, logistics, epidemics, and other responsibilities. The honor was one that was much desired, as were the many letters of commendation produced for those who served during the operation. For the navy and civilian personnel who participated during this largest evacuation of refugees known to that time, the awards and accolades were not the motivation. These were individuals who did their job and did it well. Still, it remains a particularity of such a successful operation that the U.S. Navy failed to recognize officially those who served during Operation Passage to Freedom. This first chapter in the American experience in Vietnam demonstrated U.S. resolve and epitomized the dedication of Americans in helping those in need. It was a first chapter that ended in success—one of few that would characterize the remaining American story in Vietnam.

APPENDIXES

APPENDIX A

Ship and Craft Designations and Descriptions

AF   The mission of the stores ship is to provision the ships deployed in the operation. Because of the limited time each ship was involved in the Indochina theater, only one AF was involved in Operation Passage to Freedom.

AGC   The amphibious command ship was specially designed to carry the commander of an amphibious task force and the commander of the parallel echelon of the landing force, together with their staff. It was also constructed and equipped to facilitate the planning and execution of amphibious operations. In addition to the office spaces and planning rooms, these facilities included radio equipment for handling a large volume of communications, map-making facilities for forward area map reproduction, and a photographic laboratory capable of turning out several thousand photographs per day.

AH   The hospital ship's role was to provide medical facilities in support of naval operations. Only one AH was involved during the mission, as most of the other ships possessed medical personnel to care for their ship's complement.

AKA   The assault cargo ship of the amphibious force transported supplies, personnel, and landing craft to unload them for initial assaults.

AKL   The light cargo ship was a lighter version of the cargo ship (AK) and also was charged with transporting supplies, personnel, and landing craft.

AKS   The special cargo ship was designed to serve as an advanced supply base for navy ships when facilities were not available ashore.

AO   The fleet oilers were charged with refueling ships at sea during the operation. The AO also carried mail and personnel in transit to and from the operation area.

APA   The amphibious force assault transport carried troops and landing craft for initial landings. It also evacuated wounded after the first assault phases of a landing operation.

APD   The APD was a high-speed transport, usually a converted destroyer escort, capable of about twenty-one knots maximum sustained speed. It was designed for entering and departing an objective area at relatively high speeds with raiding parties or reinforcements, underwater demolition and reconnaissance teams, or small numbers of troops and equipment on special missions. It also performed escort and convoy duties when troops or underwater demolition teams were not embarked.

AR   The repair ship was used to repair ships damaged in battle as well as provide regular maintenance to ships at sea. It also served in a logistics support role.

ARL   The light repair ship was a lighter version of the AR.

ARS   The rescue and salvage ship was used to assist ships in distress and provide any services necessary toward the recovery of disabled ships.

LCIL The light infantry landing craft was used to transport infantry from ship to shore in a combat situation.

LCM   The mechanized landing craft was much the same as the personnel and vehicle landing craft but was able to carry larger pieces of equipment.

LCU   Amphibious force LCUs were the largest noncommissioned vessels in the force. They were also used to unload cargo directly onto a beach.

LCVP The LCVP carried men, small vehicles, and light artillery to the beach during the first burst of enemy opposition.

LSD   The LSD was a landing ship dry-dock with the twofold mission of dry-docking and effecting repairs to small vessels and landing craft and of carrying to the objective area landing boats, amphibious vehicles, or amphibious trucks that could be discharged rapidly from the well deck.

LSM   The medium landing ship was smaller and more powerful than the tank landing ship. It had much the same uses, but it had an open deck. It was designed to serve complement infantry landing craft (large) (LCIL), with which it could keep pace in order to put tanks ashore immediately following the infantry.

LST   The tank landing ship was the largest amphibious force craft constructed for beaching. It carried full loads of troops and supplies directly to the beach, with bow doors and a ramp for easy access to the beach. The LST was described as a low-lying, shallow-draft, seagoing craft of compact design. Its central feature was a set of water tanks like the ballast tanks of a submarine; when the tanks were filled, they would cause the LST to sit low enough to enable it to cross any sea. The tanks would be blown out as the craft neared its destination on a hostile beach, lifting it higher in the water. It could then send off its heavily equipped men and machines.

T-AK This type of cargo ship, operated by the Marine Sea Transport Service (MSTS), was used in the same capacity as the AK.

T-AP This type of transport ship, operated by the Marine Sea Transport Service (MSTS), was used in the same capacity as the AP

YO   The fuel oil barge was a self-propelled tanker that was charged with replenishing ships with fuel while at sea.

APPENDIX B

★★★★★★★★★★★★★★★★

Ship and Craft Loading Capacity
Personnel

Type	Normal Load	Overload	Emergency Overload
AGC	198	370	1,000
APA	1,460	2,000	5,000
AKA	203	400	1,000
LSD	145	350	750
LST	170	600	1,000
LCU	—	—	200
APD	161	300	400
T-AP	1,400–2,000	3,000	5,000–7,000

APPENDIX C

★★★★★★★★★★★★★★

U.S. Ships and Craft Involved in Operation Passage to Freedom

LCU-531	August 22, 1954–September 27, 1954
LCU-539	August 22, 1954–November 12, 1954
LCU-810	August 22, 1954–September 27, 1954
LCU-877	August 22, 1954–November 12, 1954
LCU-1273	August 22, 1954–September 27, 1954
LCU-1374	August 22, 1954–September 27, 1954
LCU-1387	August 22, 1954–September 27, 1954
LCU-1396	August 22, 1954–September 27, 1954
LCU-1421	August 22, 1954–November 12, 1954
LST-47	December 14, 1954–(?)
LST-176	December 14, 1954–(?)
LST-516	August 27, 1954–November 12, 1954
LST-520	December 15, 1954–(?)
LST-535 (T)	April 1955
LST-546	December 14, 1954–(?)
LST-548 (T)	April 1955
LST-578 (T)	April 1955
LST-629 (T)	April 1955
LST-692	August 26, 1954–October 16, 1954
LST-758	August 26, 1954–September 26, 1954
LST-772	August 27, 1954–November 16, 1954
LST-803	October 24, 1954–November 14, 1954
LST-822	August 26, 1954–October 16, 1954
LST-825	August 26, 1954–October 5, 1954
LST-840	October 29, 1954–November 18, 1954

LST-845	August 26, 1954–October 6, 1954
LST-846	August 27, 1954–September 26, 1954
LST-855	August 27, 1954–November 18, 1954
LST-887	August 27, 1954–September 26, 1954
LST-901	August 27, 1954–November 7, 1954
LST-902	October 17, 1954–November 15, 1954
LST-1080	September 10, 1954–November 13, 1954
LST-1096	August 29, 1954–September 26, 1954
LST-1148	August 29, 1954–September 26, 1954
LST-1159	October 29, 1954–November 17, 1954
SS *Codington*	December 28, 1954–(?)
SS *Culucundis*	September 8, 1954–October 27, 1954
SS *Diddo*	December 25, 1954–January 1955(?)
SS *Hawaiian Bear*	September 10–14, 1954
SS *Hurricane*	September 7–15, 1954
SS *José Martí*	September 13, 1954–November 11, 1954
SS *Sea Splendor*	September 6–15, 1954
SS *Seaborne*	September 1–13, 1954
SS *Steel Marker*	December 11, 1954–(?)
SS *Steel Seafarer*	November 5, 1954–(?)
USNS *Beauregard*	September 1–14, 1954
USNS *Captain Arlo L. Olson* (T-AK-245)	December 13, 1954–(?)
USNS *Fentress* (T-AK-180)	September 7, 1954–December 28, 1954
USNS *General A. W. Brewster* (T-AP-155)	September 10, 1954–November 3, 1954
USNS *General R. L. Howze* (T-AP-134)	September 10, 1954–December 11, 1954
	December 27, 1954–February 1955(?)
USNS *General W. M. Black* (T-AP-135)	September 13, 1954–November 2, 1954
USNS *Hennepin* (T-AK-187)	September 7, 1954–December 1954
USNS *Herkimer* (T-AK-188)	(?)–January 22, 1955
USNS *Marine Adder* (T-AP-193)	September 11, 1954–November 14, 1954
USNS *Marine Lynx* (T-AP-194)	September 13, 1954–October 19, 1954(?)
USNS *Marine Serpent* (T-AP-202)	(?)
USNS *Muskingum* (T-AK-198)	September 8, 1954–October 26, 1954
USNS *Pembina* (T-AK-200)	September 9, 1954–(?)
USNS *Piscataqua* (T-AOG-80)	September 10–26, 1954
USNS *Sword Knot*	December 28, 1954–January 1955(?)
USS *Ajax* (AR-6)	August 23, 1954–September 20, 1954
USS *Diachenko* (APD-123)	(?)
USS *Algol* (AKA-54)	August 15, 1954–September 9, 1954
USS *Aludra* (AF-55)	September 21–23, 1954
USS *Andromeda* (AKA-15)	August 22, 1954–September 16, 1954
USS *Askari* (ARL-30)	October 29, 1954–November 18, 1954
USS *Atlas* (ARL-7)	August 28, 1954–September 26, 1954

USS *Balduck* (APD-132)	October 14, 1954–January 21, 1955
USS *Bayfield* (APA-33)	August 21, 1954–September 9, 1954
USS *Begor* (APD-127)	August 16, 1954–November 15, 1954
USS *Caliente* (AO-53)	August 23, 1954–September 6, 1954
USS *Calvert* (APA-32)	August 22, 1954–October 26, 1954
USS *Castor* (AKS-1)	September 9–19, 1954
USS *Cavallaro* (APD-128)	August 22, 1954–October 20, 1954
USS *Cimarron* (AO-22)	September 5, 1954–October 17, 1954
USS *Comstock* (LSD-19)	August 22, 1954–October 21, 1954
USS *Consolation* (AH-15)	September 4–27, 1954
USS *Cook* (APD-130)	January 20, 1955–(?)
USS *Current* (ARS-22)	October 25, 1954–November 17, 1954
USS *Derrick* (YO-59)	September 9, 1954–November 19, 1954
USS *Epping Forest* (LSD-4)	August 22, 1954–September 27, 1954
USS *Estero* (AKL-5)	September 16, 1954–November 12, 1954
USS *Estes* (AGC-12)	August 18, 1954–November 15, 1954(?)
USS *Faribault* (AK-179)	September 9, 1954–November 19, 1954
USS *Grapple* (ARS-7)	August 26, 1954–September 4, 1954
USS *Gunston Hall* (LSD-5)	January 10, 1955–February 28, 1955
USS *Haven* (AH-12)	September 8–10, 1954
USS *Hooper Island* (ARG-17)	(?)
USS *James E. Kyes* (DD-787)	(?)
USS *Karin* (AF-33)	August 25, 1954–October, 1954
USS *Knudson* (APD-101)	August 22, 1954–October 2, 1954
USS *Magoffin* (APA-199)	August 22, 1954–September 16, 1954
USS *Menard* (APA-201)	August 15, 1954–September 5, 1954
USS *Merapi* (AF-38)	October 6, 1954–November 19, 1954
USS *Montague* (AKA-98)	August 14, 1954–September 9, 1954
USS *Montrose* (APA-212)	August 16, 1954–September 16, 1954
USS *Mountrail* (APA-213)	August 12, 1954–September 11, 1954
USS *Pasig* (AW-3)	October 13, 1954–November 15, 1954
USS *Passumpsic* (AO-107)	September 23–24, 1954
USS *Point Cruz* (CVE-119)	(?)
USS *Reclaimer* (ARS-42)	August 26, 1954–September 19, 1954
USS *Sharps* (AKL-10)	September 10, 1954–October 17, 1954
USS *Skagit* (AKA-105)	August 22, 1954–September 20, 1954
USS *Sphinx* (ARL-24)	August 28, 1954–October 25, 1954
USS *Sussex* (AK-213)	August 25, 1954–September 19, 1954
USS *Taluga* (AO-62)	January 19, 1955–January 23, 1955
USS *Telfair* (APA-210)	August 15, 1954–September 16, 1954
USS *Tolovana* (AO-64)	October 16, 1954–November 15, 1954
USS *Tortuga* (LSD-26)	August 21, 1954–September 27, 1954
USS *Ute* (ATF-76)	September 9–11, 1954

USS *Uvalde* (AKA-88)	August 28, 1954–September 10, 1954
USS *Wantuck* (APD-125)	August 13, 1954–September 4, 1954
USS *Whetstone* (LSD-27)	August 23, 1954–November 12, 1954
USS *Zelima* (AF-49)	November 6–8, 1954
YW-130 (water barge)	August 28, 1954–November 15, 1954

Note: The information represented herein is data collected from the Task Force 90 official reports, the papers of Admiral Sabin, and available deck logs from those ships that participated in the operation. In most cases data is consistent among the sources. There are instances of inconsistent dates; in these cases deck log dates are used. The deck logs for the MSTS ships were destroyed twenty to thirty years after the operation per official retention policies. Data for those ships comes from the official records and from Task Force 90 ship deck logs that note sightings of MSTS ships in the course of their cruises. The same is true for some of the LSTs. Unfortunately, for some ships no data is available, although I was able to confirm that the ship did participate in some capacity during the operation.

NOTES

Chapter 1

1. The formation of early American foreign policy toward the Soviet Union was in part shaped by the World War II experience and the decade following that monumental event in world history. Although that perspective had undergone intensive review and revision by the time the First Indochina War ended in 1954, most American foreign policy makers accepted the analysis of American chargé d'affaires to Moscow George Kennan that he offered in his February 22, 1946, "long telegram" and his famous "Mr. X" article, "The Sources of Soviet Conduct," in *Foreign Affairs*, July 1947, which he wrote as the director of the State Department's Policy Planning Staff. Walter LaFeber, *America, Russia, and the Cold War, 1945–2002,* offers a unique insight into the development of the Cold War mentality in a European context, while George Herring, *America's Longest War: The United States and Vietnam, 1950–1975,* provides similar analysis as it relates to Vietnam. Lloyd C. Gardner, *Approaching Vietnam: From World War II through Dienbienphu, 1941–1954,* also offers a detailed history of American foreign policy during the First Indochina War that examines Cold War mentality.

2. In 1951, members of the original Indochinese Communist Party, which had been dissolved in 1945, resurfaced to organize the Dang Lao Dong Viet Nam (Vietnam Workers Party). It was at that time that the Viet Minh were disbanded and reconstituted as the Lien Hiep Quoc Dan Viet Nam or Lien Viet Front. For more information, see Robert K. Brigham, "Viet Nam Doc Lap Dong Minh Hoi [Vietnam Independence League]," in *The Encyclopedia of the Vietnam War: A Political, Social, and Military History,* ed. Spencer C. Tucker (New York: Oxford University Press, 2000). To understand the rise of Vietnamese nationalism before World War II, see William J. Duiker, *The Rise of Nationalism in Vietnam, 1900–1941.*

3. Robert Buzzanco, "Prologue to Tragedy: U.S. Military Opposition to Intervention in Vietnam, 1950–1954," *Diplomatic History* 17 (2): 201–22.

4. Ellen J. Hammer, *The Struggle for Indo-China, 1940–1954,* 313–15. For additional information on the Navarre Plan and the French political decisions in Indochina leading to their failure at the Battle of Dien Bien Phu, see Bernard B. Fall, *The Two Viet-Nams: A Political and Military Analysis,* 122–27, and Jules Roy, *The Battle of Dienbienphu,* trans. Robert Baldick.

5. For a detailed discussion of Operation Castor, see Bernard B. Fall, *Hell in a Very Small Place: The Siege of Dien Bien Phu,* 1–39.

6. Roy, *Battle of Dienbienphu,* chronicles the Viet Minh trap, as does Fall, *Hell in a Very Small Place.*

7. "Text of Address by Secretary of State Dulles on United States Policy in the Far East," *New York Times,* March 30, 1954, 4.

8. Memorandum for the Secretary's File, April 5, 1954, Conference with Congressional Leaders Concerning the Crisis in Southeast Asia, Saturday, April 3, 1954, John Foster Dulles Chronological Series, April 1954 (3), box 7, Papers of John Foster Dulles, Secretary of State, 1951–1959, Dwight D. Eisenhower Presidential Library, Abilene, Kansas [hereafter referred to as DDE Library]. See also George C. Herring and Richard H. Immerman, "Eisenhower, Dulles, and Dienbienphu, 'The Day We Didn't Go to War,' Revisited," *Journal of American History* 71 (2): 343–63.

9. Department of State to the United States Embassy, London, Telegram 5179, April 4, 1954, President–Churchill, January 1–June 30, 1954 (2), box 19, Papers of Dwight D. Eisenhower (Whitman Files), 1953–1961, International Series, DDE Library.

10. President Eisenhower's News Conference of April 7, 1954, *Public Papers of the Presidents of the United States—Dwight D. Eisenhower: Containing the Public Messages, Speeches, and Statements of the President, January 1 to December 31, 1954,* 381–90. Also parts of this significant speech were references to the Munich Analogy that cautioned against appeasement as well as the economic importance of Japan for Asia and the Pacific. Although these references have captured the attention of historians, the notion of moral obligation as it relates to America's Indochina policy has failed to garner attention in Vietnam War historiography.

11. Dulles to Department of State (President, Acting Secretary, Secretary Wilson, Admiral Radford), DULTE 2, April 22, 1954, Dulles—April 1954 (2), box 2, Dulles-Herter Series, Papers of Dwight D. Eisenhower (Whitman Files), 1953–1961, DDE Library.

12. Eisenhower to Dulles, April 23, 1954, Diaries April 1954 (1), box 6, Dwight D. Eisenhower Diaries, Papers of Dwight D. Eisenhower (Whitman Files), 1953–1961, DDE Library.

13. Dulles to Eisenhower, April 23, 1954, ibid.

14. Dulles to Acting Secretary of State, at Quai D'Orsay dinner, April 23, 1954, ibid.

15. "Points to be made with Eden At 3:30," Indochina May 1953–May 1954 (3), box 8, Subject Series, International Subseries, Papers of John Foster Dulles, Secretary of State, 1951–1959, DDE Library.

16. Memorandum of Conversation, Eden and Dulles et al., April 25, 1954, Dulles—April 1954 (1), box 2, Dulles-Herter Series, Papers of Dwight D. Eisenhower (Whitman Files), 1953–1961, DDE Library.

17. Dulles to Acting Secretary of State (Christian Herter), DULTE 5, April 25, 1954, and Memorandum of Conversation, Eden and Dulles et al., April 25, 1954, ibid.

18. Dulles (Geneva) to Acting Secretary of State, DULTE 3, April 25, 1954, ibid.

19. Dulles (London), to Acting Secretary of State, April 26, 1954, ibid.

20. Dillon (Paris) to Department of State, Incoming Telegram 4089, April 27, 1954, ibid.

21. "Text of Dulles Speech to the Nation on the Geneva Conference," *New York Times*, May 8, 1954, 4.

22. Memorandum of Conversation with the French Ambassador, Henri Bonnet, May 8, 1954, Indochina, May 1953–May 1954 (2), box 8, Subject Series, International Subseries, Papers of John Foster Dulles, Secretary of State, 1951–1959, DDE Library.

23. Dulles to United States Embassy, Paris, May 10, 1954, ibid.

24. Australian Delegation, Geneva, to Department of External Affairs, cablegram GC150 (I.6380), June 1, 1954, 19/311/217, CRS A816/29, Australian National Archives, Canberra, ACT [hereafter referred to as AA].

25. American Section Report, June 2, 1954, 250/10/7/9 PART 3, CRS A1838/2, AA.

26. Australian Delegation, Geneva, to Department of External Affairs, cablegram GC 171 (I.6610), June 7, 1954, 19/311/213, CRS A816/54, and Australian Embassy, Washington (Spender), to Department of External Affairs, cablegram 558, (6570/71), June 5, 1954, TS654/8/3/8 PART 2, CRS A1838/269, AA.

27. Memorandum for Mrs. Ann Whitman, the White House, from John W. Hanes, Jr., "United States Policy on Armed Intervention in Indochina," August 4, 1954, Dulles, John Foster—August 1954, box 4, Dulles-Herter Series, Papers of Dwight D. Eisenhower (Whitman Files), 1953–1961, DDE Library. For a detailed examination of the Geneva Conference, its participants, and a fuller examination of the agreements reached, see the seminal work of Robert Randle, *Geneva 1954: The Settlement of the Indochinese War.*

28. Agreement on the Cessation of Hostilities in Vietnam, July 20, 1954, reprinted in Marvin E. Gettleman, ed., *Viet Nam: History, Documents, and Opinions on a Major World Crisis,* 137–50.

Chapter 2

1. Holiday and Poindexter Field Trip and Inspection Report, undated, Folder 7, "Trips—Field," Box 15, series 1430, RG 469, NA.

2. Carter de Paul Airgram USOM A-20 to USOM, Saigon, February 10, 1954, ibid.

3. The Vietnamese piaster was the currency of the Republic of Vietnam. The Republic of Vietnam piaster had a value of approximately 35 piasters to $1 in U.S. currency.

4. Carter de Paul Airgram USOM A-20 to USOM, Saigon, February 10, 1954, Folder 7, "Trips—Field," Box 15, series 1430, RG 469, NA.

5. William L. Haid, Field Trip to Hue Airgram USOM A-32, February 23, 1954, ibid.

6. Ibid.

7. Richard C. Matheron Trip Report, April 6, 1954, ibid.

8. Richard C. Matheron Trip Report, July 28, 1954, Folder 3, "Reports—Field Reports," Box 3, Series 1452, RG 469, NA.

9. Paul E. Everett Memorandum, "Medical Supplies for Tay Ninh," Folder 13, "Exodus—Materials and Equipment," Box 10, Series 1447, RG 469, NA.

10. Gerald M. Strauss, Airgram, June 25, 1954, and Herman Holiday, Airgram, June 29, 1965, Folder 12, "Exodus—Evacuation Population," ibid.

11. Gerald M. Strauss, Airgrams, July 2, 6, and 9, 1954, and Telegram, USFOTO 8, July 3, 1954, ibid.; USOM response, Telegram, USFOTO 44, July 14, 1954, Folder 13, "Exodus—Materials and Equipment," ibid.

12. Confidential letter to Everett, July 13, 1954, Folder 13, ibid.

13. Hildrus A. Poindexter notes on the Hanoi-Haiphong trip, June 6–9, 1954, Folder 5, "C.C.D. Correspondence and Reports, 1953–1954—Not Classified," Box 1, Series 1455, ibid.

14. H. Reiner Memorandum, "Security—Evacuation of Effects," Folder 7, "Evacuation," Box 3, Series 1434, and Everett to Strauss, July 1, 1954, Folder 11, "Exodus," Box 10, Series 1447, ibid.

15. Everett to Heath, July 10, 1954; Joint Service Attaches to the Counselor of the Embassy, July 15, 1954; Everett to Strauss, July 16, 1954; and Carter de Paul to Strauss, July 26, 1954, Folder 13, "Exodus—Material and Equipment," Box 10, Series 1447, ibid.

16. Poindexter to Peterson, August 10, 1954, Folder 6, "Emergency Relief—Refugee—Reports—2 of 2—FY 1955," Box 11, Series 1441, and memorandum to N. Carter de Paul, July 23, 1954, Folder 12, "Exodus—Evacuation Population," Box 10, Series 1447, ibid.

17. USOM, Saigon Situation Report 6, July 28, 1954, Folder 1, "Refugees—1 of 2, 1954," Box 6, Series 1456, ibid.

18. FOA Press Release, August 5, 1954, Folder 8, "Escapee Program," Box 1, Series 1452, ibid.

19. USOM, Saigon Situation Report 6, "Evacuation Plan for North Vietnam Population," July 28, 1954, Folder 1, "Refugees—1 of 2, 1954," Box 6, Series 1456, ibid.

20. Ibid.

21. Critique of Vietnamese Plan, July 29, 1954, Folder 8, "Resettlement," Box 14, Series 1430, ibid.

22. "Outline of Functional Responsibility," Folder 2, "Refugee Registration," Box 3, Series 1452, ibid.

23. "Outline Plan for Handling Refugees," July 30, 1954, Folder 8, "Resettlement," Box 14, Series 1430, ibid.

24. "Outline of Staff Responsibilities: Staging Center—Haiphong," Folder 2, "Refugee Registration," Box 3, Series 1452, ibid.

25. Report of the Assistant to the Chief of Social Services on His Field Trip to Haiphong, July 28, 1954, Folder 3, "Reports—Field Reports," ibid.

26. Memorandum from Randall Stelly to Carter de Paul, July 28, 1954, Folder 10, "Refugee Letters," Box 2, ibid.

27. Holiday to Adler, "Refugees—North Vietnam," August 2, 1954, Folder 7, "Trips—Field," Box 15, Series 1430, ibid.

28. B. W. Rosenburg, Deputy Chief, Health and Sanitation Division, USOM, to Le Van Khai, Director General of Health and Social Action, August 2, 1954, Folder 4, "Emergency Relief—Refugee—Medical—FY 1955," Box 11, Series 1441, ibid.

29. Holiday to Kurt M. Falk, August 2, 1954, Folder 9, "Exodus—Evacuation Population," and MD and Mann response to Falk, August 3, 1954, ibid.

30. Hue Telegram, August 3, 1954, and response by Paul Q. Peterson, Chief of Health and Sanitation Division, STEM, August 4, 1954, Folder 4, "Emergency Relief—Refugee—Medical—FY 1955," Box 11, ibid.

31. Poindexter to Peterson, August 24, 1954, Folder 6, ibid.

32. FOA Press Release, August 4, 1954, Folder 8, "Escapee Program," Box 1, Series 1452, ibid.

33. Partial Record of Meeting of Department of State Representatives with Joint Chiefs of Staff, August 6, 1954, Folder 8, "PSA, Air Transports to Indochina, 1952–1954," Box 4, Records of the Office of Southeast Asian Affairs (SEA), 1950–1956, entry UD49, RG 59, NA.

34. USOM, Saigon to FOA, August 6, 1954, Folder 13, "Exodus—Materials and Equipment," Box 10, Series 1447, RG 469, NA.

35. Foreign Military Assistance Coordinating Committee Paper, February 12, 1951, Folder 1, "Indochina Agreements, 1951," Box 2, Records Relating to the Mutual Security Assistance Program (Far East), 1949–1954, entry 1393, RG 59, NA.

36. Dr. Poindexter, "Notes on the Health and Sanitation Aspect of the Refugee Operation," August 4, 1954, Folder 3, "Emergency Relief—Refugee—General—2 of 2—FY 1955," Box 11, Series 1441, RG 469, NA.

Chapter 3

1. Operation Order 2-54, August 11, 1954, Command File, Post 1 January 1946, Plans—Amphibious Groups, PHIBGRP1, Series 11, Operational Archives, Naval Historical Center, Washington, D.C. (Hereafter this document is referred to as Operation Order 2-54 and the Naval Historical Center is referred to as NHC.)

2. Annex A, "Task Organization," Operation Order 2-54.

3. Box 141, PHIBGRP1, Series 0252, 8 November 1954, Command File, Post 1 January 1946, NHC.

4. The Military Sealift Transportation Service evolved from World War II when America's armed forces competed for the services of the commercial merchant marine fleet. The details of the MSTS were worked out between the end of the war and 1949, when the organization assumed its responsibilities as the transport arm of the U.S. armed forces. Its ships were manned by civilians. For further description of the MSTS, see Robert S. Mercogliano, "Sealift: The Evolution of American Military Sea Transportation," Ph.D. dissertation, University of Alabama, 2004.

5. Tab A to Appendix II to Annex I, "Embarkation Control Plan," Operation Order 2-54.

6. Annex C, "Intelligence," Operation Order 2-54.

7. Frankum interview with Robert Mix, March 30, 2001.

8. Frankum interviews with Leo Andrade, March 9, 2001; Ray Skinner, February 13, 2001; Fred Machedo, March 5, 2001; and Louis McCluskey, February 28, 2001.

9. Frankum interview with James Chapman, February 15, 2002.

10. Appendix II to Annex C, "Intelligence," Operation Order 2-54.

11. Appendix VI to Annex I, "Debarkation Port Operations," and Tab A to Appendix VI to Annex I, "Unloading Facilities Saigon," Operation Order 2-54.

12. Annex K, "Administrative," Operation Order 2-54.

13. Annex L, "Logistics," Operation Order 2-54.

14. Annex M, "Medical," Operation Order 2-54.

Chapter 4

1. Vietnamese French Committee on Evacuation to the President of Committee on Evacuation of Government Employees; President of Committee on Evacuation of Population, and the Mayor of Hanoi, August 7, 1954, Folder 21, "Evacuation Messages," Box 2, Series 1455, RG 469, NA.

2. Diary entry dated August 8, 1954, Commander Task Force Ninety to the Chief of Naval Operation, War Diary, November 8, 1954, PHIBGRP 1, Serial 0252, Box 141, Command File, Post January 1, 1946, NHC (hereafter referred to as Task Force 90 War Diaries).

3. The following biographical information is from Box 1, Folder 1, "Biographical Data," Papers of Vice Admiral Lorenzo S. Sabin, USN, 1954–1967, NHC.

4. Ibid.

5. Letter from Admiral L. S. Sabin to Vice Admiral T. G. W. Settle, USN, Commander Amphibious Force, U.S. Pacific Fleet, August 25, 1954, Folder 2, "Correspondence, August–September 1954," Box 1, Papers of VADM Lorenzo S. Sabin, USN, 1954–1967, NHC.

6. For a description of the various ships and craft used in Operation Passage to Freedom, see Appendix A.

7. Diary entry, August 9, 1954, Task Force 90 War Diaries.

8. Diary entry, August 10, 1954, Task Force 90 War Diaries.

9. Frankum interviews with Bob Rebbetoy, September 29, 2001; Bob Raftis and Forrest Bussey, September 29, 2001; Ray Bell, September 29, 2001; and Fred Machado, March 5, 2001.

10. Frankum interview with Stan Coito, September 29, 2001.

11. Frankum interview with Mel Hone, September 29, 2001.

12. Cultural disparities include differences in language, culture, religion, and history strengthened by differences in size, skin, and hair color as well as how one views the world. It was difficult for Americans exposed to Vietnam and the Vietnamese for the first time not to notice these differences. The differences between the Americans and Vietnamese were a constant issue during the operation. See Sabin's final report on Operation Passage to Freedom, August 8–November 15, 1954, Part 1, "Narrative," PHILGRP1 Serial 4, January 3, 1955, Command File, Post 1 January 1946, NHC. While little work has been done by Americans on Vietnamese ethnography, an example of differences is explored in Gerald Cannon Hickey's monumental work *Village in Vietnam*. The issue of cultural disparity, though at a period after Operation Passage to Freedom, is also explored by Philip Catton in *Diem's Final Failure: Prelude to America's War in Vietnam*.

13. Letter from Admiral L. S. Sabin to Vice Admiral T. G. W. Settle, USN, Commander Amphibious Force, U.S. Pacific Fleet, August 25, 1954, Folder 2, "Correspondence, August–September 1954," Box 1, Papers of VADM Lorenzo S. Sabin, USN, 1954–1967, NHC.

14. Ibid.

15. Diary entry, August 23, 1954, Task Force 90 War Diaries.

16. Diary entry, August 16, 1954, Task Force 90 War Diaries. See also Frankum written interview with Carl Benning, March 13, 2001, and Frankum interviews with Leo Andrade, March 9, 2001, and Barry King, March 12, 2001.

17. Log Book of USS *Menard*, August 11, 1954, RG 24, NA, and Frankum written interview with Terry Foley, June 23, 2002.

18. Diary entry, August 12, 1954, Task Force 90 War Diaries.

19. Navy Message 150119Z, August 15, 1954, Folder 8, "PSA, Air Transports to Indochina, 1952–1954," Box 4, entry UD49, RG 59, NA.

20. Frankum written interview with Carl Benning, March 13, 2001.

21. Frankum interview with Jack Majesky, March 27, 2001.

22. Frankum written interviews with Carl Benning, March 13, 2001, and Terry Foley.

23. Log Book of USS *Menard*, August 15, 1954, RG 24, NA.

24. Frankum interview with John Ruotsala, February 9, 2001.

25. Frankum interview with Forrest Lockwood, April 16, 2001; see also diary entry, August 17, 1954, Task Force 90 War Diaries.

26. Diary entry, August 17, 1954, Task Force 90 War Diaries.

27. Frankum interviews with Stan Coito, September 29, 2001; Ray Bell, September 29, 2001; Fred Machedo, March 5, 2001; and Doug Richter, September 29, 2001. Task Force 90 War Diaries' entries for August and September discuss the issues of food for refugees and the difficulties faced by the Americans as they sought to feed the Vietnamese refugees in Operation Passage to Freedom.

28. Frankum interview with Leo Andrade, March 9, 2001.

29. Frankum interview with Jim Daniels, February 5, 2001.

30. Admiral Sabin to Admiral H. G. Hopwood, August 16, 1954, Folder 2, "Correspondence, August–September 1954," Box 1, Papers of Vice Admiral Lorenzo S. Sabin, USN, 1954–1967, NHC.

31. Diary entry, August 19, 1954, Task Force 90 War Diaries.

32. Log Book of USS *Montrose*, August 18, 1954, RG 24, NA, and Frankum interview with Ray Skinner, February 13, 2001.

33. Frankum interview with John Ruotsala, February 9, 2001. A similar incident occurred on USS *Calvert* during its August 25–28, 1954, trip. Diary entry September 2, 1954, Task Force 90 War Diaries.

34. Frankum interview with John Ruotsala, February 9, 2001.

35. Frankum interview with Eugene Mauch, February 12, 2001. Although there are no references to Dr. Mauch's story, many similar stories are told by Vietnamese of Americans' gaining their trust and confidence during the operation. This is also evident in the few films taken during the operation, which have been deposited with the Vietnam Archive at Texas Tech University.

36. Frankum interview with Eugene Mauch, February 12, 2001.

37. The issue of cleanliness was important during the operation. Many Vietnamese arrived at the embarkation point very dirty, and Americans distributed cakes of soap to them. Diary entry, August 29, 1954, Task Force 90 War Diaries.

38. Diary entry, August 18, 1954, Task Force 90 War Diaries.

39. Frankum interview with Forrest Lockwood, April 16, 2001.

40. Frankum interview with Mel Hone, April 25, 2001

41. Telegram from COMNAVPHIL to CTF-90, August 21, 1954, Folder 7, "Messages, August 24, 1954–May 1955," Box 1, Papers of Vice Admiral Lorenzo S. Sabin, USN, 1954–1967, NHC.

42. USS *Bayfield* (APA-33) to CINCPACFLT, CHINFO, and COMNAVPHIL, August 24, 1954, Folder 7, "Messages, August 24, 1954–May 1955," Box 1, Papers of Vice Admiral Lorenzo S. Sabin, USN, 1954–1967, NHC.

43. Frankum interviews with John Ruotsala, February 9, 2001, and Joe Gambone, February 23, 2001.

44. Frankum interviews with Bob Raftis and Forrest Bussey, September 29, 2001.

45. Frankum interview with James Chapman, February 15, 2002.

46. Frankum interviews with Roy Constant, February 12, 2001, and Jim Daniels, February 5, 2002.

47. Frankum interview with Willy Carrillo, January 31, 2002.

48. Sabin to Burke, "Report of Evacuation Operations in Vietnam," Part II, Chronology of Events, August 26, 1954, PHIBGRP1 Serial: 4, January 3, 1955, Box 141, Command File, Post 1 January 1946, NHC. The significant Chinese minority in Vietnam had settled there for a variety of reasons, including the need to escape persecution in China and the prospect of a better life in Vietnam. Those Chinese in the North feared Viet Minh retribution for their support of the French or their anticommunist sentiment.

Chapter 5

1. Starr to Acting Special Deputy for Refugee Affairs, August 10, 1954, Folder 9, "Reception Center," Box 2, Series 1452, RG 469, NA.

2. Evacuations through August 12, 1954, Bulletin 1, Folder 2, "Refugees—2 of 2, 1954," Box 6, Series 1456, and Meeting Notes of August 12, 1954, Folder 8, "Escapee Program, " Box 1, Series 1452, RG 469, NA.

3. Notes of Meeting at Ministere de l'Economie Nationale, August 17, 1954, Folder 8, "Escapee Program," Box 1, Series 1452, ibid.

4. Wells C. Klein to Richard Brown, August 18, 1954, Folder 10, "Refugee Letters," Box 2, ibid., and, Lavergne to STEM Staff, Bulletin #2, August 19, 1954, Folder 2, "Refugees—2 of 2, 1954," Box 6, Series 1456, ibid.

5. Report of Conference at the Red Cross School of Nursing, August 28, 1954, Folder 6, "Emergency Relief—Refugee—Reports—2 of 2—FY 1955," Box 11, Series 1441, ibid.

6. Agreement between the Government of Vietnam and Cooperative for American Remittances to Everywhere, Inc., August 9, 1954, Folder 2, "Refugees—2 of 2, 1954," Box 6,

Series 1456, and S. M. Keeny, Director, UNICEF, ARO, to Heath, August 9, 1954, Folder 10, "Refugee Letters," Box 2, Series 1452, ibid.

7. Thelen to Chief, CDD, August 18, 1954, Folder 3, "Reports—Field Reports," Box 3, ibid.

8. John P. Thelen to Chief, CDD, August 19, 1954, and August 20, 1954. Both reports in Folder 3, "Reports—Field Reports," Box 3, ibid.

9. Thelen to Holiday, August 21, 1954, Folder 3, "Reports—Field Reports," ibid.

10. Thelen to Holiday, August 24, 1954, Folder 6, "Emergency Relief—Refugee—Reports—2 of 2—FY 1955," Box 11, Series 1441, ibid.

11. Peterson to Chief, Program and Requirements Division, August 27, 1954, Folder 3, "Emergency Relief—Refugee—General—2 of 2—FY 1955," ibid.

12. Report of the Refugees Coordinating Committee, August 27, 1954, Folder 2, "Refugees—2 of 2, 1954," Box 6, Series 1456, ibid.

13. Earle to Nyland, August 30, 1954, Folder 12, "Exodus—Resettlement," Box 11, Series 1446, ibid.

14. Field Trip Report from C. A. Mann to P. E. Everett, August 10, 1954, ibid., and Field Trip Report from John A. Hackett to Captain Wyland, Chief, TCI&M Division, August 13, 1954, Folder 2, "Refugees—2 of 2, 1954," Box 6, Series 1456, ibid.

15. Kotcher to Paul Q. Peterson, Chief, Health and Sanitation Division, August 13, 1954, Folder 8, "Resettlement," Box 14, Series 1430, ibid.

16. Yergen to Peterson, August 31, 1954, Folder 6, "Emergency Relief—Refugee—Reports—2 of 2—FY 1955," Box 11, Series 1441, ibid.

17. Memorandum from the Community Development Division to Everett, August 10, 1954, Folder 5, "C.C.D. Correspondence and Reports, 1953–1954—Not Classified," Box 1, Series 1455, ibid.

18. Memorandum from Holiday to Special Deputy for Refugee Affairs, August 12, 1954, Folder 9, "Reception Center," Box 2, Series 1452, ibid.

19. Holiday to Brown, August 17, 1954, Folder 8, "Resettlement," Box 14, Series 1430, ibid.

20. D. C. Lavergne to Holiday, August 23, 1954, ibid.

21. Heath to Dulles, August 25, 1954, Folder 3, "Cables Incoming, 1954," Box 1, Series 1455, ibid.

22. Vietnam Press, August 24, 1954, Folder 2, "Refugees—2 of 2, 1954," Box 6, Series 1456, ibid.

23. Brown and Campbell to D. C. Lavergne, August 16, 1954, and Holiday to Acting Special Deputy for Refugee Affairs, August 20, 1954, Folder 3, "Reports—Field Reports," Box 3, Series 1452, ibid.

24. Dinh Trinh Chinh to Chief, Program Support Division, Field Trip to Hanoi, August 24–August 31, 1954, Folder 13, "Exodus—Materials and Equipment," Box 10, Series 1447, ibid.

25. Letter from Admiral L. S. Sabin to Admiral Felix B. Stump, August 24, 1954, OO Files, 1954, Box 8, Admiral Carney Personal File, Operational Archives, NHC. Issues regarding the Viet Minh's use of propaganda, and the role of propaganda in general, to

thwart the flow of Vietnamese from the Democratic Republic of Vietnam to the Republic of Vietnam are frequently examined during the operation. See diary entries, August 24 and 25 and September 12, 17, and 29, Task Force 90 War Diaries; Sabin to Burke, "Report of Evacuation Operations in Vietnam," Part II, Chronology of Events, November 20 and December 29, 1954, PHIBGRP1 Serial: 055, June 15, 1955, Box 141, Command File, Post 1 January 1946, NHC.

26. Frankum interview with George Dowd, March 13, 2001.

27. Frankum interview with James Chapman, February 15, 2002. See also Folder 9, "Papers on Operation Passage to Freedom, undated and 1955, Box 2, Papers of Vice Admiral Lorenzo S. Sabin, 1954–1967, NHC, for similar accounts.

28. Frankum interview with Jim Daniels, February 5, 2002.

Chapter 6

1. Admiral Sabin to Admiral Carney, Chief of Naval Operations, September 25, Folder 2, "Correspondence, August–September 1954," Box 1, Papers of VADM Lorenzo S. Sabin, Operational Archives, NHC.

2. Diary entry, September 2, 1954, Task Force 90 War Diaries.

3. Diary entry, September 1, 1954, Task Force 90 War Diaries.

4. Ibid.

5. Diary entry, September 2, 1954, Task Force 90 War Diaries.

6. Frankum interviews with Dr. Eugene Mauch, February 12, 2001, and Louis Gilbert, February 4, 2002.

7. Diary entry, September 3, 1954, Task Force 90 War Diaries.

8. Leslie H. Boyd, Acting Special Representative to Cambodia, to Everett, September 4, 1954, Folder 13, "Exodus—Materials and Equipment," Box 10, Series 1447, RG 469, NA.

9. Diary entry, September 6, 1954, Task Force 90 War Diaries.

10. Ibid.

11. Diary entry, September 4, 1954, Task Force 90 War Diaries.

12. Frankum interviews with Willy Carrillo, January 31, 2002, and John Ruotsala, February 9, 2001.

13. Frankum interviews with Fred Machado, March 5, 2001, and Eugene Mauch, February 12, 2001.

14. Frankum interview with Chester Perczynski, September 29, 2001.

15. Frankum interview with Louis Gilbert, February 4, 2002.

16. Diary entry, September 4, 1954, Task Force 90 War Diaries.

17. Diary entry, September 6, 1954, Task Force 90 War Diaries.

18. Frankum interview with Anne Peterson, March 1, 2001.

19. Diary entry, September 27, 1954, Task Force 90 War Diaries.

20. Diary entry, September 4, 1954, Task Force 90 War Diaries.

21. Diary entry, September 11, 1954, Task Force 90 War Diaries; Memorandum from G. Dickey to Admiral Sabin, September 10, 1954, Folder 2, "Correspondence, August–September 1954," Box 1, Papers of VADM Lorenzo S. Sabin, USN, 1954–1967, NHC.

22. Diary entry, September 22, 1954, Task Force 90 War Diaries.

23. USOM, Saigon, to Secretary of State John Foster Dulles, September 13, 1954, Folder 12, "Exodus—Evacuation Population," Box 10, Series 1447, RG 469, NA.

24. Sabin to Stump, September 15, 1954, Folder 2, "Correspondence, August–September 1954," Box 1, Papers of Vice Admiral Lorenzo S. Sabin, USN, 1954–1967, Operational Archives, NHC.

25. Although the medical officer is not specifically mentioned in the report, it is most likely that he was Dr. Thomas A. Dooley.

26. Cameron to Everett, Telegram 241, September 8, 1954, Folder 3, "Cables Incoming, 1954," Box 1, Series 1455, RG 469, NA.

27. STEM, Haiphong, to Lavergne, September 9, 1954, Folder 3, "Cablegrams—Incoming, 1954–1955," Box 1, Series 1452, ibid.

28. Diary entry, September 14, 1954, Task Force 90 War Diaries.

29. Diary entry, September 17, 1954, Task Force 90 War Diaries.

30. Diary entry, September 18, 1954, Task Force 90 War Diaries.

31. Stansbury to Sabin, September 14, 1954, Folder 2, "Correspondence, August–September 1954," Box 1, Papers of Vice Admiral Lorenzo S. Sabin, USN, 1954–1967, Operational Archives, NHC.

32. Andrews to Sabin, October 2, 1954, and Sabin to Stansbury, October 4, 1954, Folder 3, "Correspondence, October–December 1954," Box 1, Papers of Vice Admiral Lorenzo S. Sabin, USN, 1954–1967, Operational Archives, NHC.

33. COMPHIBGRU ONE to BUPERS, September 15, 1954, Folder 2, "Correspondence, August–September 1954," ibid.

34. Frankum interview with Roy Constant, February 12, 2001.

35. Frankum interview with Stan Coito, September 29, 2001.

36. Sabin to Stump, September 15, 1954, Folder 2, "Correspondence, August–September 1954," Box 1, Papers of Vice Admiral Lorenzo S. Sabin, USN, 1954–1967, Operational Archives, NHC.

37. Diary entry, September 21, 1954, Task Force 90 War Diaries.

38. Diary entry, September 18, 1954, Task Force 90 War Diaries.

39. Diary entry, September 21, 1954, Task Force 90 War Diaries.

40. Frankum written interview with Carl Benning, March 13, 2001.

41. Diary entry, October 2, 1954, Task Force 90 War Diaries.

42. Frankum interviews with Morris Smith, February 24 and March 12, 2001.

43. Frankum interview with Ted Zeigler, February 16, 2001.

44. Ibid.

45. Diary entry, September 25, 1954, Task Force 90 War Diaries.

46. "Ship-Days by Type through 30 September 1954," Folder 9, "Evacuation Plans," Box 1, Series 1452, RG 469, NA.

47. Diary entry, September 30, 1954, Task Force 90 War Diaries.

48. Diary entry, September 29, 1954, Task Force 90 War Diaries.

49. Diary entry, October 5, 1954, Task Force 90 War Diaries; Admiral Sabin to Admiral Carney, "Evacuation Operations in Vietnam," January 3, 1955, Part II, Chronology of

Events, Box 141, PHIBGRP1 Serial 4: January 3, 1955, Command File, Post 1 January 1946, Operational Archives, NHC.

50. Diary entry, October 5, 1954, Task Force 90 War Diaries.

51. Diary entry, October 7, 1954, Task Force 90 War Diaries.

52. Heath to Sabin, October 12, 1954, Folder 3, "Correspondence, October–December 1954," Box 1, Papers of Vice Admiral Lorenzo S. Sabin, USN, 1954–1967, Operational Archives, NHC.

Chapter 7

1. Refugee Affairs to STEM Staff, Bulletin #6, September 2, 1954, Folder 2, "Refugees—2 of 2, 1954," Box 6, Series 1456, RG 469, NA.

2. Ibid.

3. Poindexter to Lavergne, September 2, 1954, Folder 10, "Refugee Letters," Box 2, Series 1452," ibid.

4. Brown to Everett, September 2, 1954, Folder 2, "Miscellaneous—1 of 2," Box 2, ibid.

5. Diary entry, September 3, 1954, Task Force 90 War Diaries.

6. Diary entry, September 9, 1954, Task Force 90 War Diaries.

7. Holiday to Brown, September 10, 1954, Folder 3, "Miscellaneous—2 of 2," Box 2, Series 1452, RG 469, NA.

8. R. E. L. Countes to H. J. Holiday, September 3, 1954, Folder 2, "Refugees—2 of 2, 1954," Box 6, Series 1456, ibid.

9. Diary entry, September 7, 1954, Task Force 90 War Diaries.

10. O'Daniel to CINCPACFLT, September 10, 1954, Folder 21, "Evacuation Messages," Box 2, Series 1455, RG 469, NA.

11. Adler to Brown, Telegram, Haiphong 16, September 19, 1954, Folder 3, "Cables Incoming, 1954," Box 1, ibid.

12. Refugee Affairs Bulletin 11, September 14, 1954, Folder 2, "Refugees—2 of 2, 1954," Box 6, Series 1456, and Everett to Dulles, September 14, 1954, Folder 12, "Exodus—Evacuation Population," Box 10, Series 1447, RG 469, NA.

13. Dymsza to Lavergne, September 28, 1954, Folder 12, "Exodus—Resettlement," Box 11, Series 1446, ibid.

14. Acting Special Representative to Central Vietnam W. A. Dymsza to Special Deputy for Refugee Affairs, September 13, 1954, and Dymsza to Everett, September 13, 1954, ibid.

15. Notes of Resettlement of Ben Tre and Project of Resettlement of Refugees in Ben Tre, Folder 2, "Miscellaneous—1 of 2," Box 2, Series 1452, ibid.

16. Diary entry, September 12, Task Force 90 War Diaries.

17. Poindexter to Peterson, September 13, 1954, Folder 6, "Emergency Relief—Refugee—Reports—2 of 2—FY 1955," Box 11, Series 1441, RG 469, NA.

18. Bien Hoa Chief of Province Ho Bao Thanh, September 21, 1954, Folder 8, "Resettlement," Box 14, Series 1430, ibid.

19. Report of the Division Chiefs' Meeting, Bulletin 13, September 24, 1954, Folder 12, "Exodus—Resettlement," Box 11, Series 1446, ibid.

20. Notes on the Division Chiefs' Meeting, September 24, 1954, Folder 2, "Refugees—2 of 2, 1954," Box 6, Series 1456, ibid.

21. Alfred L. Cardinaux to Paul Everett, October 1, 1954, Folder 2, "Miscellaneous—1 of 2," Box 2, Series 1452, ibid.

22. Plan of Action of the Project, October 12, 1954, Folder 2, "Emergency Relief—Refugees—General, FY 1955," Box 11, Series 1441, ibid.

23. H. M. Pascal to D. C. Lavergne, "Trip to Phu-Tho and to Hospital Populaire," October 1, 1954, Folder 3, "Reports—Field Reports," Box 3, Series 1452, and "Report on the Meeting for Organization of Public Health," October 2, 1954, Folder 6, "Emergency Relief—Refugee—Reports—2 of 2—FY 1955," Box 11, Series 1441, ibid.

24. Acting Director of Mission to Division Chiefs, "Topic for Staff Meeting, Friday, October 8," October 7, 1954, Folder 1, "Meetings," Box 2, Series 1452, ibid.

25. Hilbert to Peterson, "Report of Trips," October 12, 1954, Folder 8, "Resettlement," Box 14, Series 1430, ibid.

26. STEM circular, September 22, 1954, Folder 3, "Emergency Relief—Refugee—General—2 of 2—FY 1955," Box 11, Series 1441, ibid.

Chapter 8

1. Diary entry, October 16, 1954, Task Force 90 War Diaries.

2. The Tet holiday, which is tied to the lunar new year, commenced on January 23 in 1955.

3. Diary entry, October 19, 1954, Task Force 90 War Diaries.

4. Diary entry, October 18, 1954, Task Force 90 War Diaries.

5. Embassy of Vietnam, "Viet Minh Violations of the Geneva Armistice Agreement," Folder 5, "Geneva Conference—Viet Minh Violations of the Geneva Agreements, 1955," Box 2, entry UD49, RG 59, NA.

6. Ibid. See also diary entry, September 26, 1954, Task Force 90 War Diaries.

7. Embassy of Vietnam, "Viet Minh Violations of the Geneva Armistice Agreement," Folder 5, "Geneva Conference—Viet Minh Violations of the Geneva Agreements, 1955," Box 2, entry UD49, RG 59, NA. See also diary entry, September 29, 1954, Task Force 90 War Diaries.

8. Adler to STEM, Saigon, Telegram H-41, October 27, 1954; Telegram H-42, October 27, 1954; Telegram H-45, October 28, 1954, Folder 3, "Cables Incoming, 1954," Box 1, Series 1455, RG 469, NA.

9. Ibid.

10. See Dr. Thomas Dooley, *Deliver Us from Evil: The Story of Viet Nam's Flight to Freedom.*

11. Annex I, "Testimony Taken from Refugees from Bui Chu," November 8 and 9, 1954, Embassy of Vietnam, "Viet Minh Violations of the Geneva Armistice Agreement," Folder 5, "Geneva Conference—Viet Minh Violations of the Geneva Agreements, 1955," Box 2, entry UD49, RG 59, NA.

12. Ibid.

13. Ibid.

14. Ibid.

15. Department of State, Joint Weeka 46, November 1954, Folder 12, "ICC—Indochina 2, 1954," Box 2, entry UD49, RG 59, NA.

16. "Viet Minh Compliance with Geneva Accords," Folder 12, "ICC—Indochina 2, 1954," Box 2, ibid. On the question of adherence to the Geneva Accords, one can easily make the case that all sides, in various forms, violated the spirit, if not the word, of the agreements. Although the United States did not sign the document, it did publicly announce its intention to respect the agreements as long as the North Vietnamese did the same. When evidence to the contrary mounted during the course of Operation Passage to Freedom, some U.S. action also had the appearance of violating the spirit of the agreements. Neither side was perfect; neither side was without fault.

17. Daily Intelligence Briefing No. 1,442, October 21, 1954, and Confidential message from USARMA Phnom Penh to DEPTAR Washington, October 21, 1954, Folder 12, "ICC—Indochina, 1954," Box 2, entry UD49, RG 59, NA.

18. Heath to Dulles, October 29, 1954, Folder 3, "Cables Incoming, 1954," Box 1, Series 1455, RG 469, NA.

19. Richard P. Butrick, Consul General of the United States of America to R. Douglas Stuart, United States Ambassador to Canada, November 6, 1954, and International Control Commission, Saigon 45, November 7, 1954, Folder 12, "ICC—Indochina 2, 1954," Box 2, entry UD49, RG 59, NA.

20. Sabin to Settle, October 18, 1954, Folder 3, "Correspondence, October–December 1954," Box 1, Papers of Vice Admiral Lorenzo S. Sabin, USN, 1954–1967, Operational Archives, NHC.

21. Ibid.

22. Ross to Acting Deputy for Refugee Affairs, "Field Trip—Bien Hoa—18 October," October 21, 1954, Folder 6, "Emergency Relief—Refugee—Reports—2 of 2—FY 1955," Box 11, Series 1441, RG 469, NA.

23. The Aided Self Help Housing Program provided the materials and tools necessary for the refugees to build their own dwellings. Not only was this system more economical, but it also was believed to instill a greater sense of self-ownership through the building process.

24. Bruhns to Lavergne, "Refugee Installations in North Central Vietnam," November 12, 1954, Folder 5, "Emergency Relief—Refugee—Reports—1 of 2—FY 1955," ibid.

25. South Vietnamese Director of Health Dang Ngoc Trong to General Commissioner for Refugee Affairs Mr. Doi, October 20, 1954, Folder 4, "Emergency Relief—Refugee—Medical—FY 1955," ibid.

26. Poindexter to Peterson, November 8, 1954, Folder 6, "Emergency Relief—Refugee—Reports—2 of 2—FY 1955," ibid.

27. "2nd Report on the Operation," Operation Fraternite, Jeune Chambre Internationale, Mission Medicale des Jaycees des Philippines," Folder 4, "Emergency Relief—Refugee—Medical—FY 1955," ibid.

28. Confidential memorandum on North Vietnamese Refugees, Folder 12, "ICC—Indochina 2, 1954," Box 2, entry UD49, RG 59, NA.

29. J. G. French to Paul E. Everett, "Report of Survey Made at Haiphong—October 19 through October 22," Folder 13, "Exodus—Materials and Equipment," Box 10, Series 1447, RG 469, NA.

30. Adler to STEM Saigon, Telegram, Haiphong 39, October 25, 1954, Folder 1, "Evacuation—Haiphong, 1955," Box 11, Series 1456, ibid.

31. Ely Report on the current situation of shipping, October 31, 1954, Folder 3, "Correspondence, October–December 1954," Box 1, Papers of Vice Admiral Lorenzo S. Sabin, USN, 1954–1967, Operational Archives, NHC.

32. Sabin to Admiral Will, November 15, 1954; Sabin to Admiral Settle, November 22, 1954; and Sabin to Settle, December 18, 1954, ibid.

33. Stage to Peterson, November 12, 1954, Folder 3, "Reports—Field Reports," Box 3, Series 1452, RG 469, NA.

34. Stassen to STEM, Saigon, USFOTO 565, November 5, 1954, Folder 12, "Exodus—Evacuation Population," Box 10, Series 1447, ibid.

35. CINCPACFLT to CTF 90, November 17, 1954, Folder 7, "Messages, August 24, 1954–May 1955," Box 1, Papers of Vice Admiral Lorenzo S. Sabin, USN, 1954–1967, Operational Archives, NHC.

36. Sabin to Spellman, January 1, 1955, Folder 3, "Correspondence, October–December 1954," ibid.

Chapter 9

1. Admiral Sabin to Admiral Carney, "Evacuation Operations in Vietnam," June 15, 1955: Part II, Chronology of Events, Box 141—PHIBGRP1 Serial 4: 15 June 1955, Command File, Post 1 January 1946, Operational Archives, NHC.

2. USARMA Haiphong to Department of the Army, November 16, 1954, Folder 12, "ICC—Indochina 2, 1954," Box 2, entry UD49, RG 59, NA.

3. ASTUSARMA Haiphong Telegram MC-683-54, November 20, 1954, ibid.; STEM, Haiphong Telegram 51, November 21, 1954, Folder 3, "Cables Incoming, 1954," Box 1, Series 1455, RG 469, NA.

4. November 15, 1954, Memorandum and Report titled, "Nature and Reasons for Viet Minh Cease Fire Violations," Folder 12, "ICC—Indochina 2, 1954," Box 2, entry UD49, RG 59, NA.

5. Weiner to Peterson, Trip Report, November 15, 1954, Folder 3, "Reports—Field Reports," Box 3, Series 1452, RG 469, NA.

6. Bette Moyle to R. W. Safford, Chief of Program Support, November 29, 1954, Folder 4, "Emergency Relief—Refugee—Medical—FY 1955," Box 11, Series 1441, ibid.

7. Peterson to Lavergne, December 3, 1954, ibid.

8. Stassen to STEM, Saigon, USFOTO 604 and USFOTO 605, November 16, 1954, Folder 3, "Cables Incoming, 1954," Box 1, Series 1455, RG 469, NA.

9. Ross to Chief, Community Development Division, Field Trip to Nha Trang, Khanh Hoa province, November 18, 1954, Folder 7, "Trips—Field," Box 15, Series 1430, ibid.

10. Dymsza to Leland Barrows, Director of the Mission, November 22, 1954, Folder 15, "Refugees, 1954–1956 (Administratively Controlled)," Box 3, Series 1455, ibid.

11. The CIMAVI was a general cargo transport that measured approximately one hundred meters long.

12. O'Daniel to MAAG, Haiphong, "Evacuation Policy for Civilian Material," November 30, 1954, Folder 19, "Evacuation—Commodities—Classified," Box 2, Series 1455, RG 469, NA.

13. STEM Weekly Report, December 13, 1954, Folder 7, "Weekly—Haiphong, 1954–1955—Classified," Box 5, ibid.

14. John Thelen, Problems Position Paper, Folder 2, "Miscellaneous—1 of 2," Box 2, Series 1452, ibid.

15. Official Report of the High Board for Refugees, December 6, 1954, Folder 1, "Meetings," ibid.

16. T. J. Farrell, Community Development Division, to D. C. Lavergne, Deputy Director for Resettlement and Rehabilitation, Refugee Situation Analysis, Folder 2, "Miscellaneous—1 of 2," ibid.

17. Meeting Summary, December 14, 1954, Folder 1, "Meetings," ibid.

18. Bowden telephone call, December 9, 1954, Folder 2, "Refugees—2 of 2, 1954," Box 6, Series 1456, ibid.

19. Second Interim Report of the International Commission for Supervision and Control in Vietnam, December 11, 1954–February 10, 1955, Folder 4, "ICC—Vietnam—Third Interim Report, 1955," Box 3, entry UD49, RG 59, NA.

Conclusion

1. Holiday to Barrows, January 24, 1955, Folder 15, "Refugees, 1954–1955–1956 (Administratively Controlled), Box 3, Series 1455, RG 469, NA.

2. Folder 11, "Reports on Evacuation of Refugees and Materials from Vietnam (North), ca. 1955," Box 1, Papers of Vice Admiral Lorenzo S. Sabin, 1954–1967, Operational Archives, NHC.

3. Adler to Lavergne, Field Report 48, February 1, 1955, Folder 1, "Reports—Field—Classified Nos. 17-492—12/10/1954–10/17/1955," Box 5, Series 1455, RG 469, NA.

4. Adler to Ackley, Telegram, February 1, 1955, Folder 19, "Evacuation—Commodities—Classified," Box 2, ibid.

5. Ackley, Weekly Report—Haiphong, February 4, 1955, Folder 7, "Weekly—Haiphong, 1954–1955—Classified," Box 5, ibid.

6. Report of the Evacuation Operations in Vietnam, Part I, Narrative, June 15, 1955, Command File, Post 1 January 1946, Box 141, File "PHIBGRP1 Serial 4, January 3, 1955," Operational Archives, NHC.

7. Adler to Lavergne, Mr. Ackley's Report of January 30, February 1, 1955, Folder 1, "Reports—Field—Classified Nos. 17-492—12/10/1954–10/17/1955," Box 5, Series 1455, RG 469, NA.

8. Ackley Confidential Report on Father Khue, February 3, 1955, Folder 7, "Weekly—Haiphong, 1954–1955—Classified," ibid.

9. Sabin to Vice Admiral T. G. W. Settle, Commander Amphibious Force, Pacific Fleet,

February 14, 1955, Folder 4, "Correspondence, 1955," Box 1, Papers of VADM Lorenzo S. Sabin, 1954–1967, Operational Archives, NHC.

10. Chief, Industry and Mining Division, to the Director of Mission, February 7, 1955, Folder 18, "Evacuation—Commodities, 1955 (Administratively Controlled)," Box 2, and, Haiphong Weekly Report, February 16, 1955, Folder 16, "Weekly—Haiphong, 1955 (Administratively Controlled)," Box 5, Series 1455, RG 469, NA.

11. Commander, Task Force 90.8 to CINCPACFLT, Situation Report 131, February 12, 1955, Folder 5, "Navy Situation—Classified—1954–1955," ibid.

12. Weekly Report—Haiphong, March 7, 1955, Folder 16, "Weekly—Haiphong, 1955 (Administratively Controlled)," ibid.; and USOM Saigon to USOM Haiphong, Telegram, March 11, 1955, Folder 19, "Evacuation—Commodities—Classified," Box 2, ibid.

13. Sabin Letter, March 14, 1955, Folder 4, "Correspondence, 1955," Box 1, Papers of VADM Lorenzo S. Sabin, 1954–1967, Operational Archives, NHC.

14. Weekly Report—Haiphong, March 7, 1955, and USOM Haiphong to USOM Saigon, March 14, 1955, Folder 16, "Weekly—Haiphong, 1955 (Administratively Controlled)," Box 5, Series 1455, RG 469, NA.

15. Weekly Report—Haiphong, March 29, 1955, ibid.

16. Poulin to Adler, undated, and Field Report 160, undated, ibid.

17. Protocol No. 29, Transfer of Civil Administration, Haiphong Perimeter," Folder 1, "ICC—Vietnam—Canadian Letters," Box 3, entry UD49, RG59, NA.

18. USARMA HMA-32-55, May 6, 1955, and Joint Weeka 18, May 8, 1955, Folder 8, "Collins Mission—Telegrams, May–June 1955," Box 1, ibid.

19. Dr. Thomas A. Dooley Medical Situation Report for May 8, 1955, Thomas A. Dooley Collection, Series 2—Vietnam, 1954–1956, Special Collection Library, University of Missouri at Saint Louis.

20. CTG 50.1 to CINCPACFLT, Sitrep 185, May 16, 1954, Folder 5, "Navy Situation—Classified, 1954–1955," Box 5, Series 1455, RG 469, NA.

21. Data for Weeka, June 3, 1955, Folder 14, "Reports—Weeka, 1955 (Administratively Controlled)," ibid.

22. Poulin to Adler, "First Report on the Escapee Situation at the 17th Parallel," July 1, 1955, Folder 13, "Reports—Field—General (2)—Administratively Controlled," ibid.

23. Cardinaux to Palmer, "Sabotage of Refugee Resettlement Program," August 8, 1955, Folder 15, "Refugees, 1954–1955–1956," Box 3, ibid.

24. Evans to Adler, "Field Report No. FS-752," January 27, 1956, and Thelen to Adler, Field Report No. FS-1087," May 7, 1956, Folder 2 "Field Reports—Central Vietnam—classified, 1955–1956," Box 4, ibid.

25. Roger Ackley, "Subject—Escapeee Planning in Vietnam," February 22, 1955, Folder 7, "Weekly—Haiphong, 1954–1955," Box 5, ibid.

26. Secretary of the Navy remarks, September 9, 1955, Folder 4, "Correspondence 1955," Box 1, Papers of Vice Admiral Lorenzo S. Sabin, 1954–1967, Operational Archives, NHC.

BIBLIOGRAPHY

Primary Documents

Australian National Archives, Canberra, ACT
> Department of Defence [III], Central Office (1942–1957), A816 Correspondence file,
> multiple number series (Classified 301), 1935–1958.
> Department of External Affairs, Central Office (1948–1970), A1838 Correspondence
> file, multiple number series, 1948–1989.

Dwight D. Eisenhower Presidential Library, Abilene, Kansas
> Papers of Dwight D. Eisenhower (Whitman Files), 1953–1961
>> Dulles-Herter Series
>> Dwight D. Eisenhower Diaries, April 1954 (1), box 6, April 23, 1954.
>> International Series
> Papers of John Foster Dulles, Secretary of State, 1951–1959
>> John Foster Dulles Chronological Series
>> Subject Series, International Subseries, Indochina

National Archives and Records Administration, College Park, Maryland. Records of the
Bureau of Naval Personnel. RG24.
> Deck Logs
>> LST-822
>> LST-887
>> LST-901
>> LST-1096
>> USS *Ajax* (AR-6)
>> USS *Algol* (AKA-54)
>> USS *Aludra* (AF-55)
>> USS *Andromeda* (AKA-15)
>> USS *Askari* (ARL-30)
>> USS *Balduck* (APD-132)
>> USS *Bayfield* (APA-33)
>> USS *Calvert* (APA-32)
>> USS *Current* (ARS-22)
>> USS *Gunston Hall* (LSD-5)
>> USS *Magoffin* (APA-199)

USS *Menard* (APA-201)

USS *Montague* (AKA-98)

USS *Montrose* (APA-212)

USS *Mountrail* (APA-213)

USS *Skagit* (AKA-105)

USS *Telfair* (APA-210)

USS *Uvalde* (AKA-88)

National Archives and Records Administration, College Park, Maryland. General Records
of the Department of State. RG 59.

   Bureau of Far Eastern Affairs (Files Relating to Southeast Asia and the Geneva
      Conference), 1954, entry 1200.

   Central Decimal Files (751G), 1955–1959.

   Records of the Office of Southeast Asian Affairs (SEA), 1950–1956, entry UD49.

   Records Relating to the Mutual Security Assistance Program (Far East), 1949–1954,
      entry 1393.

National Archives and Records Administration, College Park, Maryland. Records of the
Agency for International Development and Predecessor Agencies. RG 469.

   Mission to Vietnam.

      Administrative Office. Communications and Records Unit. Subject Files (Central
         Files). 1950–1954. Series 1434.

      Agriculture and National Resources Division. Subject Files, 1951–1957. Series
         1435.

      Agriculture and Natural Resources Division. Classified Subject Files, 1951–1955.
         Series 1436.

      Agricultural and Natural Resources Division. Subject Files of J. P. Gittinger,
         Assistant Agrarian Reform Specialist. Series 1437.

      Health and Sanitation Division. General Subject Files, 1951–1954. Series 1440.

      Health and Sanitation Division. Subject Files, 1951–1957. Series 1441.

      Health and Sanitation Division. Hanoi Office. Subject Files, 1951–1954. Series
         1443.

      Health and Sanitation Division. Hanoi Office. General Subject Files, 1951–1954.
         Series 1444.

      Office of the Director. Series 1430.

      Program and Requirements Division. Subject Files, 1950–1957. Series 1446.

      Program and Requirements Division. Classified Subject Files, 1950–1958. Series
         1447.

      Program and Requirements Division. General Records (General Correspondence),
         1950–1954. Series 1448.

      Program and Requirements Division. Research and Statistics Section. Subject
         Files, 1956. Series 1449.

      Program Support Division. Subject Files, 1950–1956. Series 1450.

      Public Administration Division. Subject Files, 1954–1956. Series 1451.

      Resettlement and Rehabilitation Division. Subject Files, 1953–1958. Series 1452.

Resettlement and Rehabilitation Division. Field Service. Classified Subject Files, 1954–1958. Series 1455.

Transportation, Communications, and Power Division. Subject Files, 1951–1956. Series 1456.

Naval Historical Center. Washington Naval Yard, Washington, D.C.

Command File, Post 1 January 1946.

Individual Files, Amberson, Julius, CDR (MC)—Operation Passage to Freedom.

Plans—Amphibious Groups.

PHIBGRP1, Indo-china Operation Order 2-54 Ser. 11 August 1954.

PHIBGRP1, Indo-china Operation Order 2-54 Ser. 9 November 1954.

PHIBGRP1, Ser 0252, 8 November 1954.

PHIBGRP1 Serial 4, January 3, 1955.

PHIBGRP1, Serial 2, January 5, 1955.

PHIBGRP1 Serial: 055, June 15, 1955.

Type—Amphib. Box 4.

Commander, Amphibious Force, Pacific Fleet, C/H, 1946–1960.

Type-Landing Craft LCU Squadron 1, 1955–1967.

Type MSTS/MSC; Military Sea Transportation Service (MSTS)/Military Sealift Command (MSC), Command Histories, 1950–1966 (Box).

Military Sea Transportation Service.

Serial: Diary, Historical, 1954.

Military Sealift Command/Transportation Directorate.

OO Files, 1954.

1954 Admiral Carney Personal File.

Reference File.

Operation Passage to Freedom.

Papers of VADM Lorenzo S. Sabin, USN, 1954–1967.

Biographical Data.

Correspondence, August–September 1954.

Correspondence, October–December 1954.

Correspondence, 1955.

Messages, August 24, 1954–May 1955.

Papers on Ngo Dinh Diem, undated, 1963–1964.

Papers on Operation Passage to Freedom, undated and 1955.

Report: Amphibious Group 1, Passage to Freedom, 16 November 1954–18 May 1955.

Reports on Evacuation of Refugees and Materials from Vietnam (North), ca. 1955.

The Vietnam Archive, Texas Tech University, Lubbock.

Douglas Pike Collection.

Unit 13—The Early History of Vietnam.

Ronald Frankum Collection.

Series: Operation Passage to Freedom.

LST-887.

LST-887 Association.

USS *Askari* (ARL-30).
　　USS *Askari* Association.
　　John E. Pate.
USS *Begor* (APD-127).
　　Roger Turk.
USS *Calvert* (APA-32).
　　USS *Calvert* Association.
　　James E. Chapman.
　　Roy Constant.
　　Louis Gilbert.
　　Tom McConn.
　　John Moeller.
　　Joel C. Snider.
　　Donald Thoes.
USS *Consolation* (AH-15).
　　USS *Consolation* Association.
　　William Bennett.
　　Ted Bobinski.
USS *Estes* (AGC-12).
　　USS *Estes* Association.
　　Donald I. Mayeau.
USS *Gunston Hall* (LSD-5).
　　USS *Gunston Hall* Collection.
USS *Menard* (APA-201).
　　USS *Menard* Association.
　　Carl Benning.
　　John Boland.
　　Don Bright.
　　Terry Foley.
　　Douglas Fraser.
　　Marion Hazzard.
　　Dean Hewitt.
　　Jack Majesky.
USS *Montague* (AKA-98).
　　USS *Montague* Association.
　　Stan Coito.
USS *Montrose* (APA-212).
　　USS *Montrose* Association.
　　Russ McDonald.
　　Jim Ruotsala.
　　Ray Skinner.
USS *Skagit* (AKA-105).
　　Charles R. Hackenburg.

USS *Telfair* (APA-210).

USS *Telfair* Association.

Oral History Interviews, Conducted by the Author.

Admiral Lorenzo Sabin's Staff.

Robert W. Mix, Interview Date, March 30, 2001.

John Matejceck, Interview Date, April 11, 2001.

LCU Squadron Three; Division 33.

Sheldon Friedman, Interview Date, March 20, 2001.

David M. Blemaster, Interview Date, July 13, 2001.

LST-887.

Morris Smith, Interview Date, February 24, 2001.

LST-901.

Ted Zeigler, Interview Date, February 16, 2001.

LST-1096.

Don L. Showen, Interview Date, March 6, 2001.

USS *Askari* (ARL-30).

John (Jack) Pate, Interview Date, February 15, 2001.

John P. Schenck, Interview Date, March 20, 2001.

USS *Begor* (APD-127).

Roger Turk, Interview Date, February 5, 2001.

USS *Calvert* (APA-32).

Don Thoes, Interview Date, February 16, 2001.

Dr. Ellis Fields, Interview Date, January 30, 2002.

Willy Carrillo, Interview Date, January 31, 2002.

John Moeller, Interview Date, February 1, 2002.

Louis John Gilbert, Interview Date, February 4, 2002.

Jim Daniels, Interview Date, February 5, 2002.

Tom McConn, Interview Date, February 6, 2002.

Roy J. Constant, Interview Date, February 12, 2002.

James E. Chapman, Interview Date, February 15, 2002.

John Bridgford, Interview Date, March 1, 2002.

Charles Johann, Interview Date, March 6, 2002.

Don Bergstrom, Interview Date, May 3, 2002.

USS *Consolation* (AH-15).

William Bennett, Interview Date, February 26, 2001.

Ann Ehrlinger Peterson, Interview Date, March 1, 2001.

Arthur Keller, Interview Date, March 1, 2001.

Louis McCluskey, Interview Date, March 2, 2001.

Edward K. Arndt, Interview Date, March 5, 2001.

USS *Estes* (AGC-12).

Joe Gambone, Interview Date, February 23, 2001.

USS *Menard* (APA-201).

James O'Neal Richardson, Interview Date, February 25, 2001.

Barry L. King, Interview Date, March 12, 2001.

Carl Benning, Interview Date, March 13, 2001.

Douglas R. Fraser, Interview Date, March 13, 2001.

Don Bright, Interview Date, March 14, 2001.

Jack D. Majesky, Interview Date, March 27, 2001.

Don Cook, Interview Date, August 15, 2001.

Dean Hewitt, Interview Date, August 15, 2001.

Joseph Hipskin, Interview Date, August 15, 2001.

Leo Andrade, Lieutenant USNR (ret.), Interview Date, March 9, 2002.

USS *Montague* (AKA-98).

Fred C. Machado, Interview Date, March 5, 2001.

Ray Bell, Interview Date, April 25, 2001.

Forrest D. Bussey, Interview Date, April 25, 2001.

Stan Coito, Interview Date, April 25, 2001.

Mel Hone, Interview Date, April 25, 2001.

Chester A. Perciynski, Interview Date, April 25, 2001.

Ken Pinkston, Interview Date, April 25, 2001.

Bob Raftis, Interview Date, April 25, 2001.

Robert Rebbetoy, Interview Date, April 25, 2001.

Doug Richter, Interview Date, April 25, 2001.

Gene Worrell, Interview Date, April 25, 2001.

USS *Montrose* (APA-212).

Eugene Mauch, Interview Date, February 8, 2001.

Jim Ruotsala, Interview Date, February 9, 2001.

Ray Skinner, Interview Date, February 13, 2001.

George Dowd, Interview Date, March 13, 2001.

USS *Skagit* (AKA-105).

Cecil A. Rogers, Interview Date, April 25, 2001.

USS *Telfair* (APA-210).

Forrest C. Lockwood, Interview Date, April 16, 2001.

Published Works

Acheson, Dean. *Present at the Creation: My Years in the State Department.* New York: W. W. Norton, 1969.

Alexander, Charles C. *Holding the Line: The Eisenhower Era, 1952–1961.* Bloomington: Indiana University Press, 1975.

Anderson, David L. "J. Lawton Collins, John Foster Dulles, and the Eisenhower Administration's 'Point of No Return' in Vietnam." *Diplomatic History* 12 (spring 1988): 134–48.

———. *Trapped by Success: The Eisenhower Administration and Vietnam, 1953–1961.* New York: Columbia University Press, 1991.

Arnold, James R. *The First Domino: Eisenhower, the Military, and America's Intervention in Vietnam.* New York: William Morrow, 1991.

Baldwin, Louis. Hon. *Politician: Mike Mansfield of Montana.* Missoula: Mountain Press, 1979.

Beale, John R. *John Foster Dulles: A Biography.* New York: Harper and Row, 1957.

Billings-Yun, Melanie. *Decision Against War: Eisenhower and Dien Bien Phu, 1954.* New York: Columbia University Press, 1988.

Bouscaren, Anthony T. *The Last of the Mandarins: Diem of Vietnam.* Pittsburgh: Duquesne University Press, 1965.

Brands, H. W. *Cold Warriors: Eisenhower's Generation and American Foreign Policy.* New York: Columbia University Press, 1988.

Bui Diem, with David Chanoff. *In the Jaws of History.* Boston: Houghton Mifflin, 1987.

Buttinger, Joseph. *Vietnam: A Dragon Embattled.* 2 vols. London: Pall Mall Press, 1967.

———. *Vietnam: A Political History.* New York: Praeger, 1968.

———. *Vietnam: The Unforgettable Tragedy.* New York: Horizon Press, 1977.

Buzzanco, Robert, "Prologue to Tragedy: U.S. Military Opposition to Intervention in Vietnam, 1950–1954." *Diplomatic History* 17, no. 2 (1993): 201–22.

Cable, James. *The Geneva Conference of 1954 on Indochina.* New York: Oxford University Press, 1986.

Catton, Philip E. *Diem's Final Failure: Prelude to America's War in Vietnam.* Lawrence: University Press of Kansas, 2002.

Collins, J. Lawton. *Lightning Joe: An Autobiography.* Baton Rouge: Louisiana State University Press, 1979.

Croizat, Colonel Victor J. *Journey Among Warriors: The Memoirs of a Marine.* White Mane Publishing Company, Inc., 1977.

Currey, Cecil B. *Edward Lansdale: The Unquiet American.* Boston: Houghton Mifflin, 1988.

Divine, Robert. *Eisenhower and the Cold War.* New York: Oxford University Press, 1981.

Dooley, Agnes. *Promises to Keep.* New York: Farrar, Straus, and Cudahy, 1962.

Dooley, Thomas A. *Deliver Us from Evil: The Story of Viet Nam's Flight to Freedom.* New York: Farrar, Straus, and Cudahy, 1956.

Duiker, William J. *Ho Chi Minh: A Life.* New York: Hyperion, 2000.

———. *The Rise of Nationalism in Vietnam, 1900–1941.* Ithaca, N.Y.: Cornell University Press, 1976.

Eisenhower, Dwight D. *Mandate for Change, 1953–1956.* Garden City: Doubleday, 1963.

———. *Public Papers of the Presidents of the United States—Dwight D. Eisenhower: Containing the Public Messages, Speeches, and Statements of the President, January 1 to December 31, 1954.* Washington, D.C.: Government Printing Office, 1960.

———. *The White House Years: Waging Peace, 1956–1961.* Garden City: Doubleday, 1965.

Fall, Bernard B. *Hell in a Very Small Place: The Siege of Dien Bien Phu.* New York: Da Capo, 1967.

———. "The Political-Religious Sects of Vietnam." *Pacific Affairs* 28 (September 1955): 235–53.

———. "Representative Government in the State of Vietnam." *Far Eastern Survey* 23 (August 1954): 122–25.

———. *The Two Viet-Nams: A Political and Military Analysis.* New York: Praeger, 1963.

———. *Viet-Nam Witness, 1933–1966.* New York: Praeger, 1966.

Fishel, Wesley R., ed. *Problems of Freedom: South Vietnam since Independence.* New York: Free Press of Glencoe, 1961.

Fisher, James T., *Dr. America: The Lives of Thomas A. Dooley, 1927–1961.* Amherst: University of Massachusetts Press, 1997.

Gallagher, Teresa. *Give Joy to My Youth: A Memoir of Tom Dooley.* New York: Farrar, Straus, and Cudahy, 1965.

Gardner, Lloyd C. *Approaching Vietnam: From World War II through Dienbienphu, 1941–1954.* New York: W. W. Norton, 1988.

Gettleman, Marvin E., ed. *Viet Nam: History, Documents, and Opinions on a Major World Crisis.* Fawcett Publications, 1965.

Gettleman, Marvin E., Jane Franklin, Marilyn Young, and H. Bruce Franklin, eds. *Vietnam and America.* 2nd ed. New York: Grove Press, 1995.

Greene, Daniel P. O'C. "John Foster Dulles and the End of the Franco-American Entente in Indochina." *Diplomatic History* 20 (spring 1996): 549–61.

Guhin, Michael A. *John Foster Dulles: A Statesman and His Times.* New York: Columbia University Press, 1972.

Hammer, Ellen. *A Death in November.* New York: Dutton Press, 1987.

———. *The Struggle for Indo-China, 1940–1954.* Stanford: Stanford University Press, 1966.

Herring, George C. *America's Longest War: The United States and Vietnam, 1945–1975.* 4th ed. New York: McGraw-Hill, 2002.

Herring, George C., and Richard Immerman. "Eisenhower, Dulles, and Dien Bien Phu: 'The Day We Didn't Go to War' Revisited," *Journal of American History* 71, no. 2 (1984): 343–63.

Hickey, Gerald C. *Village in Vietnam.* New Haven: Yale University Press, 1964.

Hooper, Edwin Bickford, Dean C. Allard, and Oscar P. Fitzgerald. *The United States Navy and the Vietnam Conflict. Volume 1: Setting the Stage to 1959.* Washington, D.C.: Government Printing Office, 1976.

Hoopes, Townsend. *The Devil and John Foster Dulles.* Boston: Little, Brown, 1973.

Hughes, Emmet John. *The Ordeal of Power: A Political Memoir of the Eisenhower Years.* New York: Atheneum, 1963.

Immerman, Richard H. *John Foster Dulles: Piety, Pragmatism, and Power in U.S. Foreign Policy.* Wilmington: Scholarly Resources Inc., 1999.

Jacobs, Seth. *America's Miracle Man in Vietnam: Ngo Dinh Diem, Religion, Race, and U.S. Intervention in Southeast Asia.* Durham: Duke University Press, 2004.

Kaizer, Kenneth, "Perspectives," *Vietnam Magazine* (August 2001).

Karnow, Stanley. *Vietnam: A History.* New York: Viking Press, 1983.

Krall, Yung. *A Thousand Tears Falling: The True Story of a Vietnamese Family Torn Apart by War, Communism, and the CIA.* Atlanta: Longstreet Press, 1995.

LaFeber, Walter. *American, Russia, and the Cold War, 1945–2002.* New York: McGraw-Hill, 1967, 2002.

Lancaster, Donald. *The Emancipation of French Indochina*. London: Oxford University Press, 1961.

Lederer, William J., and Eugene Burdick. *The Ugly American*. New York: W. W. Norton, 1958.

Marolda, Edward J. *The U.S. Navy in the Vietnam War: An Illustrated History*. Potomac Books, 2002.

Meade, Randoph, Jr., and Carl A. Fischer, "Mobile Logistics Support in the 'Passage to Freedom' Operation" *Naval Research Logistics Quarterly* 14 (December 1954): 258–64.

Monahan, James. *Before I Sleep: The Last Days of Doctor Tom Dooley*. New York: Farrar, Straus, and Cudahy, 1961.

Montgomery, Gayle B., and James W. Johnston. *One Step from the White House: The Rise and Fall of Senator William Knowland*. Berkeley: University of California Press, 1998.

Morgan, Joseph G. *The Vietnam Lobby: The American Friends of Vietnam, 1955–1975*. Chapel Hill: University of North Carolina Press, 1997.

Nguyen, Cao Ky. *Twenty Years and Twenty Days*. New York: Stein and Day, 1976.

O'Daniel, John W. *The Nation That Refused to Starve: The Challenge of the New Vietnam*. New York: Coward-McCann, 1960.

Olson, Gregory A. *Mansfield and Vietnam: A Study in Rhetorical Adaptation*. East Lansing: Michigan State University Press, 1995.

Prados, John. *The Sky Would Fall: Operation Vulture—The U.S. Bombing Mission in Indochina, 1954*. New York: Dial Press, 1983.

Race, Jeffrey. *War Comes to Long An: Revolutionary Conflict in a Vietnamese Province*. Berkeley: University of California Press, 1972.

Randle, Robert F. *Geneva 1954: The Settlement of the Indochinese War*. Princeton: Princeton University Press, 1969.

Redmond, Daniel M. "Getting Them Out," *Proceedings of the U.S. Naval Institute* (August 1990): 44–51.

Roy, Jules, *The Battle of Dienbienphu*. Trans. Robert Baldick. New York: Harper and Row Publishers, 1965.

Samuels, Gertrude. "Passage to Freedom in Viet Nam," *The National Geographic Magazine* (57:6 (June 1955): 858–74.

Scigliano, Robert. *South Vietnam: Nation under Stress*. Boston: Houghton Mifflin, 1963.

Simpson, Howard R. *Dien Bien Phu: The Epic Battle America Forgot*. Washington, D.C.: Brassey's, 1994.

Warner, Denis. *The Last Confucian*. New York: Macmillan, 1963.

Weisner, Louis A. *Victims and Survivors: Displaced Persons and Other War Victims in Viet-Nam, 1954–1975*. Westport: Greenwood Press, 1988.

INDEX

Adler, Michael, 23, 33, 161, 175
Adler, Robert, 124
Amberson, Julius, 90
Andrade, Leo, 51, 75
ANZUS, 10
Australia, 10, 193

Barrows, Leland, 196
Bell, Ray, 62
Benning, Carl, 70–71, 134
Bidault, Georges, 7–8, 10–11
Brown, Richard R., 36, 109, 144–145
Bui Chu Province, 18–20, 136, 160, 162–163, 167, 181–182

Can Tho, 149
Canada, 166, 190
Cap St. Jacques, 33, 54, 93–94, 104–106, 134, 143–144, 147–149, 151–152, 170, 189, 194
CARE. *See* Cooperative for American Remittances to Everywhere, Inc. (CARE)
Carney, Robert B., 37–38, 58, 61, 65, 68, 76, 125, 176, 189
Carrillo, Willy, 92
Catholic World Service, 99
Chapman, James, 52, 92, 113
Churchill, Winston, 7, 9
Cogny, René, 63, 188, 199
Coito, Stan, 62, 132

Constant, Roy, 132
Cooperative for American Remittances to Everywhere, Inc. (CARE), 99, 157
Cooperative American Remittances to Everywhere, 98–99, 157, 171–172

Danang. *See* Tourane
Daniels, Jim, 75, 113
DDT, 24, 36, 137–138, 144, 177, 187
   use of, 79, 85, 117
de Castries, Christian Marie Ferdinand de la Croix, 4
de Paul, Carter, 18–19, 25
Diem, Ngo Dinh. *See* Ngo Dinh Diem
Dien Bien Phu, 4–10
Dillon, C. Douglas, 7, 9, 11
Do Son Peninsula, 41, 45, 66, 77–78, 204–205
Doi, Ngo Ngoc. *See* Ngo Ngoc Doi
Dooley, Thomas A, 162, 187, 197–198, 204
Dowd, George, 112
Dulles, John Foster, 6–11, 108
Dymsza, William. A., 150, 184–185

Eden, Sir Anthony, 8–10
Eisenhower, Dwight D., 1–2, 6–8, 11
Ely, Paul Henri Romuald, 7, 63, 97, 176, 186
Everett, Paul, 24, 36–37

Foley, Terry, 66

France
  Admiral Sabin's concerns of, 63–64
  as obstacles to Passage to Freedom,
      51–55, 73–74, 78–79, 82, 85, 87, 90,
      94, 110, 114, 119, 125, 133, 135, 145,
      188
  and Cambodian Refugees, 165
  departure from Haiphong, 203–204
  at Dien Bien Phu, 4–10
  in the First Indochina War, 2–5
  and Geneva Conference, 5–12
  and POWs, 68
  relocation of French Union troops, 23,
      65, 104, 110, 113, 128, 176, 189–191
  and ships involved in Operation, 162,
      205
  and transportation of Viet Minh to the
      North, 138, 166
  and United Action, 7
  and Viet Minh violations of Geneva
      Conference, 167, 173–174, 195
  Vietnamese Resettlement involvement,
      21–22, 33–37, 58, 65–67, 76, 91–92,
      103, 152, 161–162, 164, 172, 182,
      185–186, 189–191,204–206
  Vinh Operation, 182, 188–189, 247
  and Violation of Geneva Accords
      (1954), 164

Gambiez, Jean (General), 97–98
Gano, Roy A. (Admiral), 44, 64–65, 121,
      128–129, 133
Geneva Conference (1954)
  and Canada, 166, 190
  and France, 5–12
  and Poland, 165–166, 174
  and Final Accords, 12–14,124, 175
Giap, Vo Nguyen. See Vo Nguyen Giap

Haid, William L., 18–20
Heath Donald R. (Ambassador), 24, 59,
      61, 66, 99, 108, 116, 141, 145, 167–
      168, 177

Hilbert, Morton S., 156
HMS Warrior, 116, 120, 124, 168
Ho Chi Minh, 4–5
Holiday, Herman J., 101, 196–197
  in Bien Hoa, 153, 169
  and condition of Refugee Camps, 33–
      35
  and Resettlement, 107, 109–110
  and Thailand Field Trip, 17, 22
Hone Mel, 62, 85

Kennan, George F., 1–2
Kotcher, Emil, 104–105

Laniel, Joseph, 5, 11
Lavergne, Daly C., 97–98, 108, 148, 150,
      154, 184
Lockwood, Forrest, 72, 82

Machedo, Fred, 51
Majesky, Jack, 71
Matheron, Richard C., 20–21, 25
Mauch, Eugene, 81, 117
McCluskey, Louis, 51
Mennonite Central Committee, 157
Military Sea Transportation Service
      (MSTS), 41, 55–56, 59, 61, 67, 77–78,
      83, 91, 116–117, 121–125, 128, 130,
      134–135, 137, 147, 159, 175, 178, 180,
      186, 188–189, 193–195, 200
Mix, Robert, 49
Montagnards, 150, 177
MSTS. See Military Sea Transportation
      Service (MSTS)
My Tho, 98, 149, 171

National Catholic Welfare Conference,
      157
Navarre Plan, 3
Navarre, Henri, 3–4, 8
NCWC. See National Catholic Welfare
      Conference
Ngai, Vu Thi. See Vu Thi Ngai

Ngo Dinh Diem, 28, 37, 97, 108, 113, 115,
    199, 207
  and Admiral Sabin, 141
  opposition to, 185, 196, 203, 206
  and refugees as supporters, 102, 206
  and request for US Assistance, 59
  and Thomas A. Dooley, 197
  and the 100,000th Refugee, 133, 168
Ngo Ngoc Doi, 108, 113, 142, 148, 156
Ngo Van Cuong
  and complaints regarding passage on
    USS Montrose, 129–130
Nguyen Van Thoai, 97–98
Nung (Chinese), 14, 104, 116, 127, 128,
    194

O'Daniel, John (General), 58–59, 61, 63–
    64, 66, 68, 79, 87, 93, 97, 113, 120,
    122, 124–125, 129, 134, 138, 140, 145,
    147–148, 176, 186, 188,
Operation Brotherhood, 170, 172
Operation Castor, 4
Operation Exodus, 14
Operation Order 2–54, 40–57
Operation Trojan Horse, 201
Operation Vautour (Vulture), 7

Pays Montagnard du Sud, 177
Peterson, Anne, 123
Peterson, Paul Q., 102, 106
Phat Diem Province, 136, 160, 167, 172–
    174, 179, 181–183, 188
Philippines Jaycees, 157, 170–172
Pleven, Réne, 9
PMS. See Pays Montagnard du Sud
Poindexter, Hildrus A., 23, 38, 176
  and Cap St. Jacques Refugee Camp,
    105, 152, 170
  and Hue Field Trip, 36
  and Thailand Field Trip, 17
  and Tourane Field Trip, 25–26
Poland, 165–166, 174
  and Shipping, 138, 166, 201

Poulin, Norman, 202
  press coverage, 54, 61–63, 129, 167–
    168, 172, 195
  and AP, 87–88, 168
  negative coverage, 129–130

Querville, Jean Marie (Admiral), 63, 94,
    205

Radio Hanoi, 111
Red Cross
  American, 72, 171–172
  Vietnamese, 71, 101–102, 157
  refugee camps
    at Ban Me Thuot, 183
    at Ben Tre, 151, 171
    at Bien Hoa, 98, 103–104, 143, 149,
      152–154, 168–169, 171, 184, 191–193,
      206
    at Camp de la Pagoda, 138–139, 197
    at Cap St. Jacques, 93, 104–106, 143–
      144, 151–152, 170
    in Central Vietnam, 156, 169
    at Gia Kiem, 183
    at Go Vap, 35, 100, 171
    at Haiduong, 175
    at Haiphong, 34, 64, 109–110, 116, 122,
      138–140, 147, 160, 181, 187–189,
      197–199, 203
    at Hanoi, 34, 109–110
    at Nha Trang, 104, 184
    at Phu Tho, 155–156, 170
    at Ponte de Rach-Dua, 104
    at the Saigon Hippodrome, 100–102,
      146
    at Tay Ninh, 206
    in Thailand, 17
    at Thu Dau Mot, 28, 149, 171
Rittenhouse, B. N. (Captain), 53, 66, 69,
    76–77, 90, 92–94, 115, 122, 133–134,
    140, 152
Ross, Walter, 168–169, 184
Ruotsala, Jim, 72, 79

Sabin, Lorenzo, 40, 42, 45, 49, 54–55, 57,
    91–95, 97, 122–130, 134, 136–138,
    141, 147–148, 158–159, 161, 175–180,
    189, 194, 199–200, 202, 207
  and his arrival in Indochina, 76–79
  and Cardinal Spellman, 130
  and issues with first ships, 83–87
  and logistical support, 121
  and operation press coverage, 167–168
  and problems with French, 145
  and problems with South Vietnamese,
    143
  and refugee conditions, 90
  and restrictions to US personnel, 82
  and his transfer of command, 115–117
  and the Viet Minh threat, 120
  and Operation Order 2–54, 59–70
  and the 100,000ᵗʰ Refugee, 133
Salley, R. Bruce, 18
Skinner, Ray, 51
Smith, Morris, 137
Son Tay Province, 23, 112, 160
Special Technical and Economic Mission,
    17, 19–21, 24–25, 33, 36, 58, 63, 79,
    94, 97–99, 104–106, 108–111, 114,
    118, 135, 138, 142–146, 148–154,
    156–157, 161, 168–170, 174, 177,
    183–184, 188, 193,
Special Technical and Economic Mission
    (STEM)
  Agricultural and Natural Resources,
    153
  Community Development Division,
    17–18, 23, 35, 101, 106–107, 146, 168,
    198
  Health and Sanitation Division,
SS Codington, 191, 195
SS Culucundis, 175
SS José Martí, 176
Stassen, Harold, 22, 27, 36, 177, 184
Strauss, Gerald, 22, 24–25, 63
Stump, Felix B., 58, 61–63, 65, 67–68, 76–

    77, 82, 86–87, 92, 115–116, 122–126,
    128, 130, 133, 145, 147–148, 176, 178,

Tachen Islands, 60, 200
Teall, A. E., 45, 47, 140
Thelen, John P., 100–102, 146, 148, 184
Thoai, Nguyen Van. See Nguyen Van
    Thoai
Tourane, 21, 25–26, 36, 54–5, 64–66, 68–
    69, 77, 83, 86, 91, 121–126, 128, 133,
    135, 147, 169, 177, 186, 189, 205
Truman Doctrine, 2
typhoons, 52, 116
  Grace, 67–68, 77
  Helen, 67, 77
  Ida, 93–95
  Nancy, 140–141
  Pamela, 172

UNICEF. See United Nations
    International Children's Emergency
    Fund
United Action, 66, 10–11
United Kingdom
  and involvement in Operation, 115–116
  and United Action, 10
United Nations International Children's
    Emergency Fund, 99, 157
United States Overseas Mission [USOM],
    17–19, 22–24, 27–28, 34–36, 38, 99,
    101–102, 104, 153, 155–156, 168–169,
    175, 182, 183, 188, 190–191, 193,
    196–204, 206–207
USNS Beauregard, 116, 121
USNS Captain Arlo L. Olson (T-AK-245),
    191, 194–195
USNS Fentress (T-AK-180), 128, 181, 191
USNS General A. W. Brewster (T-AP-155),
    128, 134, 159, 162, 204–205
USNS General R. L. Howze (T-AP-134),
    128, 140, 191, 193–195, 197

USNS *General W. M. Black* (T-AP-135), 128, 140, 159

USNS *Hennepin* (T-AK-187), 172, 187, 191

USNS *Herkimer* (T-AK-188), 180, 191

USNS *Marine Adder* (T-AP-193), 128, 133, 138, 180, 200, 202–203, 205

USNS *Marine Serpent* (T-AP-202), 137, 195, 198, 200, 203

USNS *Marine Lynx* (T-AP-194), 128, 134, 174, 181

USNS *Muskingum* (T-AK-198), 135

USNS *Pembina* (T-AK-200), 135, 137

USNS *Sword Knot*, 191, 195, 200–201

USOM. *See* United States Overseas Mission

USS *Ajax* (AR-6), 44, 64–65, 77, 215

USS *Algol* (AKA-54), 43, 82, 90, 215

USS *Andromeda* (AKA-15), 42, 77, 124, 215

USS *Bayfield* (APA-33), 43, 87–90, 216

USS *Begor* (APD-127), 42, 66, 69, 126, 216

USS *Calvert* (APA-32), 42, 52, 75, 91–92, 100, 113, 124, 132, 216

USS *Comstock* (LSD-19), 43, 66, 87, 120, 216

USS *Consolation* (AH-15), 51, 122–123, 216

USS *Estes* (AGC-12), 40, 42, 62, 66–69, 133, 168, 177, 216,

USS *Gunston Hall* (LSD-5), 194–195, 199, 216,

USS *Haven* (AH-12), 44, 65, 68, 122, 216

USS *Menard* (APA-201), 43, 51, 66, 68–69, 71–76, 79, 81, 91, 101, 122, 216

USS *Montague* (AKA-98), 43, 62–63, 66, 68, 75, 79, 81, 84–85, 121, 132, 216

USS *Montrose* (APA-212), 42, 51, 66, 72, 79, 81–83, 112, 116–117, 121, 124, 129, 216

USS *Reclaimer* (ARS-42), 44, 65, 83, 216

USS *Skagit* (AKA-105), 42, 91, 117, 124, 216

USS *Telfair* (APA-210), 42, 66, 72, 82–83, 124, 216

USS *Uvalde* (AKA-88), 79, 86, 217

USS *Wantuck* (APD-125), 42, 68, 77, 122, 217

USS *Whetstone* (LSD-27), 43, 87, 94, 217

Viet Nam Doc Lap Dong Minh Hoi (Vietnam Independence League; Viet Minh), 2–3

and Forces in Cambodia, 165–166

and the Quin Hon Regrouping Area, 146

and threats to Refugees, 20, 135–136, 161–165, 173–174

and threats to US ships, 126, 174, 186–187

and violation of the Geneva Accords (1954), 127, 163–167, 182, 191

Vietnamese Relief Committee, 33

Vo Nguyen Giap, 3

and Dien Bien Phu, 4–5

Vu Thi Ngai, 201

Vung Tau. *See* Cap St. Jacques

Weiner, Daniel, 23, 38, 183

Winn, Walter C., 46, 76, 94, 116, 118–119, 124–125, 127–128, 138–139, 145, 147–148, 186, 202

Yergan, Laura, 105

Zeigler, Ted, 137